MathFlare

Name: _______________________

Class: ___________

Teacher: _______________________

Introduction

As parents and educators, we recognize the pivotal role mathematics plays in shaping a child's academic journey and future success. Yet, the path to mathematical proficiency can often seem daunting, fraught with challenges and complexities. That's where the transformative power of MathFlare Workbooks shine through, illuminating the way forward with clarity, precision, and purpose.

Introducing MathFlare Workbooks – a beacon of guidance, a testament to excellence, and a catalyst for achievement. Crafted with meticulous care and expertise, MathFlare Workbooks stand as paragons of educational excellence, designed to nurture young minds, ignite a passion for learning, and develop a deep-rooted understanding of mathematical concepts.

Picture this: your child eagerly delves into the pages of Mathflare Workbook, greeted by a step-by-step guide illuminated with vivid examples that demystify complex mathematical concepts. With each turn of the page, they embark on a journey of discovery, encountering thoughtfully curated practice questions that reinforce learning and hone problem-solving skills. And when they unveil the answers to those very questions, a sense of accomplishment blossoms within them – a tangible reward for their hard work and dedication.

But MathFlare Workbooks are more than just tools for learning; they are pathways to comprehension, fostering a deep-seated understanding of mathematical concepts through a sequential, logical flow. From fundamental principles to advanced problem-solving strategies, every chapter builds upon the last, ensuring a robust foundation upon which future knowledge can be constructed.

As parents, we yearn for nothing more than to see our children thrive, to witness the spark of inspiration ignited within them as they conquer academic challenges with confidence and poise. MathFlare Workbooks serve as partners in this noble endeavor, offering not just practice questions, but the keys to unlocking a world of opportunity.

And for teachers, MathFlare Workbooks stand as invaluable allies in the quest to cultivate mathematical proficiency in the classroom. With answers readily available, instructors can focus on guiding and nurturing their students, confident in the knowledge that MathFlare Workbooks provide a solid framework upon which to build.

In the pages of MathFlare Workbooks, we find not just the promise of academic excellence, but the seeds of a brighter tomorrow. So let us embrace the power of mathematics, let us champion the journey of learning, and let us pave the way for a generation of young minds poised to shape the world. With MathFlare Workbooks as our guide, the possibilities are infinite, and the future, bright.

Table of Contents

MathFlare
MATH WORKBOOK
Grade 2
Step by Step Guide and Essential Practice with Answers
Addition
Subtraction
Multiplication
Place Value and Expanded Notations
Geometry
MathFlare Publishing

MathFlare
MATH WORKBOOK
Grade 2-3
Step by Step Guide and Essential Practice with Answers
Addition
Subtraction
Multiplication and Division
Place Value and Expanded Notations
Geometry
MathFlare Publishing

MathFlare
MATH WORKBOOK
Grade 3
Step by Step Guide and Essential Practice with Answers
Multiplication and Division
Decimals
Place Value and Expanded Notations
Fractions and Geometry
MathFlare Publishing

MathFlare
MATH WORKBOOK
Grade 1
Step by Step Guide and Essential Practice with Answers
Counting and Numbers
Addition and Subtraction
Place Value and Expanded Notations
Understanding Time
MathFlare Publishing

MathFlare
MATH WORKBOOK
Grade 1-2
Step by Step Guide and Essential Practice with Answers
Counting and Numbers
Addition and Subtraction
Place Value and Expanded Notations
Understanding Time
MathFlare Publishing

MathFlare
MATH WORKBOOK
Grade 3-4
Step by Step Guide and Essential Practice with Answers
Addition Subtraction
Multiplication Division
Place Value and Expanded Notations
Fractions and Geometry
MathFlare Publishing

MathFlare
MATH WORKBOOK
Grade 4
Step by Step Guide and Essential Practice with Answers
Addition Subtraction
Multiplication Division
Place Value and Expanded Notations
Fractions and Geometry
MathFlare Publishing

MathFlare
MATH WORKBOOK
Grade 4-5
Step by Step Guide and Essential Practice with Answers
Multiplication Division
Place Value and Expanded Notations
Fractions and Geometry
Unit Conversion
MathFlare Publishing

MathFlare
Grade 5
MATH WORKBOOK
Step by Step Guide and Essential Practice with Answers
Multiplication Division
Place Value and Expanded Notations
Fractions and Geometry
Unit Conversion
MathFlare Publishing

MathFlare
Grade 5-6
MATH WORKBOOK
Step by Step Guide and Essential Practice with Answers
Multiplication Division
Place Value and Expanded Notations
Fractions and Geometry
Units and Statistics
MathFlare Publishing

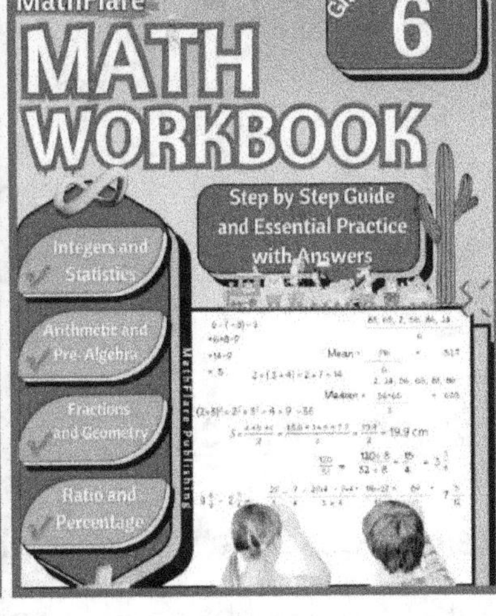
MathFlare
Grade 6
MATH WORKBOOK
Step by Step Guide and Essential Practice with Answers
Integers and Statistics
Arithmetic and Pre-Algebra
Fractions and Geometry
Ratio and Percentage
MathFlare Publishing

MathFlare
Grade 6-7
MATH WORKBOOK
Step by Step Guide and Essential Practice with Answers
Arithmetic and Pre-Algebra
Ratio, Percent Proportion
Geometry
Statistics
MathFlare Publishing

MathFlare
Grade 7
MATH WORKBOOK
Step by Step Guide and Essential Practice with Answers
Pre-Algebra
Ratio, Percent Proportion
Geometry
Statistics
MathFlare Publishing

MathFlare
Grade 7-8
MATH WORKBOOK
Step by Step Guide and Essential Practice with Answers
Pre-Algebra
Ratio, Percent Proportion
Geometry and Cartesian Plane
Statistics
MathFlare Publishing

MathFlare
Grade 8-9
MATH WORKBOOK
Step by Step Guide and Essential Practice with Answers
Pre-Algebra
Ratio, Proportion and Percentage
Linear Equations
Geometry and Cartesian Plane
MathFlare Publishing

MathFlare
Grade 8
MATH WORKBOOK
Step by Step Guide and Essential Practice with Answers
Pre-Algebra
Percentage
Linear Equations
Geometry
MathFlare Publishing

Chapter. 01

Addition and Subtraction

Addition with Regrouping

When we do addition, we combine numbers. But sometimes, when we're adding numbers, we might need to regroup. Regrouping means we have to move a number from one place to another, usually to the next column, to get the right answer.

For Example: Let's take an example of adding 533 and 579 together:

$$
\begin{array}{r}
5\ 3\ 3 \\
+\ \underline{5\ 7\ 9} \\
\end{array}
$$

First, we start by adding the digits in the ones place: 3 + 9 = 12. We write down the 2 in the ones place and carry over the 1 to the tens place.

$$
\begin{array}{r}
1\ \ \ \\
5\ 3\ 3 \\
+\ \underline{5\ 7\ 9} \\
2 \\
\end{array}
$$

Now, we add the digits in the tens place, along with the carry-over: 2 + 8 + 1 = 11. We write down the 1 in the tens place and carry over the 1 to the hundreds place.

$$
\begin{array}{r}
1\ 1\ \ \\
5\ 2\ 2 \\
+\ \underline{5\ 8\ 9} \\
1\ 2 \\
\end{array}
$$

Now, we add the digits in the hundreds place, along with the carry-over: 5 + 5 + 1 = 11. We write down the 1 in the tens place and carry over the 1 to the hundreds place.

$$\begin{array}{r} 1\ 1 \\ 5\ 2\ 2 \\ +\ 5\ 8\ 9 \\ \hline 1\ 1\ 1\ 2 \end{array}$$

This process of carrying over helps us accurately add numbers, especially when they're larger.

Subtraction with Regrouping

Subtraction is a key math operation where we find the difference between two numbers. Sometimes, when we subtract, we might need to regroup, which means borrowing from the next column.

Let's take an example of subtracting 436 from 563:

First, we start by subtracting the digits in the ones place: 3 - 6.

Since 3 is less than 6, we need to regroup. We borrow 1 from the tens place, making it 5 tens instead of 6, and add it to the ones place.

So, 3 becomes 13, and then we subtract 6.

$$\begin{array}{r} 5\ \ 6\ 13 \\ -\ 4\ \ 3\ \ 6 \\ \hline 7 \end{array}$$

Now, we subtract the tens place digits: 5 - 3 = 2

$$\begin{array}{r} 5 \\ 5\ \ \cancel{6}\ 13 \\ -\ 4\ \ 3\ \ 6 \\ \hline 2\ 7 \end{array}$$

Now, we subtract the hundreds place digits: 5 - 4 = 1

$$
\begin{array}{r}
5 \\
5\ \cancel{6}\ 13 \\
-\ 4\ 3\ 6 \\
\hline
1\ 2\ 7
\end{array}
$$

This process of regrouping or borrowing helps us accurately subtract numbers, especially when the top digit is smaller than the bottom one.

Let's solve problems from exercises:

$$
\begin{array}{r}
714 \\
+\ 797 \\
\hline
1{,}511
\end{array}
\qquad
\begin{array}{r}
980 \\
-\ 896 \\
\hline
84
\end{array}
$$

Word Problems

Word problems are like little puzzles that help us use addition in real-life situations.

For instance:

1. Jake has 6 carrots. He gets 2 more carrots. How many carrots does he have now?

To find out how many carrots he has now, we add the number of carrots he started with (6) to the number of carrots he got (2).

So, we add 6 + 2, which equals 8. Jake now has 8 carrots in total!

2. Jake saved up 4 dollars to buy pencils. He spent 2 dollars on it. How much money does he have left?

To solve this problem, we need to start with the number of dollars Jake started with and subtract the number of dollars he spent on the pencils.

So, we subtract 2 from 4, which equals 2: Jake has 2 dollars left after buying the pencils.

We need to understand what the problem is asking and what information it provides. Then, we can use addition or subtraction, depending on whether we're combining or taking away objects, to find the answer.

Let's solve problems from exercises:

Leo has 100 hats, and 14 more hats are added to the collection. How many hats does Leo have in total?

$$
\begin{array}{r}
100 \\
+\ 14 \\
\hline
114
\end{array}
$$

Leo has 100 Hats

14 more hats are added

Leo has 114 hats in total

A recipe needs 67 cups of sugar. Christine added 18 cups of   sugar. How many cups of sugar are still needed?

$$
\begin{array}{r}
67 \\
-\ 18 \\
\hline
49
\end{array}
$$

Recipe call for 67 cups of suger

Christine adds 18 cups

cups are still needed

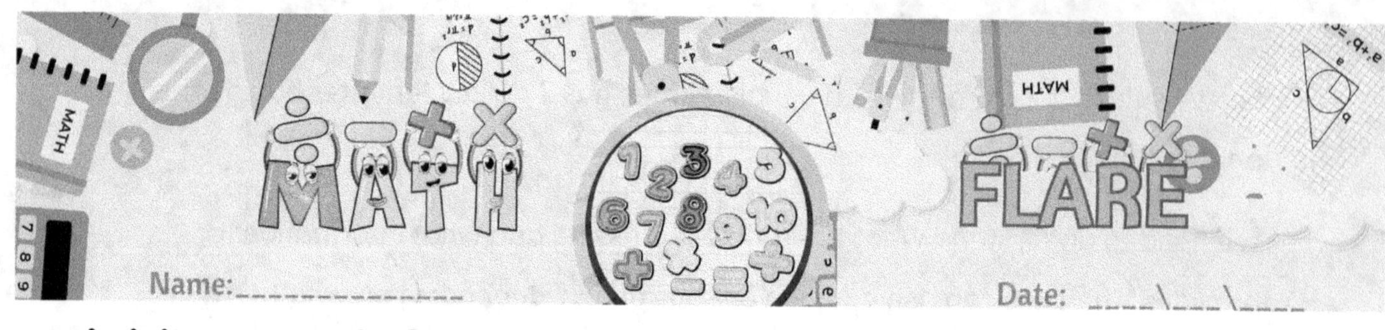

Addition with Regrouping

Find the sum.

1) 714 + 797 1,511	2) 881 + 849 1,730	3) 897 + 927	4) 551 + 959
5) 875 + 376	6) 421 + 889	7) 754 + 778	8) 784 + 789
9) 126 + 989	10) 157 + 973	11) 911 + 599	12) 298 + 876
13) 511 + 999	14) 732 + 689	15) 845 + 295	16) 582 + 869
17) 531 + 579	18) 242 + 998	19) 112 + 999	20) 424 + 798

21) 333 + 897	22) 172 + 989	23) 344 + 966	24) 554 + 657
25) 991 + 679	26) 817 + 399	27) 125 + 988	28) 361 + 879
29) 554 + 868	30) 435 + 789	31) 295 + 969	32) 175 + 985
33) 792 + 419	34) 916 + 699	35) 631 + 989	36) 772 + 368
37) 944 + 496	38) 796 + 617	39) 519 + 895	40) 832 + 578

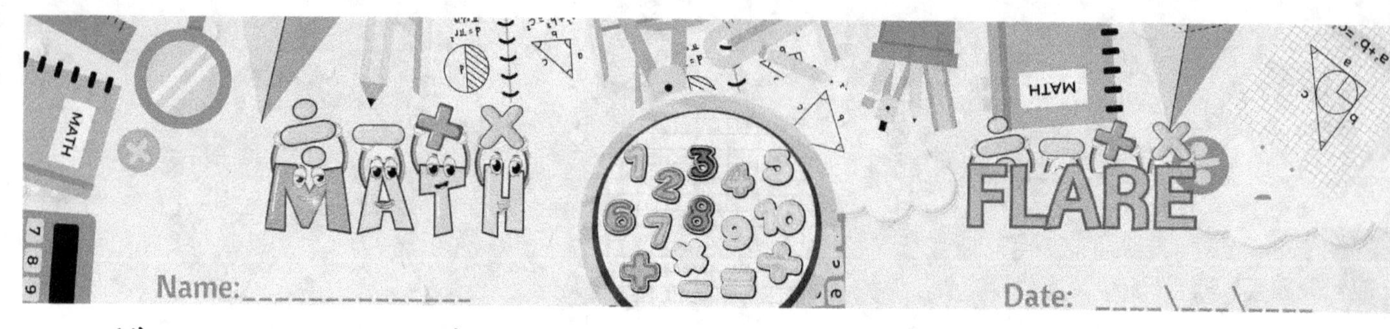

Name: _________________   Date: ____________

41)	42)	43)	44)
723 + 598	291 + 979	472 + 939	975 + 978

45)	46)	47)	48)
884 + 279	343 + 779	467 + 774	555 + 969

49)	50)	51)	52)
315 + 796	391 + 929	125 + 985	123 + 998

53)	54)	55)	56)
899 + 594	424 + 788	762 + 748	713 + 499

57)	58)	59)	60)
972 + 859	995 + 217	179 + 972	312 + 799

61) 443 + 968	62) 724 + 698	63) 742 + 569	64) 855 + 377
65) 851 + 879	66) 397 + 833	67) 824 + 997	68) 553 + 778
69) 154 + 988	70) 372 + 879	71) 887 + 357	72) 311 + 799
73) 415 + 999	74) 334 + 776	75) 718 + 498	76) 885 + 485
77) 274 + 849	78) 581 + 599	79) 321 + 789	80) 738 + 583

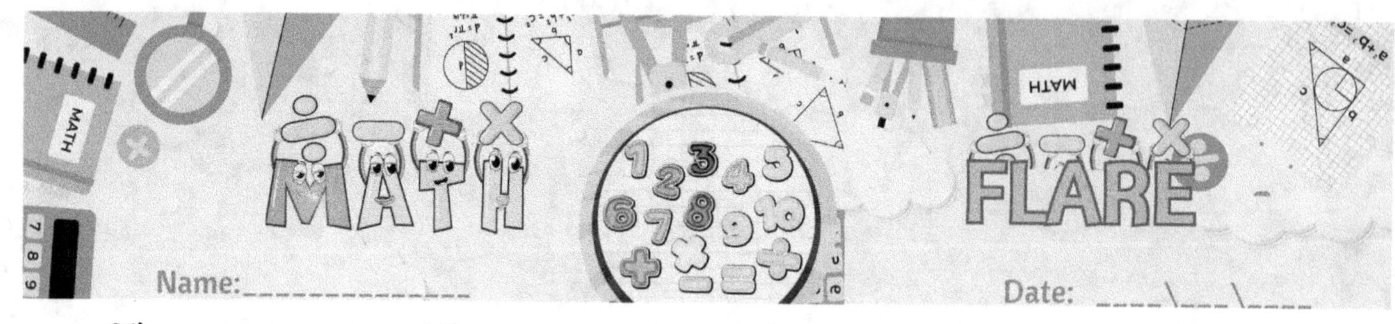

81) 868 + 949	82) 452 + 679	83) 614 + 597	84) 413 + 898
85) 163 + 998	86) 631 + 499	87) 691 + 489	88) 723 + 588
89) 297 + 838	90) 332 + 979	91) 632 + 578	92) 945 + 989
93) 858 + 665	94) 426 + 896	95) 557 + 653	96) 923 + 998
97) 239 + 874	98) 488 + 784	99) 783 + 748	100) 391 + 969

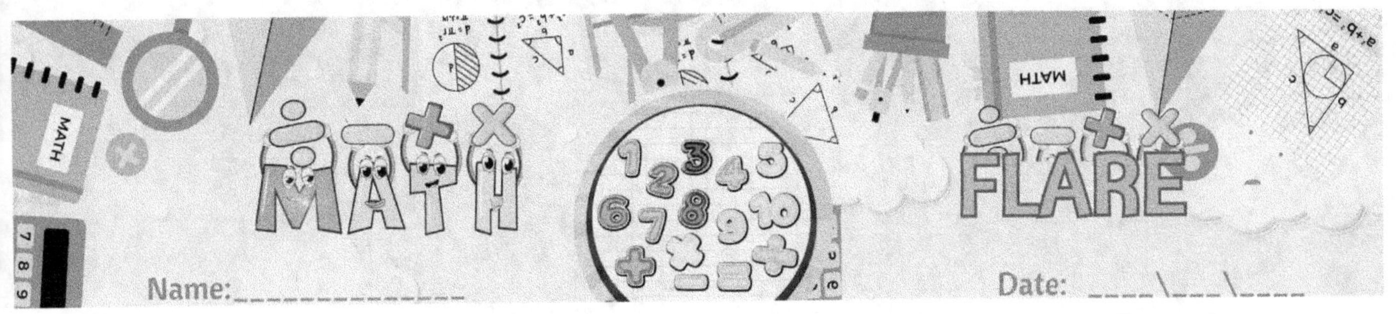

101) 317 + 894	102) 375 + 996	103) 781 + 839	104) 218 + 994
105) 467 + 767	106) 314 + 799	107) 212 + 898	108) 551 + 859
109) 983 + 467	110) 811 + 599	111) 738 + 989	112) 761 + 599
113) 968 + 699	114) 295 + 886	115) 697 + 443	116) 815 + 595
117) 548 + 663	118) 139 + 972	119) 237 + 993	120) 313 + 799

Subtraction with Regrouping

Find the difference.

1) 980
  − 896
    84

2) 980
  − 897
    83

3) 420
  − 243

4) 830
  − 694

5) 350
  − 189

6) 380
  − 292

7) 930
  − 767

8) 530
  − 258

9) 720
  − 643

10) 220
  − 162

11) 640
  − 259

12) 780
  − 199

13) 920
  − 733

14) 970
  − 197

15) 450
  − 274

16) 310
  − 157

17) 360
  − 293

18) 700
  − 571

19) 940
  − 887

20) 280
  − 197

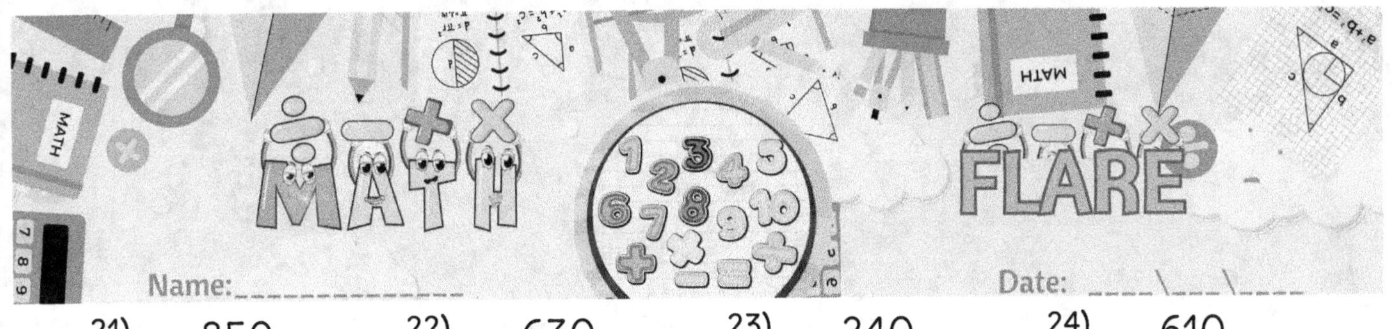

21) 850 - 474	22) 630 - 493	23) 240 - 167	24) 610 - 473
25) 630 - 495	26) 510 - 228	27) 920 - 233	28) 470 - 383
29) 330 - 276	30) 880 - 598	31) 520 - 496	32) 480 - 393
33) 810 - 399	34) 250 - 173	35) 280 - 196	36) 420 - 347
37) 760 - 484	38) 330 - 164	39) 680 - 196	40) 970 - 583

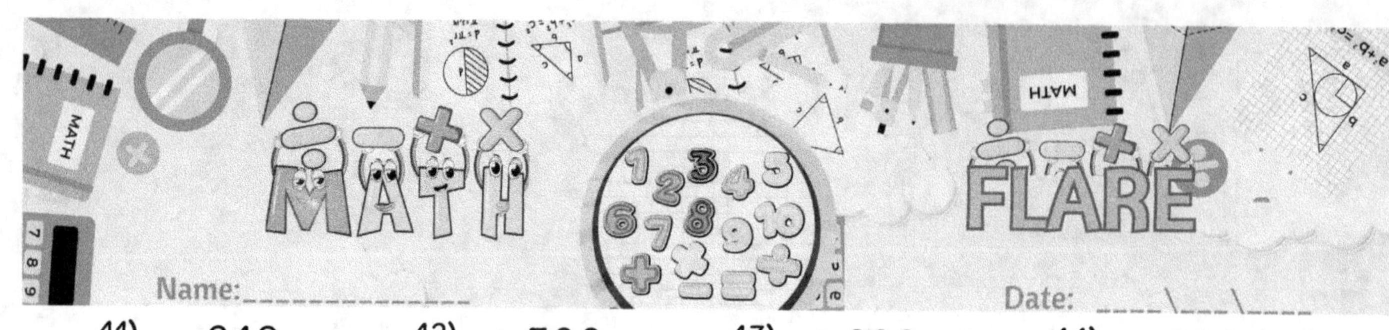

41) 240
  − 194
	42) 500
	  − 359
		43) 980
		  − 895
			44) 200
			  − 186

45) 410
  − 123
	46) 770
	  − 692
		47) 230
		  − 144
			48) 240
			  − 183

49) 250
  − 198
	50) 850
	  − 668
		51) 330
		  − 197
			52) 760
			  − 673

53) 440
  − 374
	54) 610
	  − 392
		55) 870
		  − 388
			56) 960
			  − 193

57) 980
  − 497
	58) 520
	  − 198
		59) 380
		  − 297
			60) 250
			  − 193

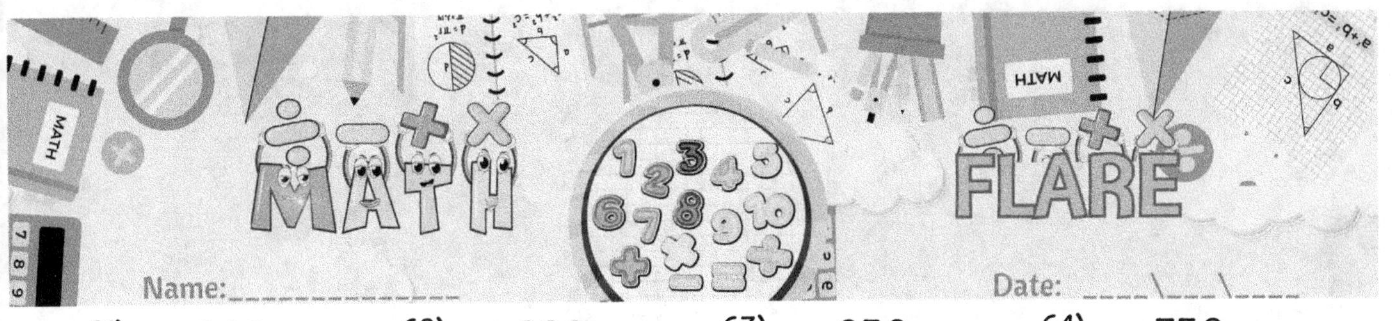

61) 260 − 198	62) 820 − 141	63) 250 − 199	64) 750 − 274
65) 510 − 181	66) 930 − 161	67) 370 − 199	68) 300 − 248
69) 640 − 399	70) 330 − 145	71) 420 − 373	72) 270 − 187
73) 970 − 697	74) 980 − 893	75) 760 − 477	76) 730 − 646
77) 610 − 177	78) 650 − 477	79) 950 − 896	80) 960 − 393

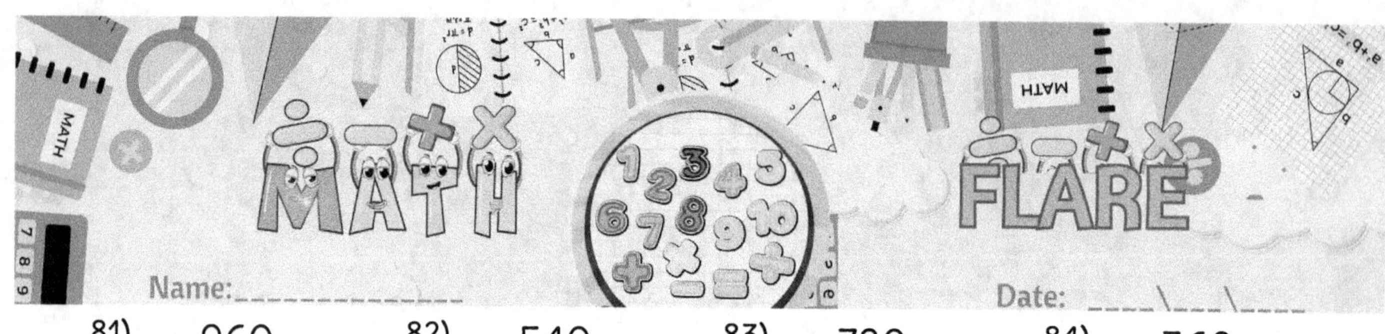

81)   960
    - 673
    ______

82)   540
    - 493
    ______

83)   720
    - 582
    ______

84)   360
    - 297
    ______

85)   660
    - 591
    ______

86)   570
    - 498
    ______

87)   550
    - 399
    ______

88)   920
    - 795
    ______

89)   980
    - 496
    ______

90)   470
    - 183
    ______

91)   340
    - 255
    ______

92)   510
    - 279
    ______

93)   470
    - 285
    ______

94)   670
    - 197
    ______

95)   200
    - 173
    ______

96)   740
    - 271
    ______

97)   310
    - 181
    ______

98)   760
    - 478
    ______

99)   680
    - 194
    ______

100) 940
    - 266
    ______

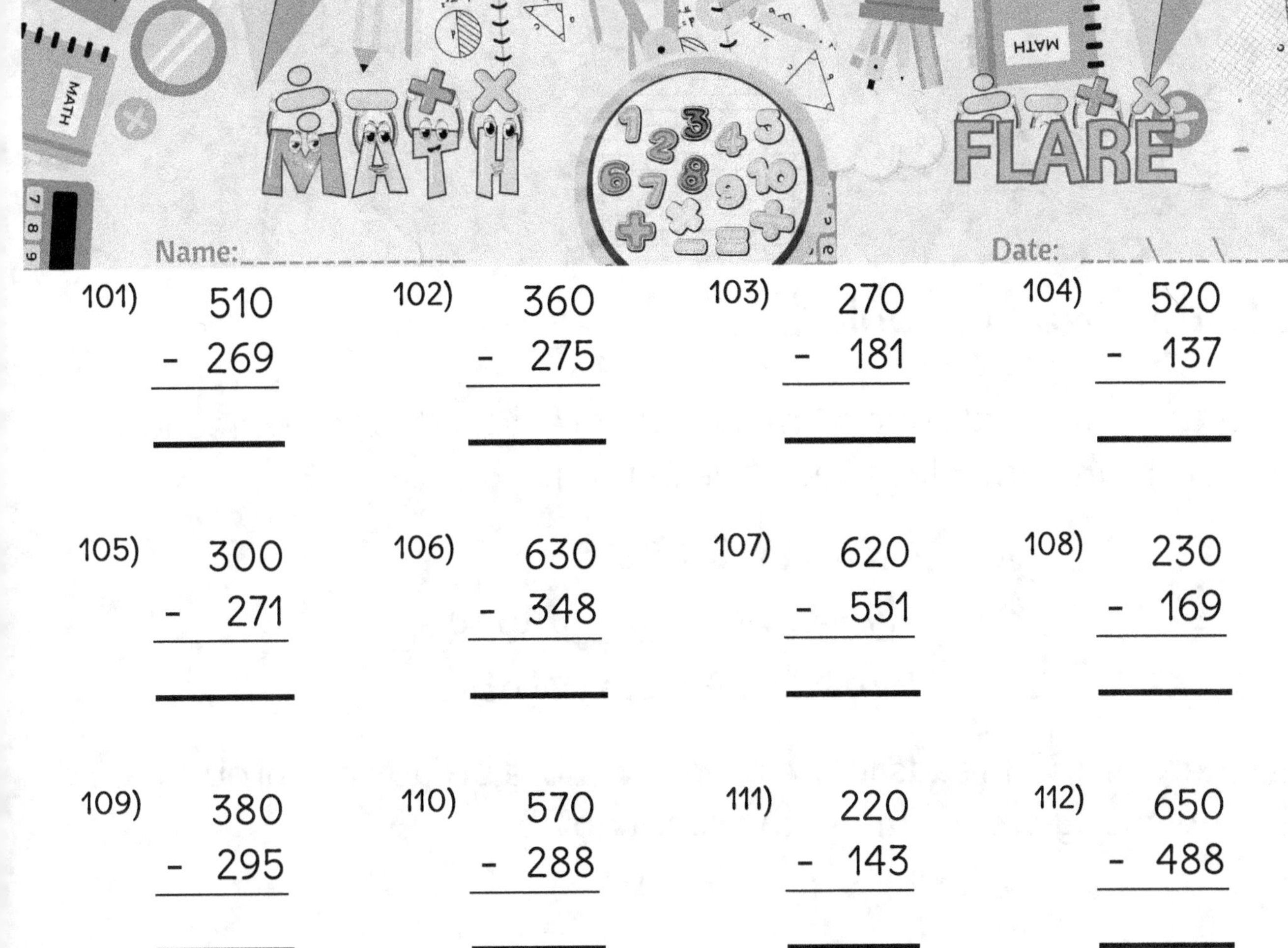

101)   510
    - 269

102)   360
    - 275

103)   270
    - 181

104)   520
    - 137

105)   300
    - 271

106)   630
    - 348

107)   620
    - 551

108)   230
    - 169

109)   380
    - 295

110)   570
    - 288

111)   220
    - 143

112)   650
    - 488

113)   240
    - 176

114)   650
    - 381

115)   770
    - 382

116)   540
    - 196

117)   660
    - 183

118)   510
    - 359

119)   420
    - 359

120)   880
    - 591

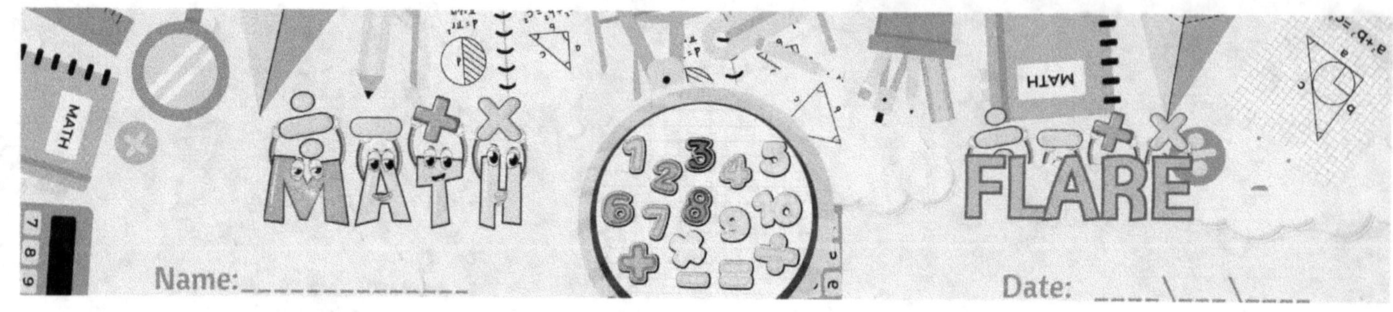

Addition Word Problems

1) Leo has 100 hats and 14 more hats are added to the collection. How many hats does Leo have in total?

$$
\begin{array}{r}
100 \\
+\ 14 \\
\hline
114
\end{array}
$$

Leo has 100 Hats

14 more hats are added

Leo has 114 hats in total

2) There are 32 breads in the room. 15 more breads are brought in. How many breads are in the room now?

3) Matthew has 50 red marbles and 3 blue marbles in a jar. How many marbles does Matthew have in total?

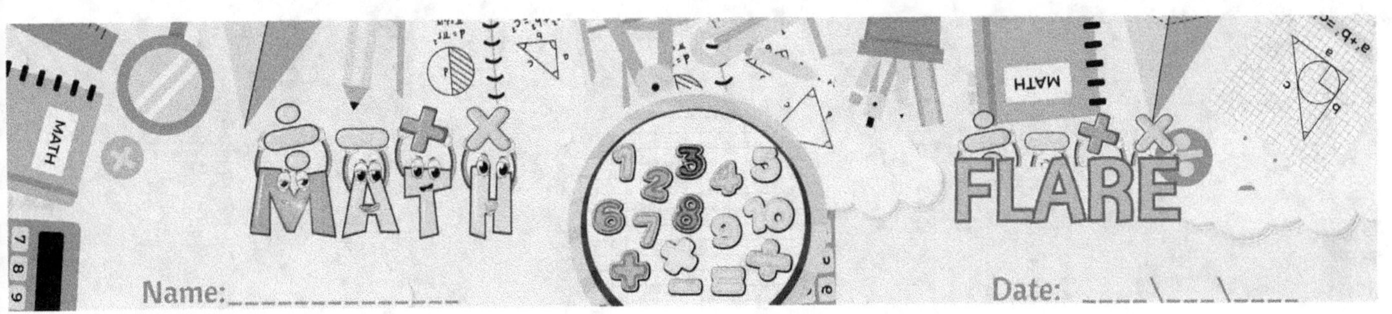

4) There are 28 toothbrushes in the bag. If 69 more toothbrushes are added, how many toothbrushes are in the bag now?

5) There are 71 sticks on the shelf. Layla puts 67 more sticks on the shelf. How many sticks are there on the shelf now?

6) Owen has 5 pants. He gets 90 more pants. How many pants does he have now?

7) Noah has 70 rocks. He gets 76 more rocks. How many rocks does he have now?

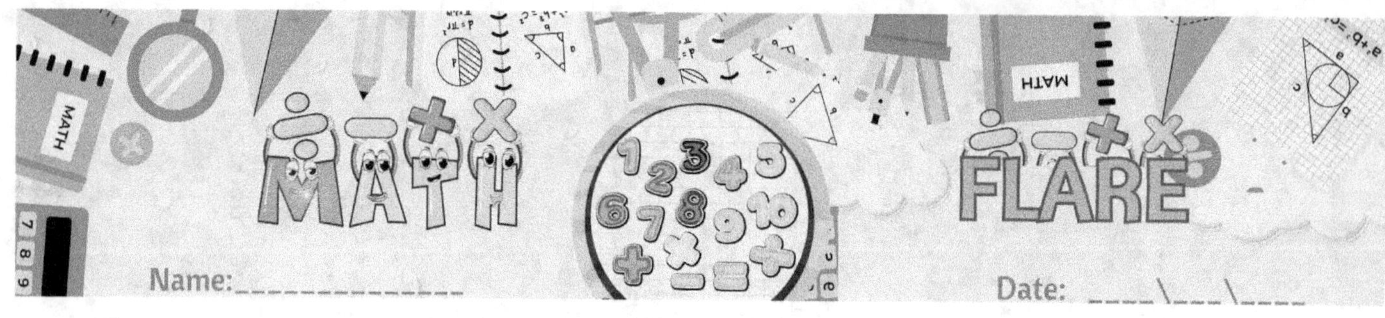

8) Sebastian has 56 apples and 51 oranges in a basket. How many fruits does Sebastian have in total?

9) Ethan has 28 pencils. He finds 9 more pencils. How many pencils does he have now?

10) William has 32 red candies and 50 green candies. If William puts all the candies in a basket, how many candies are in the basket in total?

11) Thomas had 17 dollars and earned 32 more dollars. How much money does Thomas have now?

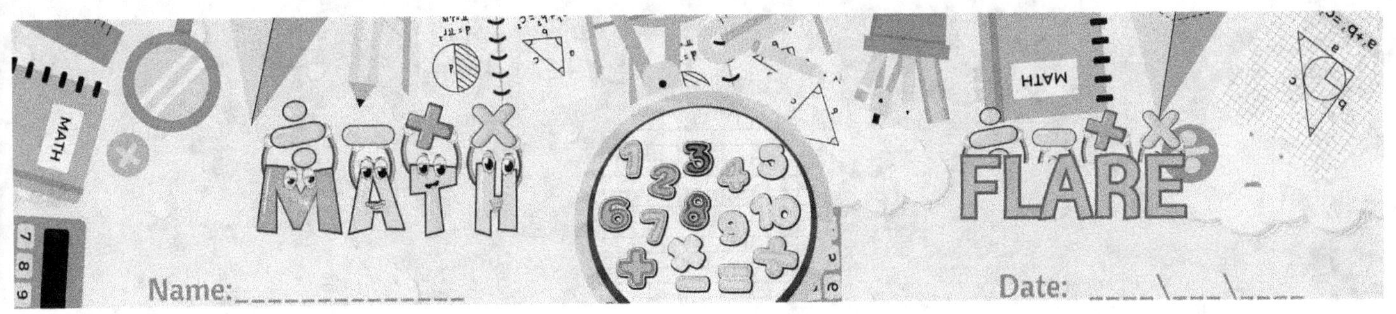

12) A bakery sold 60 cupcakes in the morning and 51 cupcakes in the afternoon. How many cupcakes did the bakery sell in total?

13) Claire has 21 plates. She gets 35 more plates. How many plates does Claire have now?

14) Wesley has 20 balls. He buys 53 more balls. How many balls does she have now?

15) Aria bought 26 cookies and later bought 75 cookies. How many cookies does Aria have now?

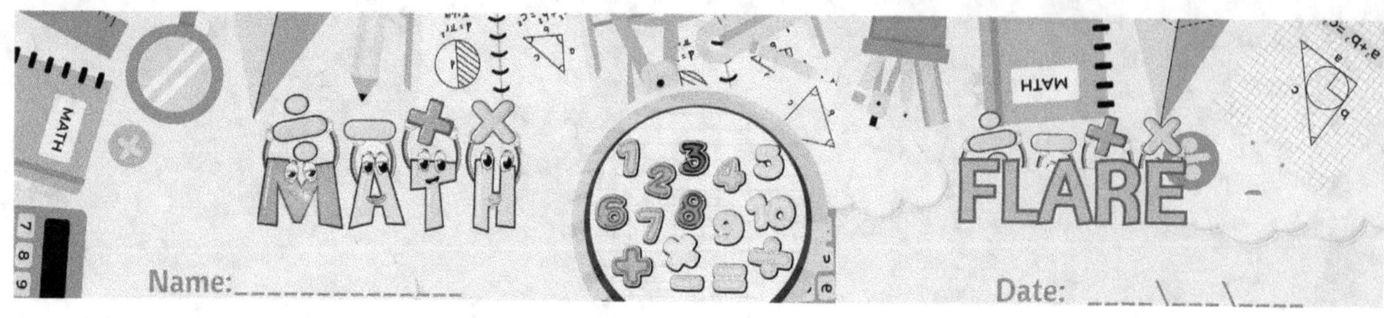

16) A bus made 76 stops in the morning and 28 stops in the afternoon. How many stops did the bus make in total?

17) Leah planted 41 flowers in the morning and 4 flowers in the afternoon. How many flowers did Leah plant?

18) Yesterday, Molly earned $9, and today, Molly earned $15. How much money did Molly earn in total?

19) Henry has 26 calendars. He gets 88 more calendars as a gift. How many calendars does Henry have now?

20) Ariana has 55 vitamins. Her friend gives her 99 more vitamins. How many vitamins does Ariana have now?

21) Michael has 20 bags. He finds 86 more bags. How many bags does he have now?

22) Jade has 96 scrubs in a bag. If Jade adds 43 more scrubs to the bag, how many scrubs does Jade have in total?

23) At the store, Robert bought 22 compasses. Later, Skylar bought 73 compasses from the same store. How many compasses were bought in total?

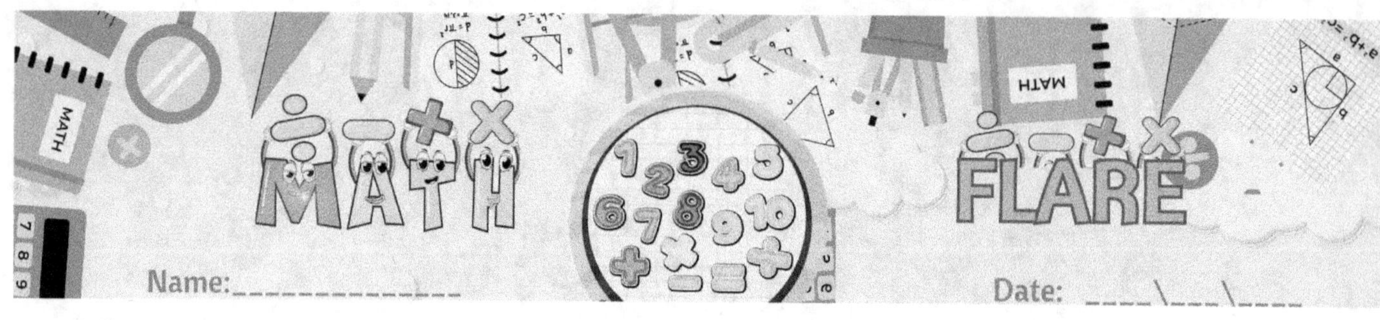

24) Sadie has 74 liters of water in a container. She pours in 95 more liters of water. How much water is in the container now?

25) Hazel watched 45 movies last week and 53 movies this week. How many movies did Hazel watch altogether?

26) There are 13 cats in the ground. 84 more cats come to play. How many cats are in the ground now?

27) Diego has 14 tables. He finds 81 more tables on the ground. How many tables does Diego have now?

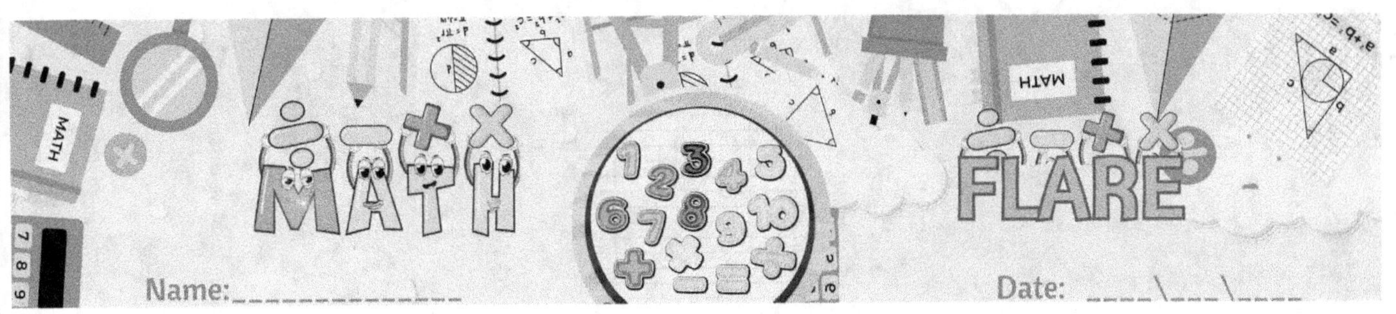

28) There are 59 crows on a tree. 68 more crows land on the tree. How many crows are on the tree now?

29) Oliver made 55 cookies and Bella made 82 cookies. How many cookies were made in total?

30) There were 95 people in line at the store. After 16 more people joined the line, how many people are in the line now?

31) Sebastian has 83 computers and buys 75 more computers. How many computers does Sebastian have in total?

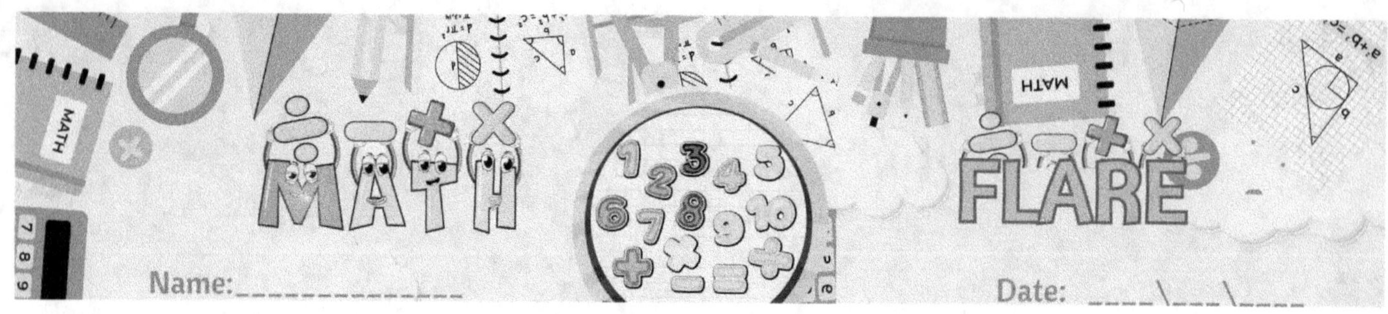

32) Harper walked 44 miles yesterday and 96 miles today. How many miles did Harper walk in total?

33) Justin filled a tank with 91 gallons of gas and then added 78 more gallons. How many gallons of gas are in the tank now?

34) Cooper spent 49 dollars on Monday and 67 dollars on Tuesday. How much money did Cooper spend in total?

Subtraction Word Problems

1) A recipe needs 67 cups of sugar. Christine added 18 cups of sugar. How many cups of sugar are still needed?

$$
\begin{array}{r}
67 \\
-18 \\
\hline
49
\end{array}
$$

Recipe call for 67 cups of suger
Christine adds 18 cups
cups are still needed

2) Elizabeth baked a 41 cookies. 14 of them were chocolate chip cookies and the rest were oatmeal raisin cookies. How many oatmeal raisin cookies did Elizabeth bake?

3) There are 31 dogs in a park. If 12 leave, how many dogs are left in the park?

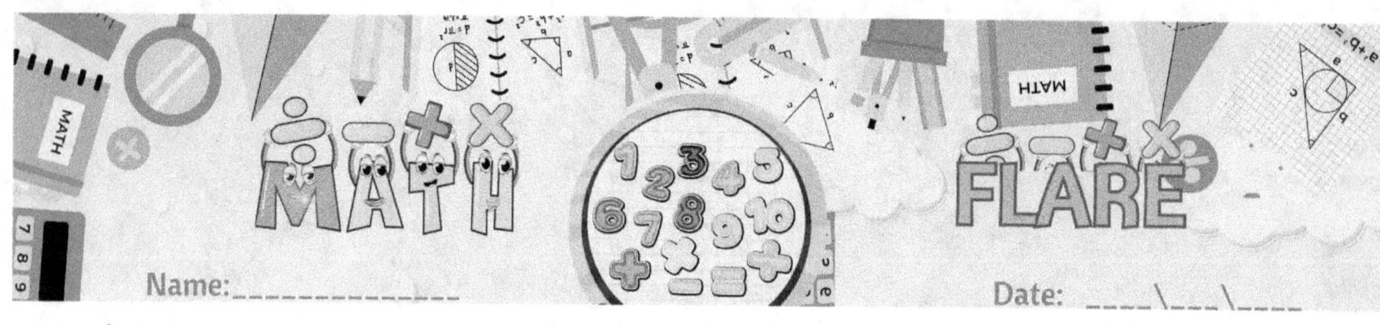

4) Ryan has 17 red notebooks and 9 green notebooks. How many more red notebooks does Ryan have than green notebooks?

5) Marin bought compasses for 62 dollars but later found out it was on sale for 6 dollars less. How much did she overpay for compasses?

6) Lotions costs 74 dollars. If you paid $69. How much change will you get back?

7) A cake recipe requires 15 cups of sugar. Jackie only has 7 cups of sugar. How many more cups of sugar does Jackie need?

8) A small bag of chips has 42 chips in it. Robert ate 19 chips. How many chips are left in the bag?

9) A cake recipe calls for 94 cups of flour. 14 cups of flour have already been added. How many more cups of flour are needed?

10) Matthew has 46 dollars. He needs to buy toothpastes that costs 46 dollars. How much money will he have left after buying the toothpastes?

11) Ellen has 52 mirrors. She lost 13 of them. How many mirrors does Ellen have left?

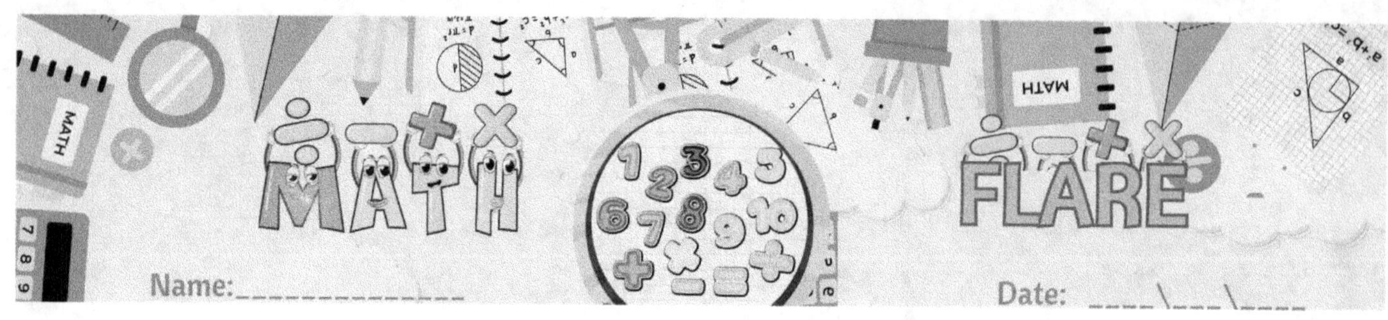

12) If you have 8 flowers and you give away 1, how many flowers do you have left?

13) Michele and Amy went shopping for bats. They had 27 dollars to spend but 8 dollars ended up being spent. How much money do they have left?

14) Andrew is 80 years old and Gary is 22 years old. What is the difference in their ages?

15) Lisa and Jackie had 32 deodorants altogether. Jackie gave 17 deodorants to Steven. How many deodorants do they have left?

Name:________________________   Date: ____________

16) There are 47 fish in a tank. If 28 leave, how many fish are left in the tank?

17) There are 67 turtles in a pond. If 23 leave, how many turtles are left in the pond?

18) Michael has 99 dollars. He wants to buy scalpels that costs 81 dollars. How much more money does he need to buy the scalpels?

19) There are 21 cars in a parking lot. Robert took 18 cars out of the lot. How many cars are still in the lot?

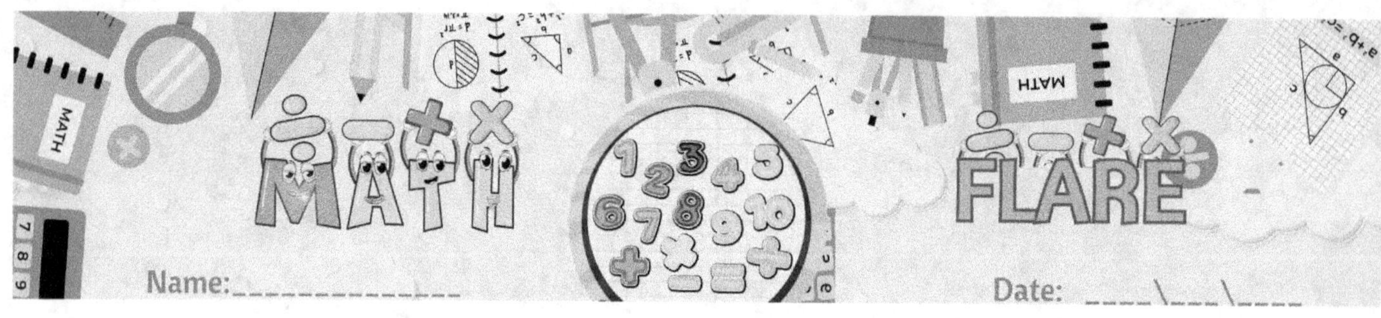

20) Ellen has 14 dollars. She wants to buy shirts, which costs 83 dollars. How much more money does she need to buy it?

21) Joseph saved up 19 dollars to buy bananas. He spent 17 dollars on it. How much money does he have left?

22) Charles had 37 dresses. He gave 32 dresses to Amanda. How many dresses does Charles have left?

23) A pack of gum had 24 pieces. Marin took 24 pieces of gum. How many pieces of gum are left in the pack?

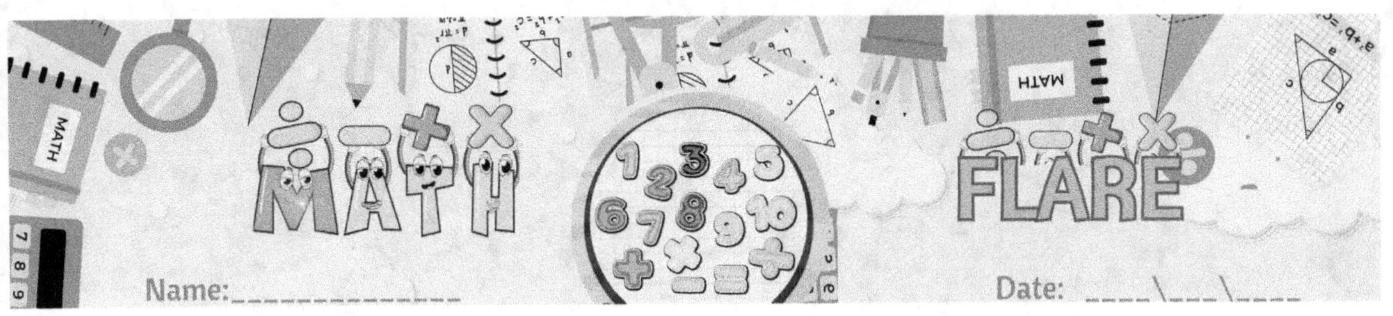

24) Jennifer had 6 dollars. She spent 6 dollars on violins. How much money does Jennifer have left?

25) Pens originally cost 64 dollars, but it is now on sale for 6 dollars. How much money can you save by buying it on sale?

26) Richard had 19 dollars. He spent 5 dollars on a radios. How much money does Richard have left?

27) If brushes costs 91 dollars and you have 77 dollars, how much more money do you need to buy it?

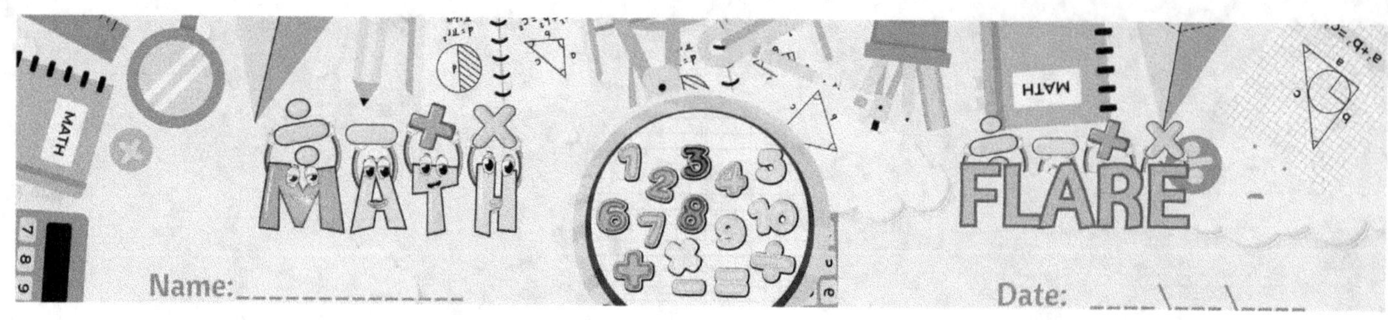

28) A pizza has 58 slices. Linda ate 43 slices. How many slices of pizza are left?

29) Allan has 66 hats. He traded 54 of them with his friend. How many hats does Allan have now?

30) A cotton swabs costs $35 and a pen costs $1. How much more expensive is the cotton swabs than the pen?

31) Linda and Ellen went on a shopping spree and bought 21 gauzes. After returning home, they realized that they didn't need 6 of them. How many gauzes did they end up keeping?

Chapter. 02

Multiplication and Division

Multiplication

Multiplication is an easy way of adding numbers together quickly. Instead of adding the same number repeatedly, we use multiplication to find the total much faster.

For instance, rather than adding 2 + 2 + 2 + 2 + 2, we can multiply 2 by 5 to get the same result: 2 x 5 = 10.

Here, the first number (2) is called the multiplicand, second number (5) is the multiplier. The answer we get, in this case, 10, is called the product.

Let's think of multiplication as repeated addition.

Take 2 x 5, for example. It means adding 2 together five times, which we can illustrate as: 2 + 2 + 2 + 2 + 2 = 10

Multiplication can also be visualized as groups of objects. Imagine we have 2 groups, each containing 5 oranges.

To find the total number of oranges, we multiply the number of groups (2) by the number of oranges in each group (5):

2 groups of 5 oranges = 10 oranges

Expressed as multiplication: 2 x 5 = 10

In summary, multiplication offers various ways to approach it: through repeated addition or by envisioning groups of objects. It's a powerful tool that makes solving math problems much quicker and more efficient!

We can also use the following table to quickly remember multiplication facts. The intersection of two points shows the product of two numbers.

For instance, the product of 5 x 6 = 30, or 6 x 5 = 30.

	1	2	3	4	5	6	7	8	9	10
1	1	2	3	4	5	6	7	8	9	10
2	2	4	6	8	10	12	14	16	18	20
3	3	6	9	12	15	18	21	24	27	30
4	4	8	12	16	20	24	28	32	36	40
5	5	10	15	20	25	30	35	40	45	50
6	6	12	18	24	30	36	42	48	54	60
7	7	14	21	28	35	42	49	56	63	70
8	8	16	24	32	40	48	56	64	72	80
9	9	18	27	36	45	54	63	72	81	90
10	10	20	30	40	50	60	70	80	90	100

Let's solve problems from exercises:

$$
\begin{array}{r}
11 \\
\times\ 4 \\
\hline
44
\end{array}
\qquad
\begin{array}{r}
20 \\
\times\ 4 \\
\hline
80
\end{array}
$$

Commutative Property of Multiplication

The commutative property of multiplication is a special rule in math that tells us the order of the numbers being multiplied doesn't affect the result.

For instance, let's take 2 x 5. If we switch the order of the numbers, multiplying 5 by 2 instead, we'll still end up with the same answer: 2 x 5 = 10, or 5 x 2 = 10.

So, whether we multiply 2 by 5 or 5 by 2, we get 10. That's the commutative property of multiplication in action!

Division

Division is like the opposite of multiplication. It's all about sharing or distributing items equally among a certain number of groups or people.

When we divide one number by another, we're essentially splitting a number into equal parts. We're figuring out how many groups of a certain size can be made from that number.

For instance, let's divide 20 by 4.

When we divide 20 by 4, we're essentially asking, "How many groups of size 4 can we make from 20?"

Now, there are several parts or terms involved in the division process:

- **Dividend:** This is the number being divided, which in this case, is 20.

- **Divisor:** This is the number we're dividing by, which is 4.

- **Quotient:** This is the answer we get after dividing. It tells us how many groups of divisors can be made from the dividend. In this case, the answer is 5.

So, when we divide 20 by 4, we found out that 5 groups of 4 can be made from 20.

Let's solve problems from exercises:

$$
\begin{array}{r}
8 \\
3\overline{)24} \\
-24 \\
\hline
0
\end{array}
$$

Multiplication and Division Word Problems:

A garden has eight rows of flowers and 15 flowers in each row. How many flowers are there in total?

$$
\begin{array}{r}
15 \\
\times\ 8 \\
\hline
120
\end{array}
$$

15   rows of flowers
× 8   flowers in each row
120   there are 120 flowers in total

Nolan read a book that had 1,122 pages in 17 days. If he read the same number of pages each day, how many pages did he read per day?

$$
\begin{array}{r}
66 \\
17\overline{)1122} \\
-102 \\
\hline
102 \\
102 \\
\hline
0
\end{array}
$$

Nolan read 66 pages per day.

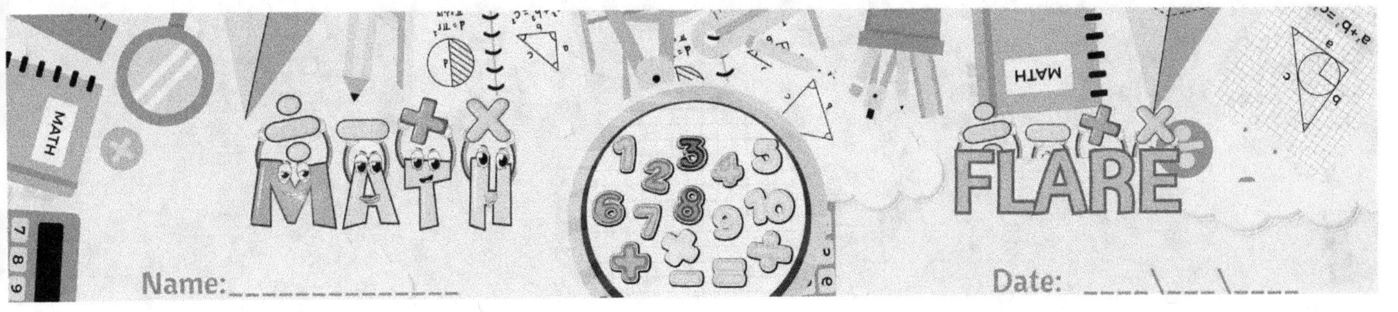

Multiplication

Find the product.

1)   7
  × 3
   21

2)   11
  × 3
   33

3)   0
  × 7

4)   10
  × 1

5)   3
  × 5

6)   2
  × 10

7)   10
  × 2

8)   11
  × 1

9)   1
  × 2

10)   12
  × 9

11)   7
  × 4

12)   6
  × 4

13)   3
  × 6

14)   8
  × 8

15)   6
  × 7

16)   1
  × 4

17) 12 × 7	18) 7 × 12	19) 3 × 9	20) 4 × 8
21) 1 × 7	22) 2 × 9	23) 4 × 12	24) 5 × 5
25) 3 × 7	26) 4 × 10	27) 9 × 7	28) 9 × 9
29) 2 × 6	30) 10 × 9	31) 9 × 5	32) 4 × 3
33) 6 × 2	34) 11 × 2	35) 5 × 11	36) 3 × 11

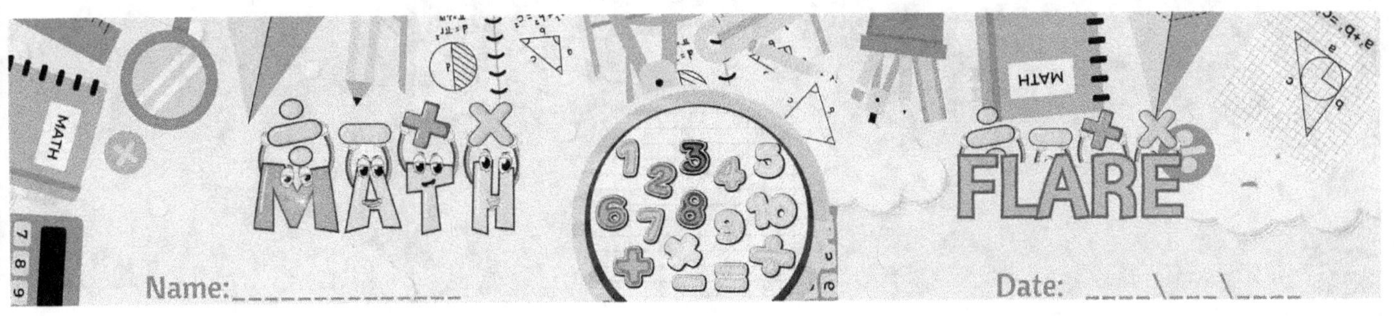

37) 1 × 3	38) 5 × 10	39) 3 × 3	40) 8 × 4
41) 11 × 10	42) 11 × 7	43) 11 × 8	44) 8 × 9
45) 8 × 1	46) 7 × 5	47) 5 × 7	48) 9 × 6
49) 0 × 6	50) 6 × 8	51) 4 × 2	52) 3 × 10

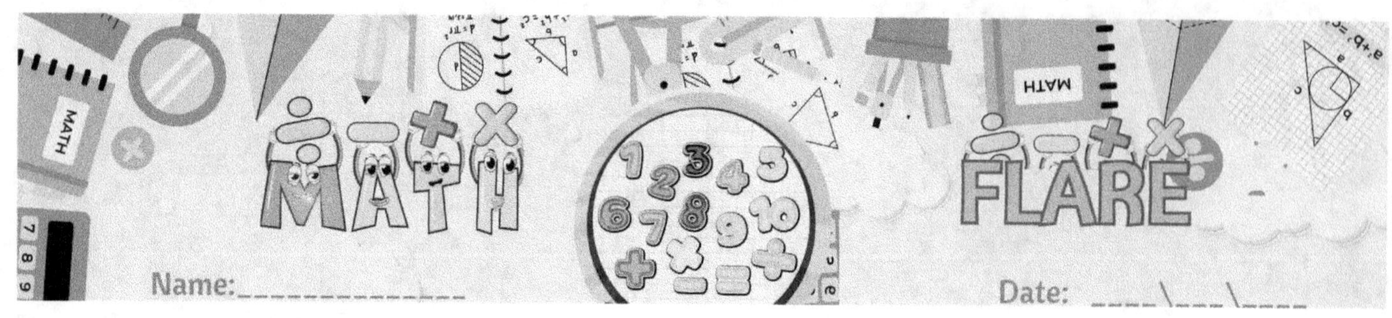

Multiplication: 2 x 1

Find the product.

1)   11
 × 4
 44

2)   20
 × 4
 80

3)   20
 × 3

4)   11
 × 3

5)   15
 × 1

6)   36
 × 1

7)   71
 × 1

8)   22
 × 4

9)   12
 × 4

10) 30
 × 3

11) 33
 × 3

12) 22
 × 3

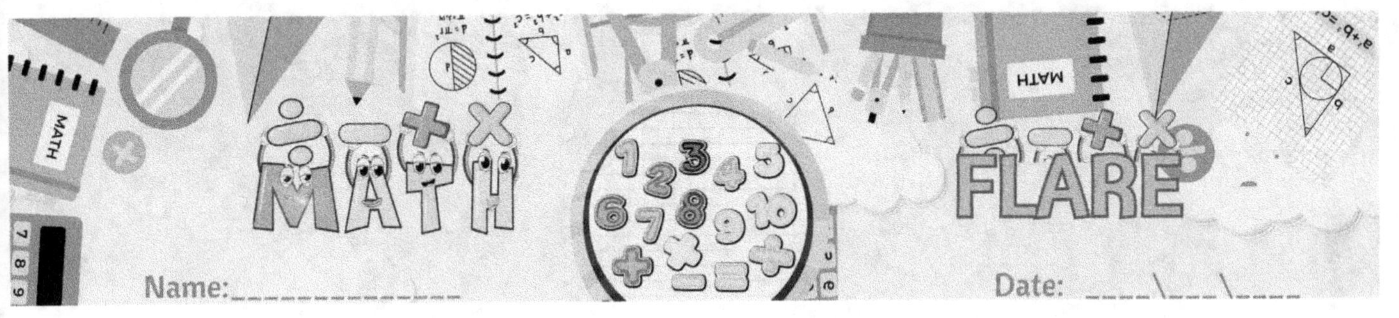

13)　11　× 5

14)　40　× 2

15)　12　× 3

16)　10　× 4

17)　10　× 5

18)　33　× 2

19)　23　× 3

20)　13　× 3

21)　21　× 2

22)　32　× 3

23)　14　× 2

24)　21　× 4

25)　13　× 2

26)　24　× 2

27)　16　× 1

28)　31　× 3

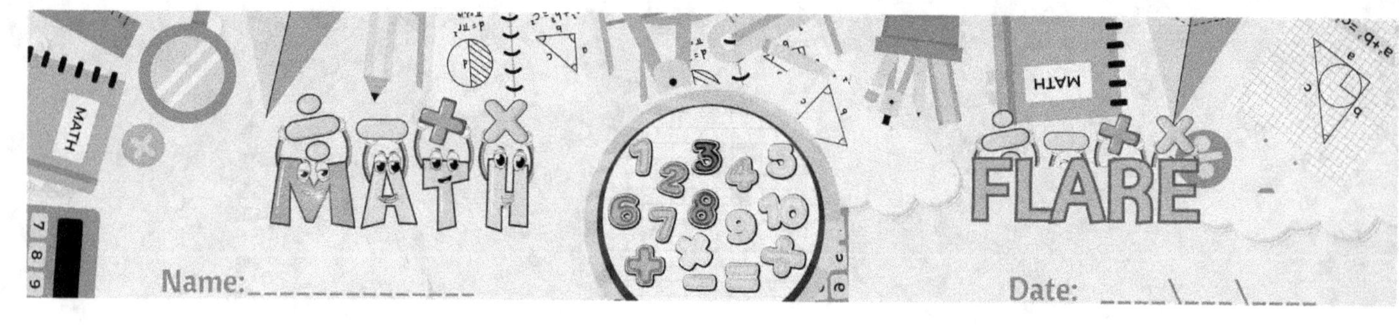

Name:_______________   Date: _______________

29)   41
   × 2

30)   74
   × 1

31)   32
   × 2

32)   31
   × 2

33)   10
   × 3

34)   25
   × 1

35)   64
   × 1

36)   43
   × 2

37)   91
   × 1

38)   34
   × 2

39)   42
   × 2

40)   12
   × 2

41)   11
   × 2

42)   10
   × 2

43)   20
   × 2

44)   44
   × 2

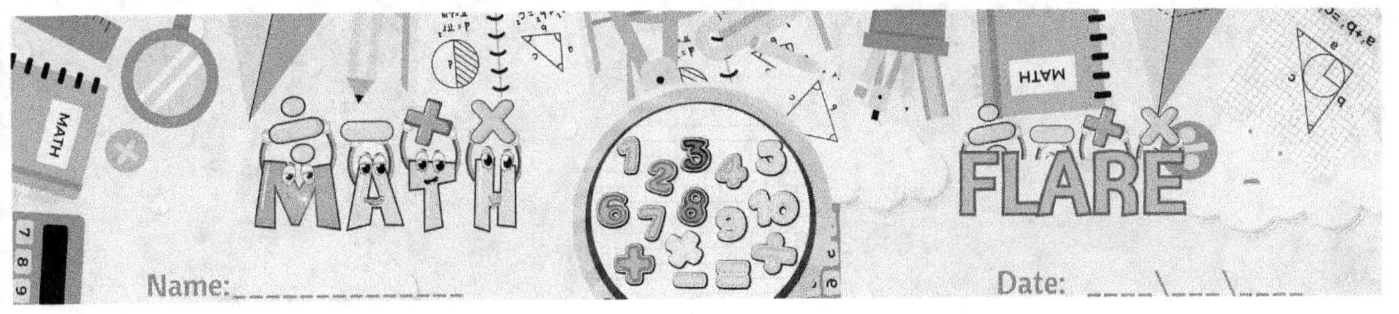

45) 23 × 2	46) 84 × 1	47) 85 × 1	48) 37 × 1
49) 67 × 1	50) 21 × 3	51) 41 × 1	52) 38 × 1
53) 30 × 2	54) 52 × 1	55) 77 × 1	56) 94 × 1
57) 12 × 1	58) 48 × 1	59) 22 × 2	60) 83 × 1

61)   92
 × 1

62)   19
 × 1

63)   11
 × 1

64)   28
 × 1

65)   18
 × 1

66)   69
 × 1

67)   26
 × 1

68)   89
 × 1

69)   98
 × 1

70)   45
 × 1

71)   70
 × 1

72)   10
 × 1

73)   53
 × 1

74)   99
 × 1

75)   75
 × 1

76)   93
 × 1

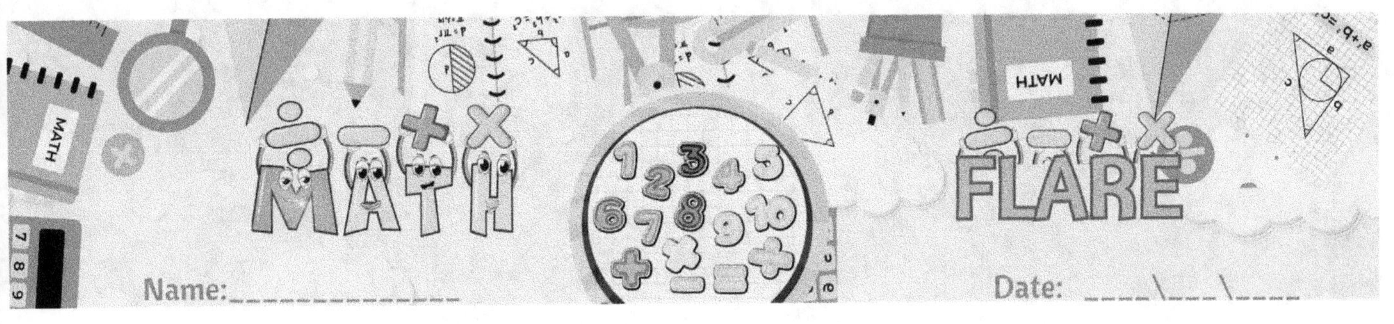

77) $\begin{array}{r} 62 \\ \times\ 1 \\ \hline \end{array}$	78) $\begin{array}{r} 82 \\ \times\ 1 \\ \hline \end{array}$	79) $\begin{array}{r} 86 \\ \times\ 1 \\ \hline \end{array}$	80) $\begin{array}{r} 68 \\ \times\ 1 \\ \hline \end{array}$
81) $\begin{array}{r} 66 \\ \times\ 1 \\ \hline \end{array}$	82) $\begin{array}{r} 24 \\ \times\ 1 \\ \hline \end{array}$	83) $\begin{array}{r} 22 \\ \times\ 1 \\ \hline \end{array}$	84) $\begin{array}{r} 61 \\ \times\ 1 \\ \hline \end{array}$
85) $\begin{array}{r} 78 \\ \times\ 1 \\ \hline \end{array}$	86) $\begin{array}{r} 42 \\ \times\ 1 \\ \hline \end{array}$	87) $\begin{array}{r} 40 \\ \times\ 1 \\ \hline \end{array}$	88) $\begin{array}{r} 50 \\ \times\ 1 \\ \hline \end{array}$
89) $\begin{array}{r} 20 \\ \times\ 1 \\ \hline \end{array}$	90) $\begin{array}{r} 80 \\ \times\ 1 \\ \hline \end{array}$	91) $\begin{array}{r} 13 \\ \times\ 1 \\ \hline \end{array}$	92) $\begin{array}{r} 60 \\ \times\ 1 \\ \hline \end{array}$

93) 76 × 1	94) 32 × 1	95) 14 × 1	96) 47 × 1
97) 95 × 1	98) 54 × 1	99) 55 × 1	100) 57 × 1
101) 81 × 1	102) 44 × 1	103) 23 × 1	104) 34 × 1
105) 17 × 1	106) 87 × 1	107) 31 × 1	108) 35 × 1

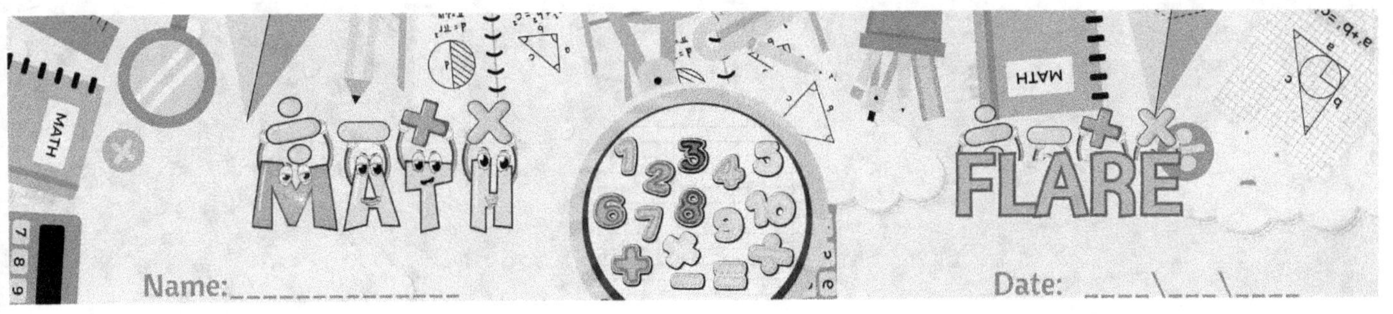

Division

Find the quotient.

1)
$$\begin{array}{r} 6 \\ 1\overline{)6} \\ -6 \\ \hline 0 \end{array}$$

2) $7\overline{)21}$

3) $2\overline{)8}$

4) $4\overline{)40}$

5) $4\overline{)12}$

6) $2\overline{)4}$

7) $9\overline{)81}$

8) $10\overline{)10}$

9) $3\overline{)15}$

10) $4\overline{)16}$

11) $9\overline{)36}$

12) $7\overline{)56}$

13) $10\overline{)90}$

14) $8\overline{)24}$

15) $8\overline{)48}$

16) $9\overline{)54}$

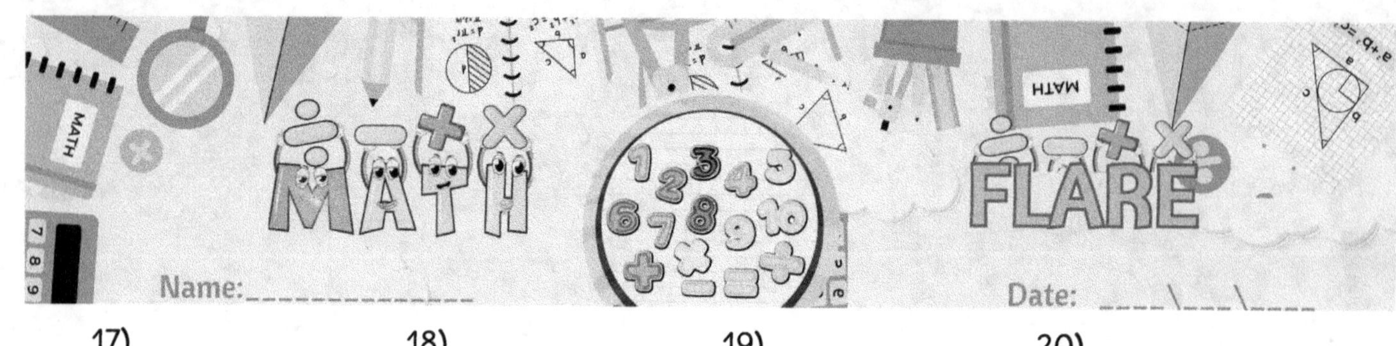

17) 8)64

18) 3)12

19) 4)8

20) 3)24

21) 2)16

22) 4)32

23) 10)20

24) 8)40

25) 5)45

26) 8)72

27) 10)70

28) 6)12

29) 5)30

30) 2)6

31) 9)90

32) 3)27

33) 5)10

34) 9)63

35) 5)15

36) 8)32

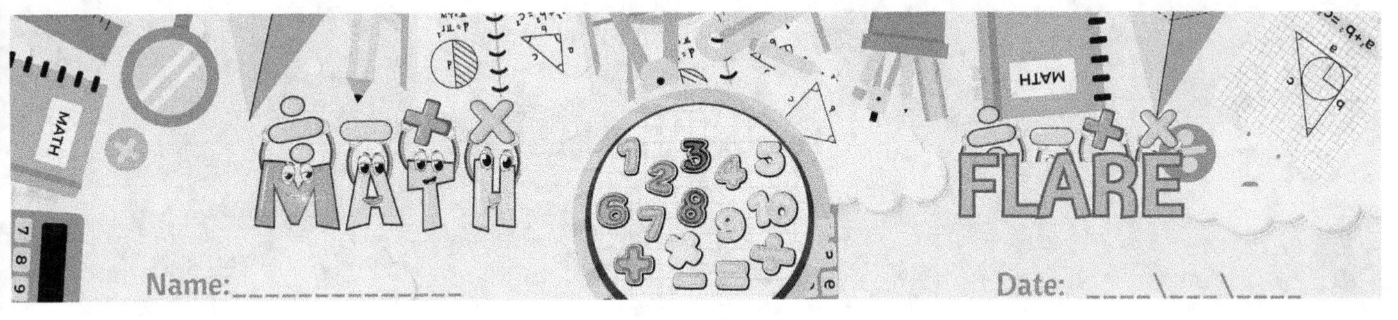

37) 1)2̅

38) 4)2̅8̅

39) 5)3̅5̅

40) 6)3̅0̅

41) 7)1̅4̅

42) 9)4̅5̅

43) 7)7̅0̅

44) 4)2̅4̅

45) 7)7̅

46) 6)4̅8̅

47) 6)5̅4̅

48) 7)2̅8̅

49) 7)4̅9̅

50) 9)1̅8̅

51) 2)2̅

52) 9)7̅2̅

Long Division (double digit)

Find the quotient.

1)

$$8$$
$$3\overline{)24}$$
$$-24$$
$$0$$

2)

$$7\overline{)462}$$

3)

$$7\overline{)14}$$

4)

$$5\overline{)380}$$

5)

$$7\overline{)84}$$

6)

$$6\overline{)396}$$

7)

$$4\overline{)372}$$

8)

$$4\overline{)264}$$

9)

$$7\overline{)70}$$

10)

$$1\overline{)9}$$

11)

$$9\overline{)459}$$

12)

$$9\overline{)675}$$

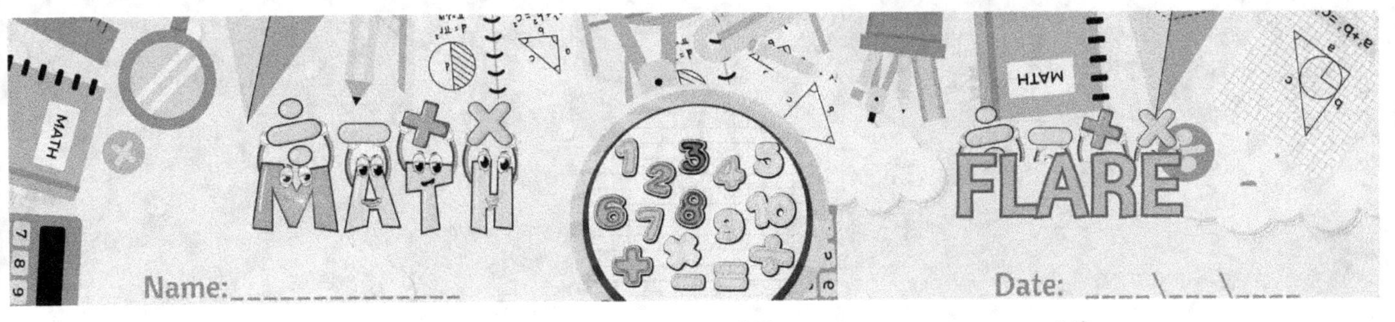

13)   11$\overline{)616}$

14)   3$\overline{)162}$

15)   10$\overline{)570}$

16)   9$\overline{)225}$

17)   5$\overline{)190}$

18)   7$\overline{)455}$

19)   2$\overline{)56}$

20)   5$\overline{)445}$

21)   4$\overline{)248}$

22)   9$\overline{)405}$

23)   5$\overline{)110}$

24)   10$\overline{)140}$

25)   10$\overline{)500}$

26)   6$\overline{)282}$

27)   10$\overline{)790}$

28)   2$\overline{)128}$

29) 4)¯336

30) 10)¯960

31) 10)¯800

32) 12)¯1,152

33) 5)¯95

34) 5)¯450

35) 5)¯305

36) 7)¯224

37) 9)¯144

38) 10)¯80

39) 10)¯320

40) 5)¯335

41) 9)¯54

42) 9)¯270

43) 6)¯324

44) 5)¯475

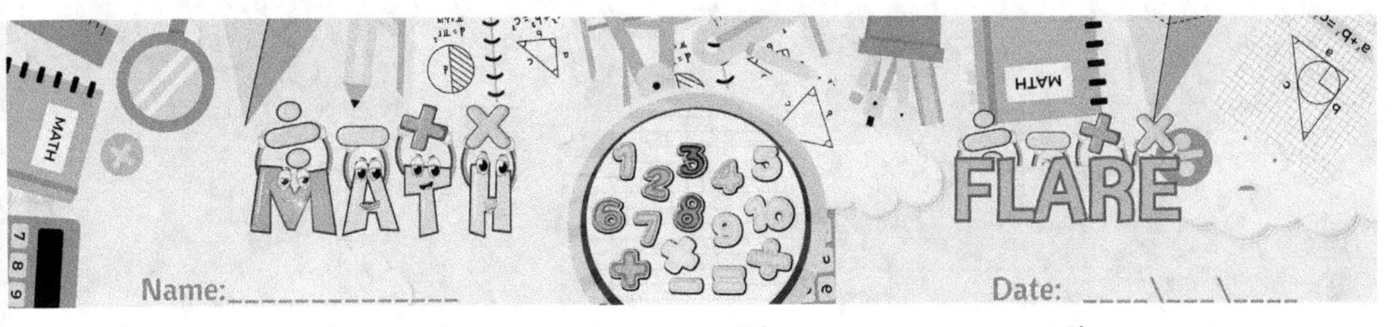

45) $5\overline{)150}$

46) $6\overline{)234}$

47) $2\overline{)98}$

48) $8\overline{)592}$

49) $2\overline{)36}$

50) $11\overline{)1,023}$

51) $10\overline{)200}$

52) $12\overline{)204}$

53) $9\overline{)612}$

54) $12\overline{)1,176}$

55) $10\overline{)1,000}$

56) $6\overline{)72}$

57) $3\overline{)234}$

58) $2\overline{)136}$

59) $10\overline{)110}$

60) $9\overline{)720}$

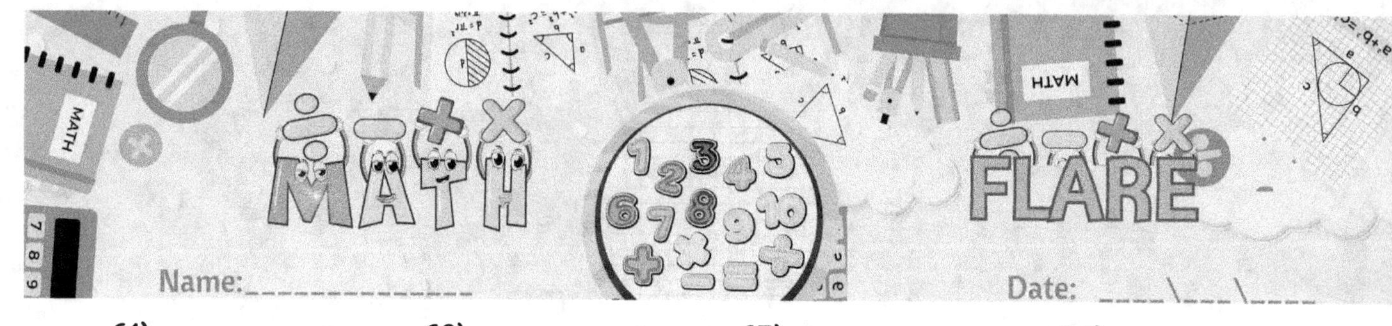

61)

$$7\overline{)280}$$

62)

$$4\overline{)100}$$

63)

$$10\overline{)370}$$

64)

$$2\overline{)66}$$

65)

$$6\overline{)48}$$

66)

$$4\overline{)96}$$

67)

$$4\overline{)216}$$

68)

$$5\overline{)470}$$

69)

$$7\overline{)525}$$

70)

$$7\overline{)245}$$

71)

$$2\overline{)70}$$

72)

$$10\overline{)390}$$

73)

$$3\overline{)87}$$

74)

$$6\overline{)582}$$

75)

$$11\overline{)1,067}$$

76)

$$5\overline{)45}$$

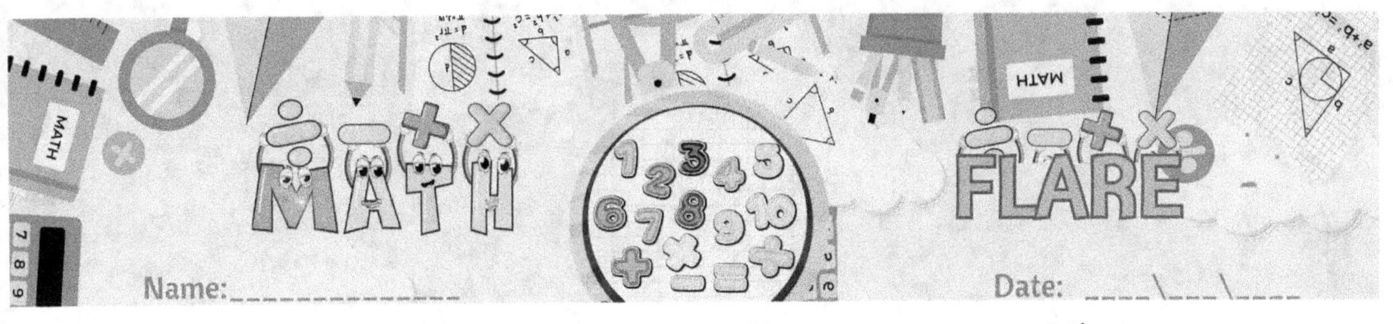

77) 5⟌200

78) 11⟌803

79) 5⟌185

80) 7⟌532

81) 9⟌189

82) 5⟌215

83) 7⟌371

84) 5⟌460

85) 7⟌21

86) 5⟌220

87) 3⟌240

88) 11⟌506

89) 10⟌710

90) 6⟌528

91) 8⟌480

92) 8⟌160

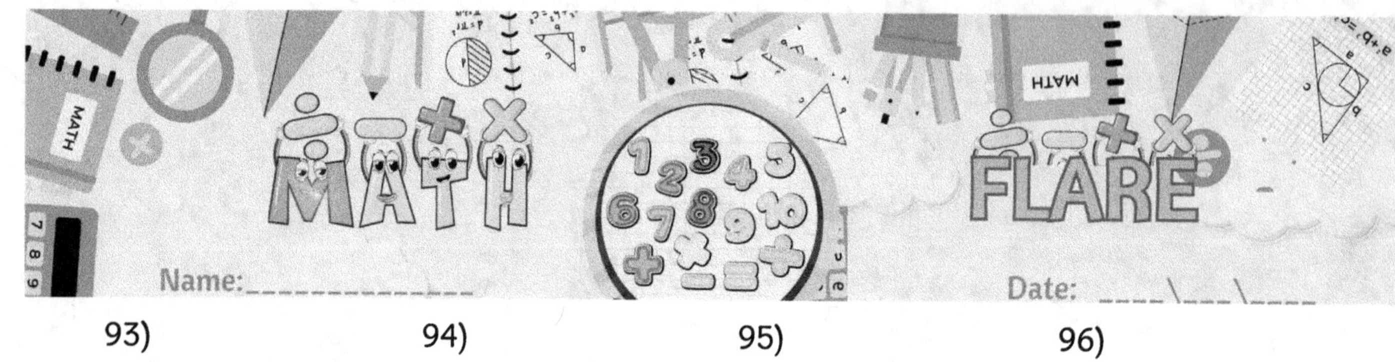

93)

3)270

94)

10)360

95)

8)520

96)

2)148

97)

10)900

98)

8)768

99)

10)130

100)

2)200

101)

5)455

102)

3)237

103)

9)90

104)

7)336

105)

5)310

106)

12)756

107)

11)836

108)

5)180

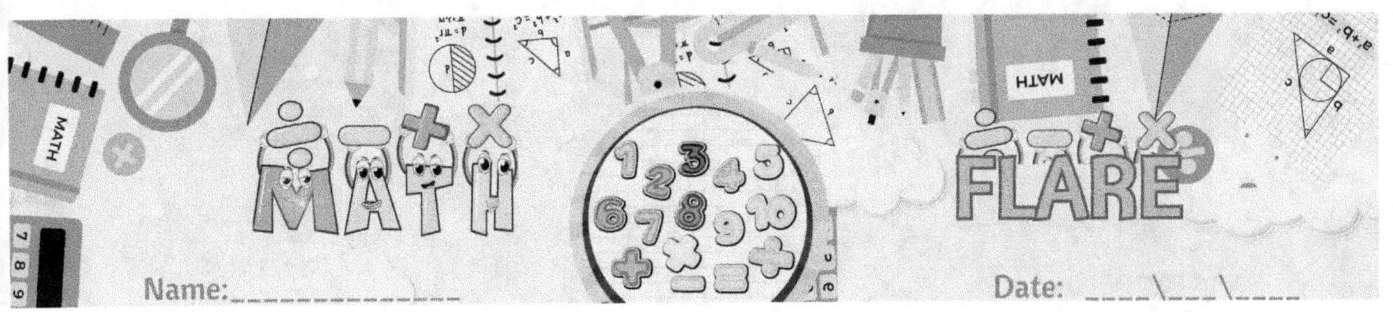

Multiplication Word Problems

1) A garden has eight rows of flowers and 15 flowers in each row. How many flowers are there in total?

    15   rows of flowers
    x 8   flowers in each row
    120   there are 120 flowers in total

2) Luna has 17 jars of jam. Each jar has nine ounces of jam. How many ounces of jam does Luna have in all?

3) Mia has 20 containers of paint. Each container holds 10 liters of paint. How many liters of paint does Mia have in total?

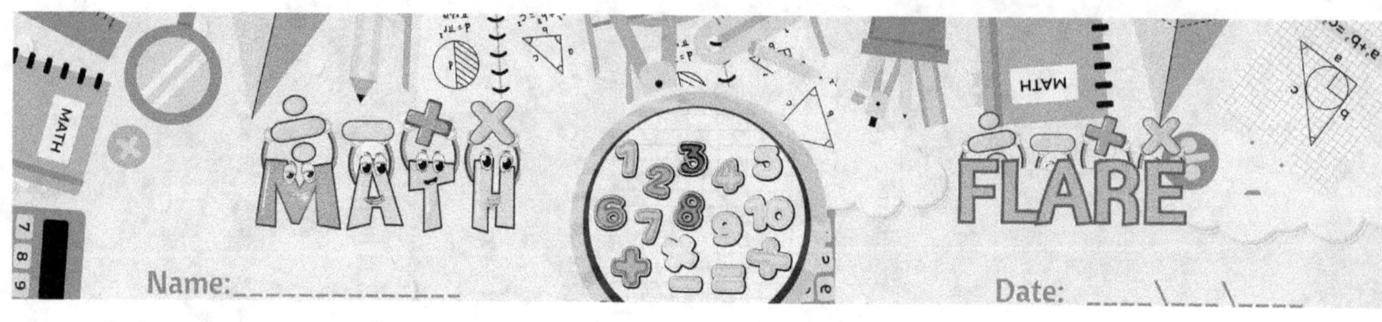

4) Michael can make 13 sandwiches in 1 hour. How many sandwiches can he make in 14 hour?

5) If a train travels at eight miles per hour for 13 hours, how far will it go?

6) Adalyn has nine books on each shelf, and there are 10 shelves. How many books does Adalyn have in total?

7) If a boat travels at 18 miles per hour for 17 hours, how far will it go?

8) Noah can type 18 words per minute. How many words can Noah type in two minutes?

9) Bella baked 18 batches of cookies. Each batch had nine cookies. How many cookies did Bella bake in all?

10) There are 15 pencils in each pack. If Everly buys 12 packs, how many pencils will Everly have?

11) A bookshelf can hold 10 books. If there are nine bookshelves in a room, how many books can the room hold in total?

12) Ellie has 14 vases of flowers. Each vase has 20 flowers. How many flowers does Ellie have in all?

13) A box contains 11 bottles of juice, and each bottle contains 20 ounces of juice. How many ounces of juice are there in total?

14) There are five seats on a bus. If 18 buses are needed to transport a group of people, how many people can the group consist of at most?

15) David can ride 12 miles in one hour. How far can he ride in 16 hours?

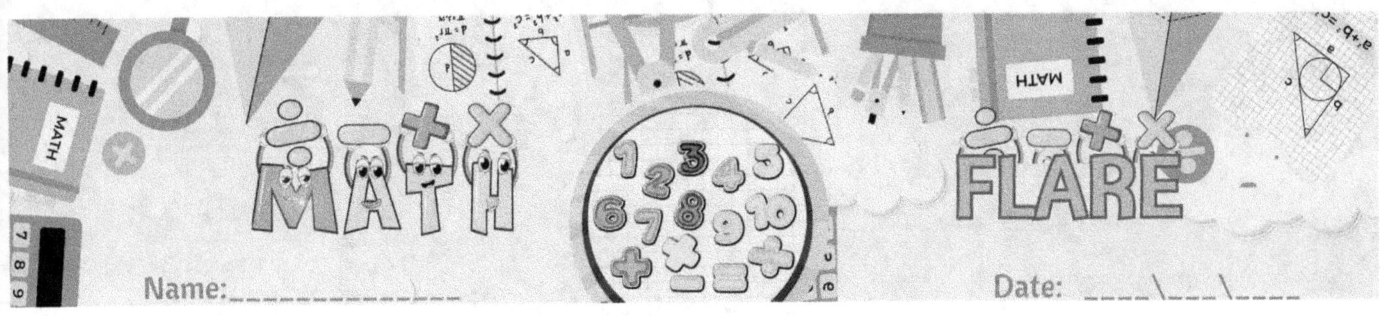

16) Miles can lift three pounds of weight. How many pounds of weight can he lift in 14 repetitions?

17) Josiah can catch five fish per hour. How many fish can Josiah catch in nine hours?

18) William can lift 19 pounds of weight. How many pounds of weight can William lift in total if he lifts for three sets?

19) Serenity has four books. Each book has 10 pages. How many pages does Serenity have in all?

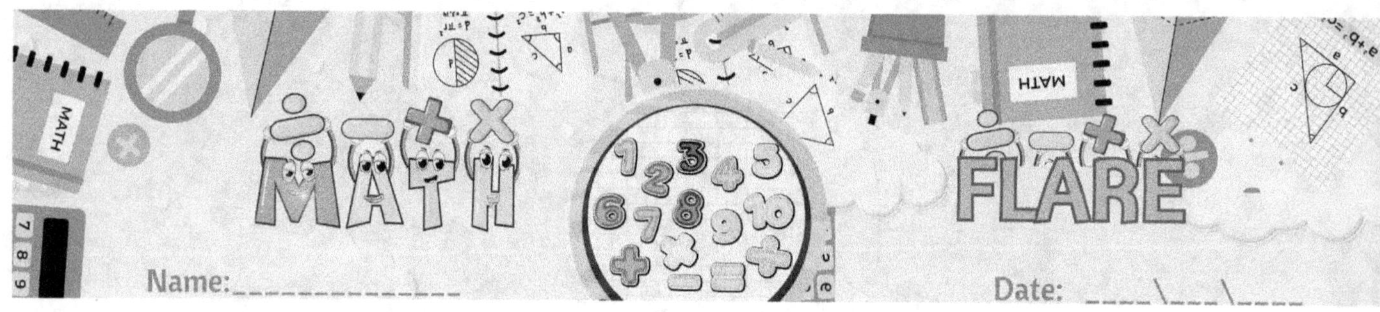

20) Xavier earns 15 dollars per hour. How much will Xavier earn after working for six hours?

21) There are two flosses in each bag. If Isabelle buys four bags, how many flosses will Isabelle have?

22) There are two shelves in Isaac's bookcase. Six books can fit on each shelf. How many books can the bookcase hold in total?

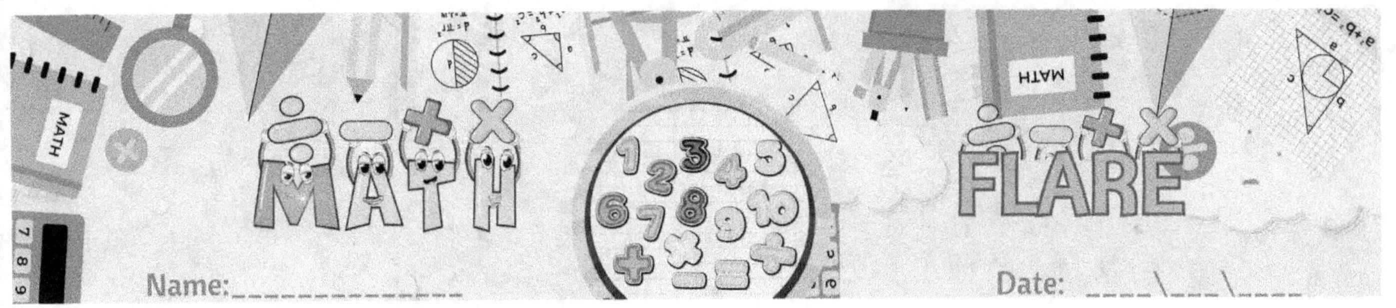

Division Word Problems

1) Nolan read a book that had 1,122 pages in 17 days. If he read the same number of pages each day, how many pages did he read per day?

$$17 \overline{)1122} = 66$$

Nolan read 66 pages per day.

$$\begin{array}{r} 66 \\ 17\overline{)1122} \\ -102 \\ \hline 102 \\ 102 \\ \hline 0 \end{array}$$

2) Madelyn bought 15 cookies for a total of $1,050. How much did each cookies cost?

3) If Isabella has 462 cakes and wants to divide them equally among 11 friends, how many cakes will each friend get?

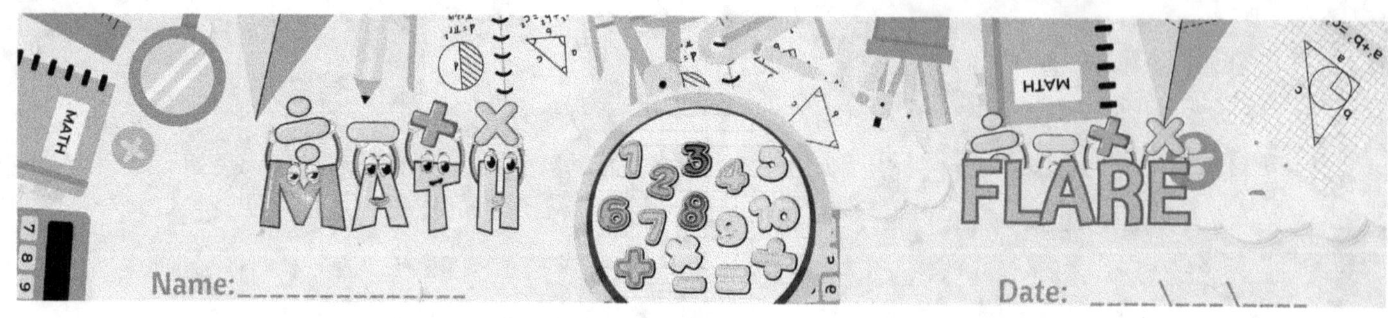

4) At a restaurant, nine friends decided to divide the bill equally. If each person paid $100, then what was the total bill?

5) Madison made 60 cookies for a bake sale. She put the cookies in bags, with six cookies in each bag. How many bags did she have for the bake sale?

6) A box of candies has 405 candies. If nine children each get an equal number of candies, how many candies will each child get?

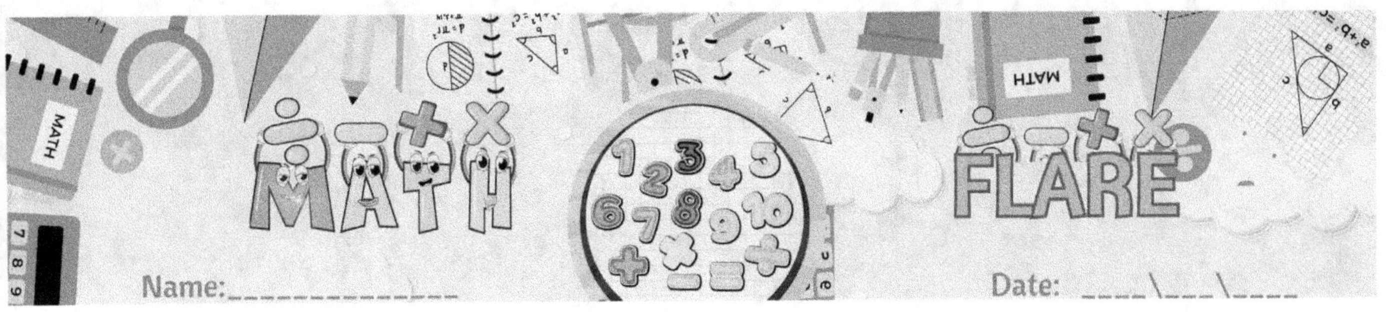

7) Paisley has $144 and she wants to buy three scarves that cost the same amount. How much does each scarves cost?

8) If a field is 39 acres and it is divided into three equal parts, how many acres is each part?

9) Hunter scored 252 points in seven games. What is his average score per game?

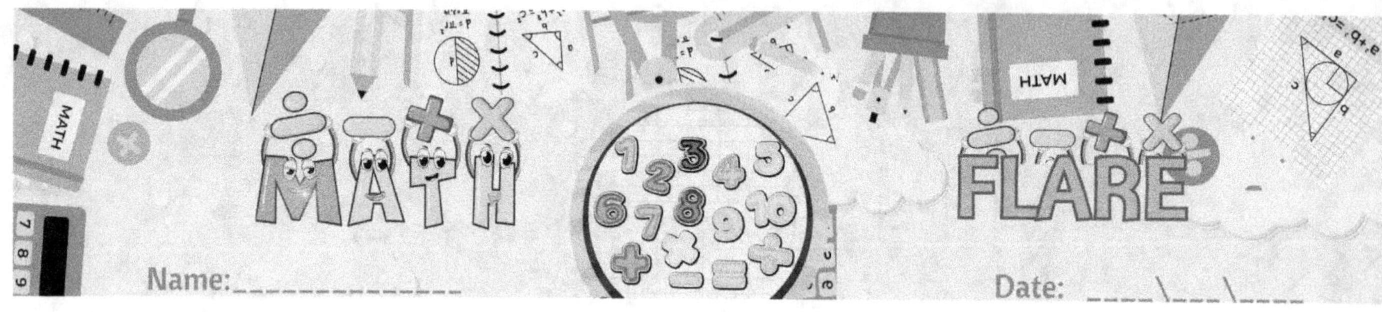

10) A recipe calls for 720 cups of sugar to make 12 cookies. How much sugar is needed to make 1 cookie?

11) Isaac is reading a book with 190 pages. If Isaac wants to read the same number of pages every day, how many pages would Isaac have to read each day to finish in five days?

12) A pool is 340 meters long. If it is divided into 17 equal parts, how long is each part?

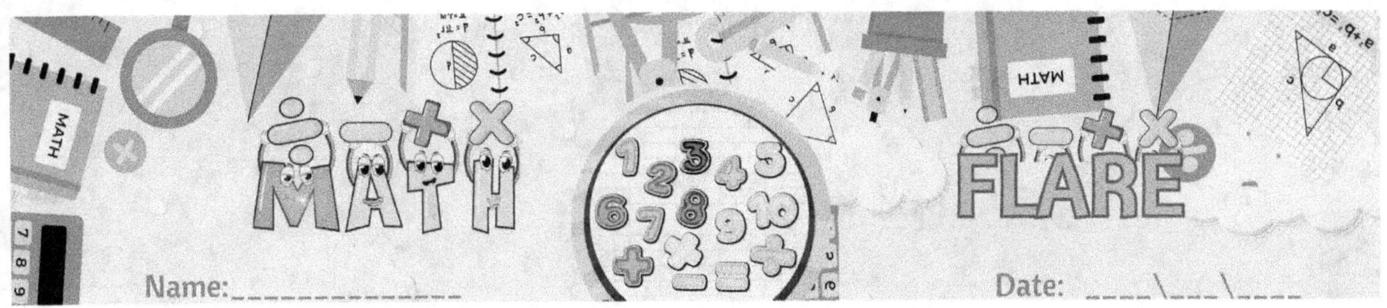

13) Jade can run 1,843 miles in 19 hours. How many miles can she run in 1 hour?

14) A box contains 708 candy bars. If each candy bar has 12 calories, how many calories are there in the box?

15) A car can travel 585 miles on nine gallons of gas. How many miles can it travel on 1 gallon of gas?

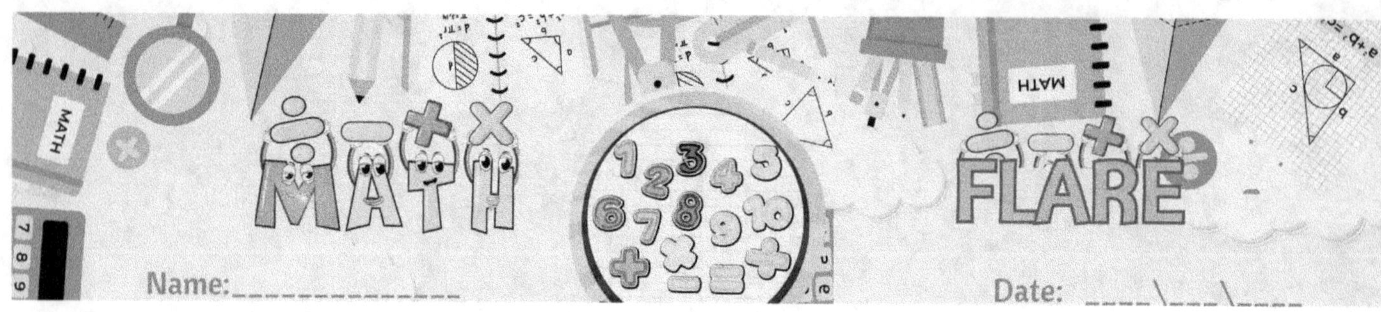

16) Serenity baked 34 cakes for a party. If she wants to divide them into 17 equal portions, how many cakes will each portion have?

17) Addison has 560 cookies and wants to divide them equally into 20 bags. How many cookies will be in each bag?

18) If a rope is 549 meters long and you want to cut it into nine equal pieces, how long will each piece be?

Name:_________________   Date: ____________

19) If a garden is 30 feet long and it is divided into six equal parts, how long is each part?

20) If a box contains 392 needles and each person can have eight needles, how many people can be served from that box?

21) How many nine cm pieces of pipe can you cut from a pipe that is 459 cm long?

Chapter. 03

Decimals

Adding Decimals

Adding decimals is like adding whole numbers, but we must align the decimal points carefully. For instance, when adding 49.88 and 45.78:

Step 1: Align the decimal points.

$$
\begin{array}{r}
49.88 \\
+\ 45.78 \\
\hline
\end{array}
$$

Step 2: Start adding from the rightmost digit (the ones place) and move to the left.

Add 8 and 8: 8 + 8 = 16. Write down 6 in the ones place and carry over 1 to the tenths place.

$$
\begin{array}{r}
49.88 \\
+\ 45.78 \\
\hline
6
\end{array}
$$

Step 3: Add the tenths place.

Add 1 (carried over from the previous step), 8, and 7: 1 + 8 + 7 = 16. Write down 6 in the tenths place and carry over 1 to the hundredths place.

$$
\begin{array}{r}
49.88 \\
+\ 45.78 \\
\hline
66
\end{array}
$$

Step 4: Continue adding digits to the left until you reach the leftmost digit:

$$
\begin{array}{r}
49.88 \\
+\ 45.78 \\
\hline
9566
\end{array}
$$

<u>Step 5: Finally, write the sum with the decimal point directly below the decimal points in the original numbers.</u>

$$49.88$$
$$+\ 45.78$$
$$95.66$$

Subtracting Decimals

Subtracting decimals follows a process like adding decimals, except instead of adding the numbers, we subtract them.

Let's solve more problems:

$$10.26 \qquad 87.11$$
$$+\ 80.45 \qquad -\ 11.31$$
$$90.71 \qquad 75.80$$

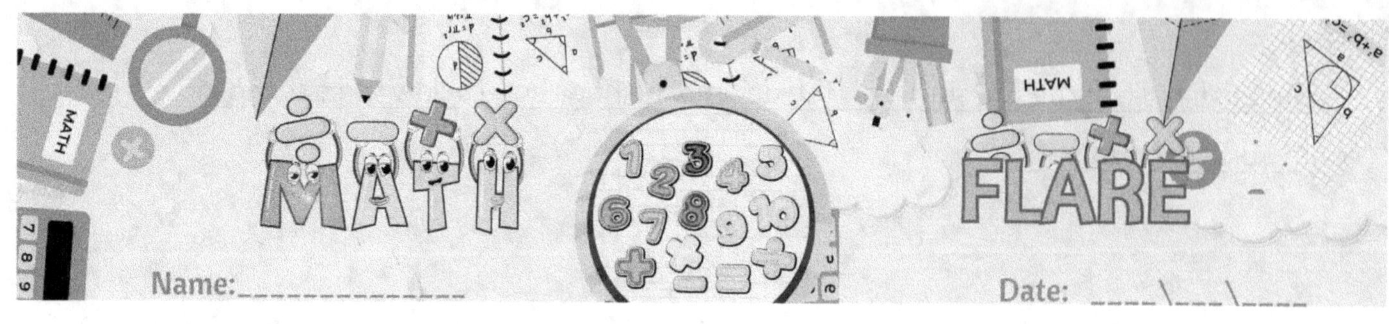

Adding Decimals

Find the sum.

1)   49.88
  + 45.78
    95.66

2)   10.26
  + 80.45
    90.71

3)   49.19
  + 99.52

4)   31.74
  + 52.03

5)   10.87
  + 39.33

6)   75.97
  + 18.19

7)   91.23
  + 88.13

8)   88.77
  + 17.40

9)   58.61
  + 54.95

10)   66.09
  + 33.46

11)   97.44
  + 54.02

12)   50.98
  + 64.16

13)   10.80
  + 86.05

14)   34.57
  + 25.27

15)   49.48
  + 36.42

16)   64.56
  + 15.03

17)   80.15
  + 18.72

18)   40.93
  + 13.42

19)   98.10
  + 39.18

20)   13.31
  + 34.99

21) 60.88 + 84.73	22) 78.69 + 41.30	23) 12.49 + 93.83	24) 74.20 + 82.30
25) 66.47 + 28.86	26) 22.65 + 52.73	27) 80.08 + 96.94	28) 41.75 + 95.85
29) 94.79 + 46.09	30) 79.66 + 63.13	31) 74.95 + 16.47	32) 12.55 + 74.44
33) 74.76 + 70.94	34) 38.02 + 82.51	35) 57.20 + 85.35	36) 19.29 + 29.44
37) 51.65 + 41.09	38) 72.57 + 22.70	39) 75.32 + 19.68	40) 61.67 + 16.96

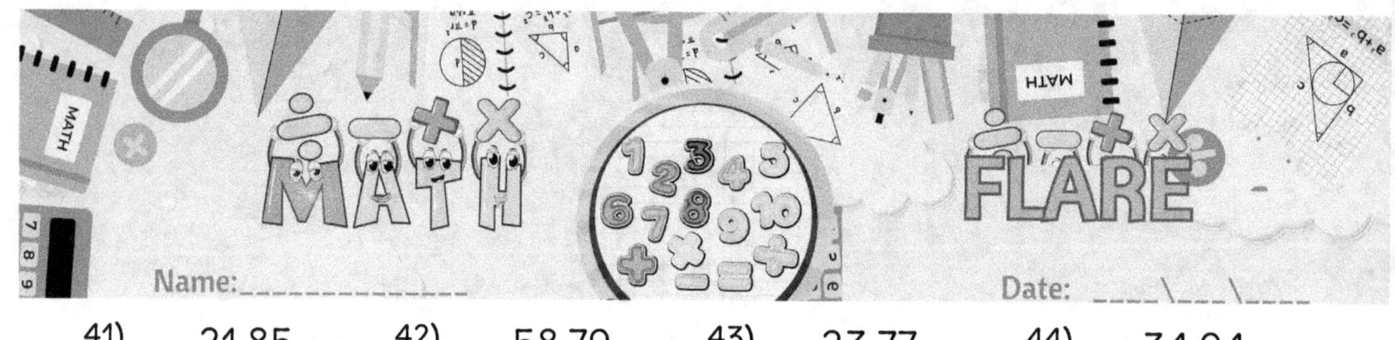

41) 21.85 + 52.26	42) 58.79 + 30.62	43) 23.77 + 21.83	44) 34.94 + 83.20
45) 76.96 + 45.07	46) 18.62 + 62.01	47) 59.51 + 50.16	48) 60.04 + 54.40
49) 82.18 + 14.25	50) 66.53 + 41.54	51) 65.80 + 91.68	52) 35.09 + 81.11
53) 19.58 + 93.21	54) 11.09 + 48.99	55) 34.37 + 29.05	56) 30.53 + 85.11
57) 84.40 + 72.70	58) 51.29 + 32.68	59) 57.68 + 81.92	60) 60.68 + 62.93

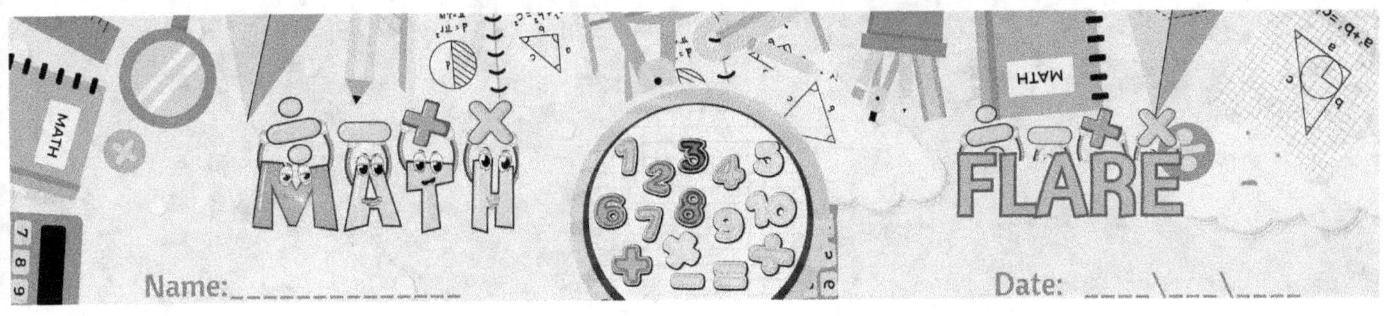

Subtracting Decimals

Find the difference.

1)   87.11
   - 11.31
   ____
      75.80

2)   42.86
   - 41.05
   ____
       1.81

3)   88.25
   - 42.47
   ____

4)   31.86
   - 14.72
   ____

5)   25.16
   - 15.51
   ____

6)   88.82
   - 22.15
   ____

7)   76.07
   - 57.09
   ____

8)   24.14
   - 13.77
   ____

9)   67.87
   - 21.09
   ____

10)   83.66
   - 73.85
   ____

11)   90.62
   - 30.53
   ____

12)   80.56
   - 30.35
   ____

13)   99.41
   - 26.33
   ____

14)   92.36
   - 80.02
   ____

15)   57.43
   - 37.85
   ____

16)   85.48
   - 77.16
   ____

17)   82.65
   - 54.00
   ____

18)   44.23
   - 11.33
   ____

19)   94.70
   - 83.61
   ____

20)   85.69
   - 53.52
   ____

21)
$$65.25 - 15.92$$

22)
$$94.76 - 43.13$$

23)
$$97.62 - 19.01$$

24)
$$86.14 - 73.08$$

25)
$$73.59 - 46.78$$

26)
$$85.31 - 73.80$$

27)
$$64.83 - 32.71$$

28)
$$26.35 - 16.56$$

29)
$$67.86 - 49.52$$

30)
$$56.37 - 35.22$$

31)
$$93.27 - 79.24$$

32)
$$64.35 - 20.54$$

33)
$$90.98 - 58.24$$

34)
$$78.29 - 74.91$$

35)
$$92.65 - 11.49$$

36)
$$43.80 - 38.50$$

37)
$$31.92 - 12.69$$

38)
$$97.75 - 16.07$$

39)
$$82.16 - 54.29$$

40)
$$65.33 - 34.18$$

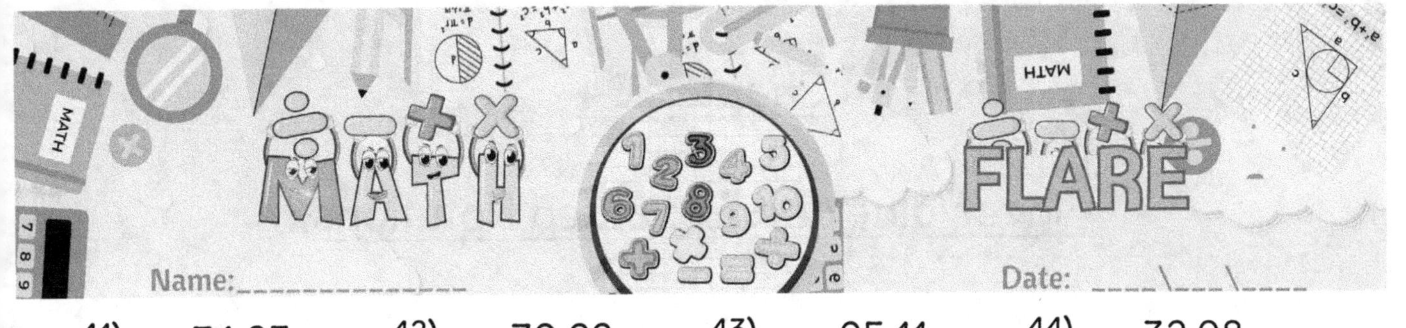

41)   74.23
    − 15.86
    ____

42)   70.22
    − 14.51
    ____

43)   95.11
    − 33.67
    ____

44)   32.98
    − 19.62
    ____

45)   45.60
    − 17.59
    ____

46)   94.91
    − 35.85
    ____

47)   97.03
    − 31.94
    ____

48)   34.56
    − 21.41
    ____

49)   28.48
    − 25.37
    ____

50)   76.07
    − 34.00
    ____

51)   77.67
    − 61.78
    ____

52)   93.38
    − 35.89
    ____

53)   70.12
    − 15.97
    ____

54)   70.46
    − 63.76
    ____

55)   80.70
    − 56.31
    ____

56)   92.03
    − 86.46
    ____

57)   91.57
    − 91.54
    ____

58)   79.94
    − 49.42
    ____

59)   64.53
    − 17.83
    ____

60)   82.96
    − 65.61
    ____

Chapter. 04

Place Value and Expanded Notations

Place value tells us the value of a digit in a number based on where it's placed.

Imagine we have the number 45,643. It has five digits: 4, 5, 6, 4, and 3.

Now, each digit holds a special place. Let's break down the number 45,643:

- The first digit, 4, is in the ten thousands place.

- The second digit, 5, is in the thousands place.

- The third digit, 6, is in the hundreds place.

- The fourth digit, 4, is in the tens place.

- The fifth digit, 3, is in the ones place.

When we add these values together, we find the value of the entire number:

$$40000 + 5000 + 600 + 40 + 3 = 45,643$$

Expanded notation helps us see the individual value of each digit in a number and how they contribute to the overall value of the number. It's like breaking down a big puzzle into smaller pieces to understand it better!

So, in expanded notation, we can write 45,643 as: 40000 (from ten thousand place) + 5000 (from thousands place) + 600 (from the hundreds place) + 40 (from the tens place) + 3 (from the ones place).

Let's solve some problems:

Place value of the underlined digit:

$$13.027 = \underline{\text{3 ones}}$$

Expanded notations:

7,409.3   7 thousands + 4 hundreds + 9 ones + 3 tenths

52,374   5 ten thousands + 2 thousands + 3 hundreds + 7 tens + 4 ones

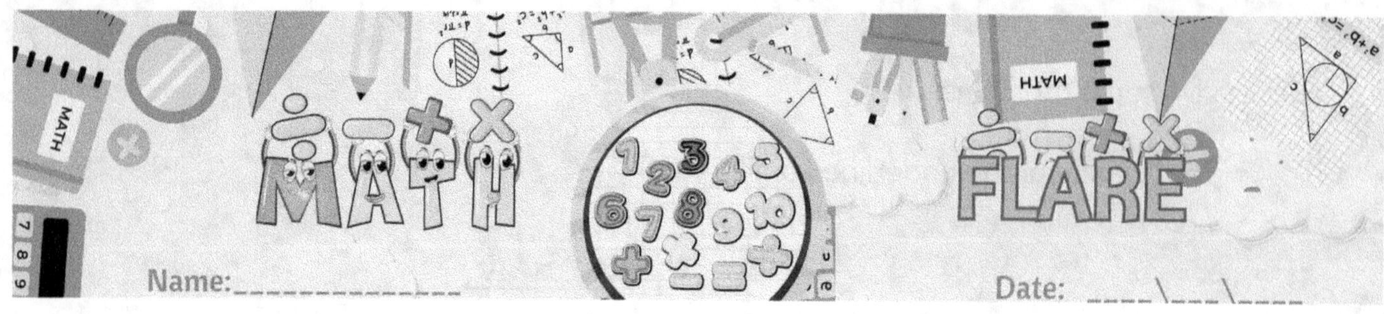

Place Value

Determine the place value of the underlined digit.

1) 1<u>3</u>.027 =   3 ones

2) 1<u>2</u>,903 =

3) 789.7<u>9</u> =

4) <u>8</u>,160.1 =

5) 61,8<u>5</u>8 =

6) 2,14<u>8</u> =

7) 4,091.<u>1</u> =

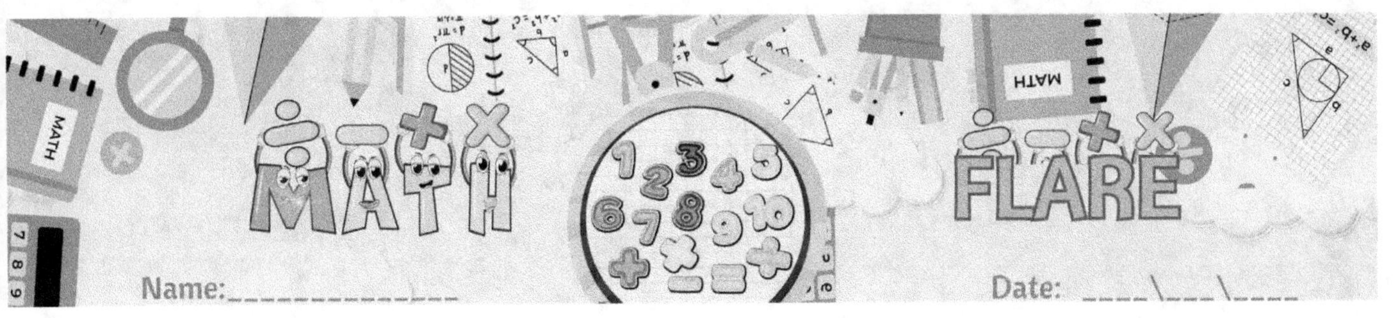

8) 8,911.<u>5</u> = _______________________________

9) 49.1<u>7</u>9 = _______________________________

10) 63,<u>5</u>04 = _______________________________

11) 987.5<u>4</u> = _______________________________

12) 73,<u>9</u>54 = _______________________________

13) 75,8<u>1</u>1 = _______________________________

14) 82.<u>1</u>3 = _______________________________

15) 2,<u>0</u>75.6 = _______________________________

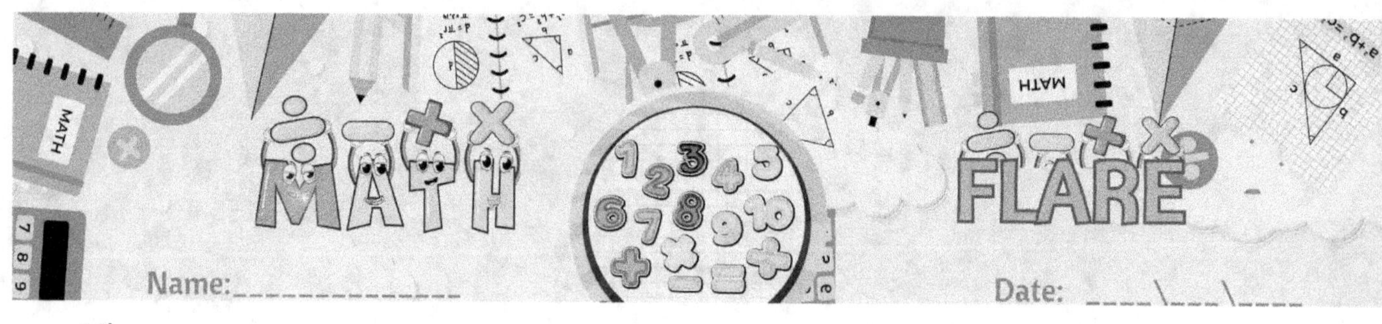

16) 908.2<u>4</u> = ___________________________

17) 59.<u>9</u>38 = ___________________________

18) 43.1<u>3</u>7 = ___________________________

19) 53,<u>6</u>42 = ___________________________

20) <u>4</u>75.52 = ___________________________

21) 83.<u>1</u>36 = ___________________________

22) 60.61<u>1</u> = ___________________________

23) 74.45<u>8</u> = ___________________________

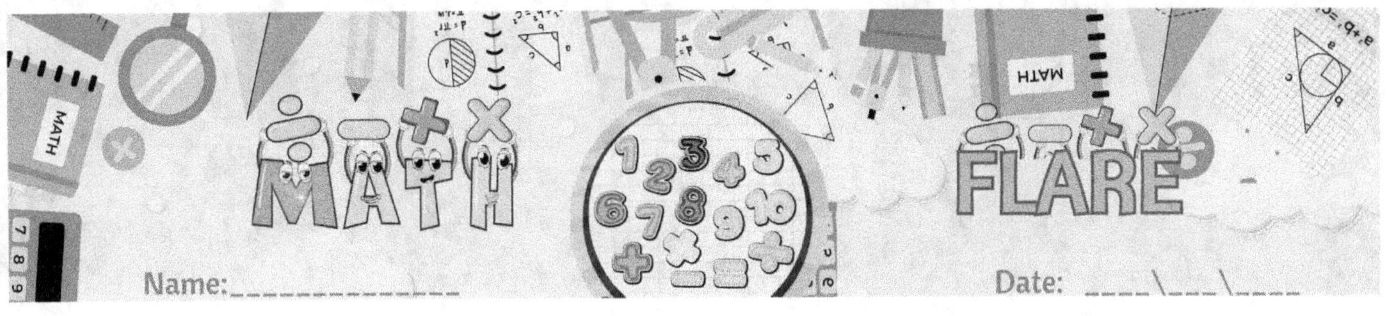

24) 55.93<u>9</u> = _______________________________

25) 5<u>5</u>.207 = _______________________________

26) 8<u>5</u>,259 = _______________________________

27) 13,2<u>2</u>8 = _______________________________

28) <u>1</u>,447 = _______________________________

29) 539.<u>2</u>7 = _______________________________

30) 74,<u>2</u>22 = _______________________________

31) <u>2</u>,036.6 = _______________________________

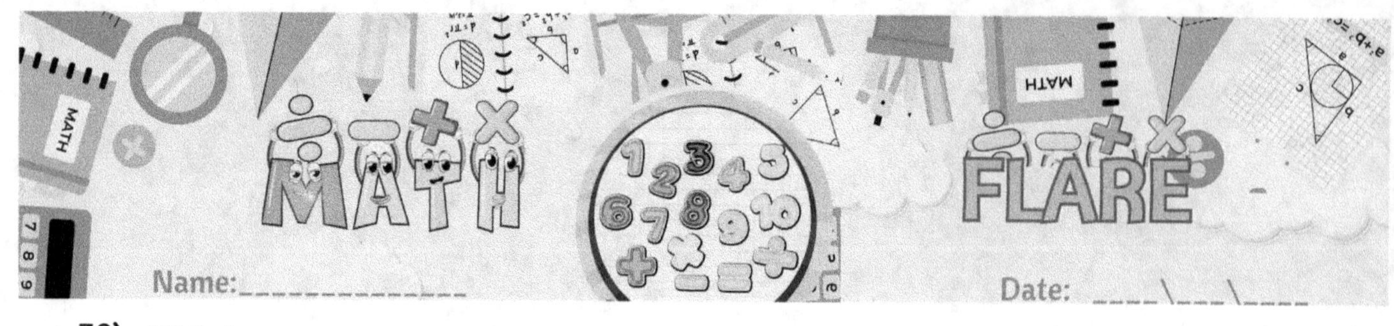

32) 498.<u>4</u> = _______________________________

33) <u>3</u>,905.1 = _______________________________

34) 8,09<u>0</u>.6 = _______________________________

35) 2,4<u>8</u>6.5 = _______________________________

36) <u>9</u>,257.6 = _______________________________

37) 6<u>9</u>1.62 = _______________________________

38) <u>1</u>8.345 = _______________________________

39) 19,34<u>8</u> = _______________________________

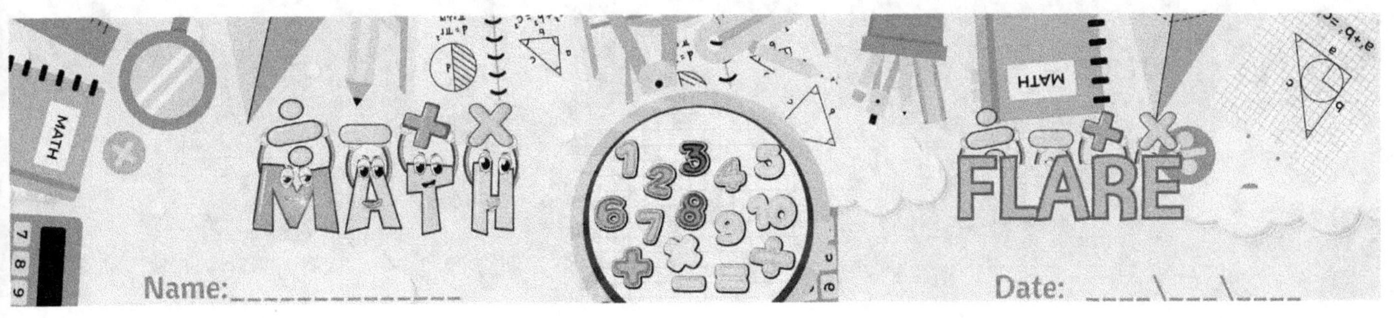

40) 7,434.7 = _______________________________

41) 38.349 = _______________________________

42) 997.49 = _______________________________

43) 643.29 = _______________________________

44) 510.2 = _______________________________

45) 5,853.5 = _______________________________

46) 60,412 = _______________________________

47) 22.614 = _______________________________

48) 461.2<u>2</u> = _______________________

49) <u>2</u>,931.8 = _______________________

50) 9<u>9</u>.046 = _______________________

51) <u>1</u>,947.7 = _______________________

52) 3<u>7</u>,413 = _______________________

53) 758.2<u>7</u> = _______________________

54) 2,0<u>3</u>7.9 = _______________________

55) 4,531.<u>1</u> = _______________________

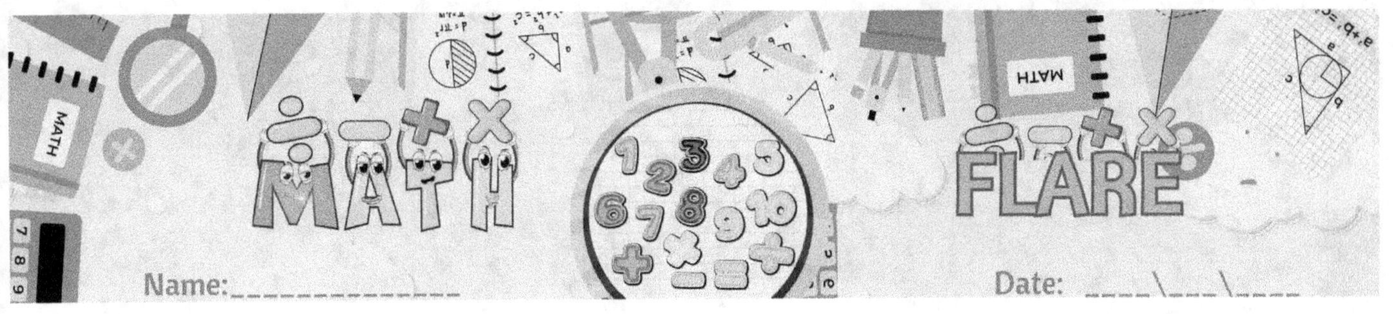

56) 52,4_15 = _______________________________

57) 38,4_44 = _______________________________

58) 33.0_4 = _______________________________

59) 363.9_4 = _______________________________

60) 76.59_7 = _______________________________

61) 1,8_25.1 = _______________________________

62) _36,441 = _______________________________

63) 451._88 = _______________________________

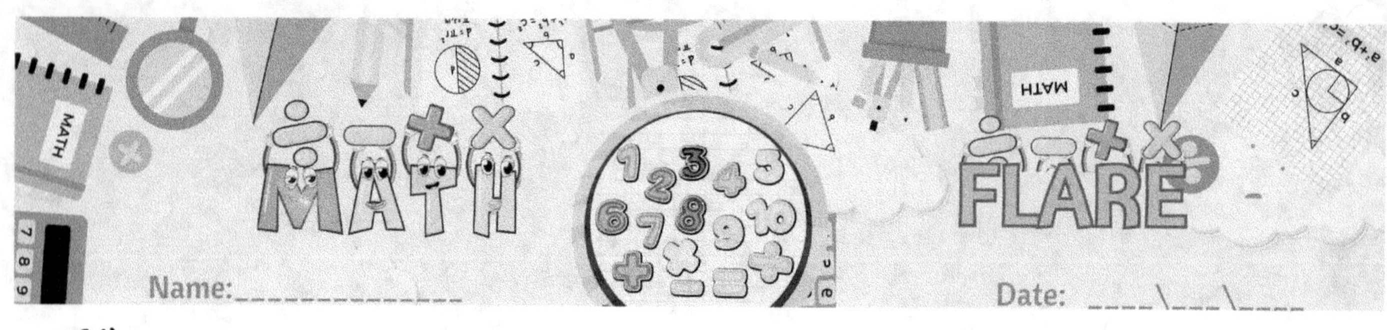

64) 74.956 = _______________________

65) 531.38 = _______________________

66) 58,914 = _______________________

67) 44.903 = _______________________

68) 949.04 = _______________________

69) 6,726.5 = _______________________

70) 28.18 = _______________________

Place Value: Expanded Notation

Provide the expanded notation for each value.

1) ___7,409.3___   7 thousands + 4 hundreds + 9 ones + 3 tenths

2) __________   6 hundreds + 9 tens + 9 ones + 2 tenths + 4 hundredths

3) __________   1 hundred + 4 tens + 4 ones + 2 tenths + 3 hundredths

4) __________   4 hundreds + 8 tens + 3 ones + 1 hundredth

5) __________   6 thousands + 6 hundreds + 3 ones + 5 tenths

6) __________   6 thousands + 5 hundreds + 2 tens + 2 ones + 9 tenths

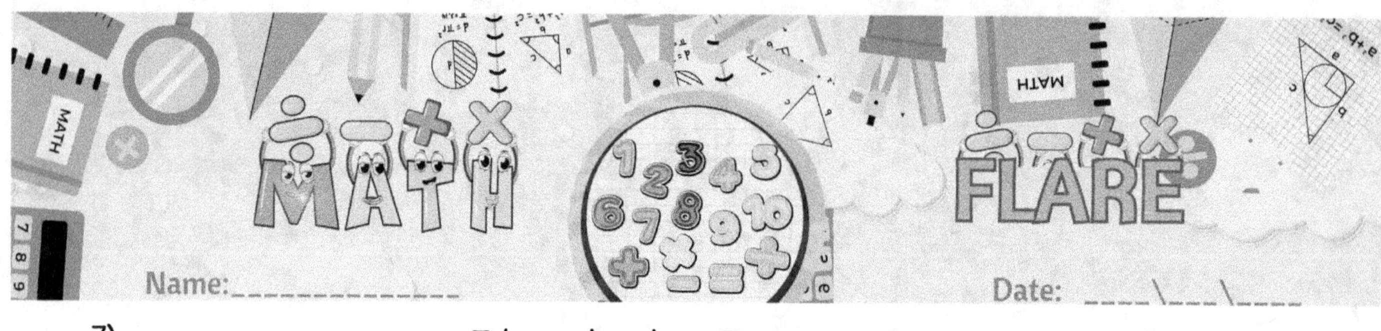

7) __________________ 7 hundreds + 3 tens + 6 ones + 7 tenths + 7 hundredths

8) __________________ 6 thousands + 9 hundreds + 1 ten + 7 ones + 6 tenths

9) __________________ 9 tens + 2 ones + 5 tenths + 1 hundredth + 5 thousandths

10) __________________ 6 thousands + 5 hundreds + 7 tens + 7 ones + 9 tenths

11) __________________ 5 hundreds + 1 ten + 1 one + 9 tenths + 1 hundredth

12) __________________ 3 ten thousands + 9 thousands + 7 hundreds + 1 ten + 4 ones

13) __________________ 8 hundreds + 5 ones + 7 tenths + 5 hundredths

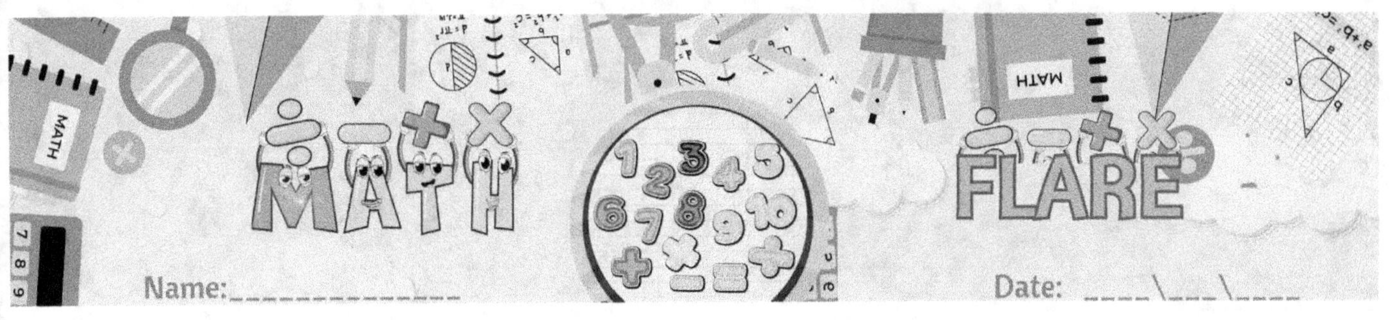

14) ___________________ 1 thousand + 8 hundreds + 8 ones + 5 tenths

15) ___________________ 6 ten thousands + 3 thousands + 2 hundreds +
2 tens + 4 ones

16) ___________________ 2 tens + 9 ones + 2 tenths + 7 hundredths + 8
thousandths

17) ___________________ 9 tens + 6 ones + 7 tenths + 2 hundredths + 4
thousandths

18) ___________________ 1 hundred + 2 tens + 8 ones + 6 tenths + 4
hundredths

19) ___________________ 2 thousands + 9 hundreds + 5 tens + 1 one + 2
tenths

20) ___________________ 1 ten thousand + 4 thousands + 3 hundreds +
2 tens + 2 ones

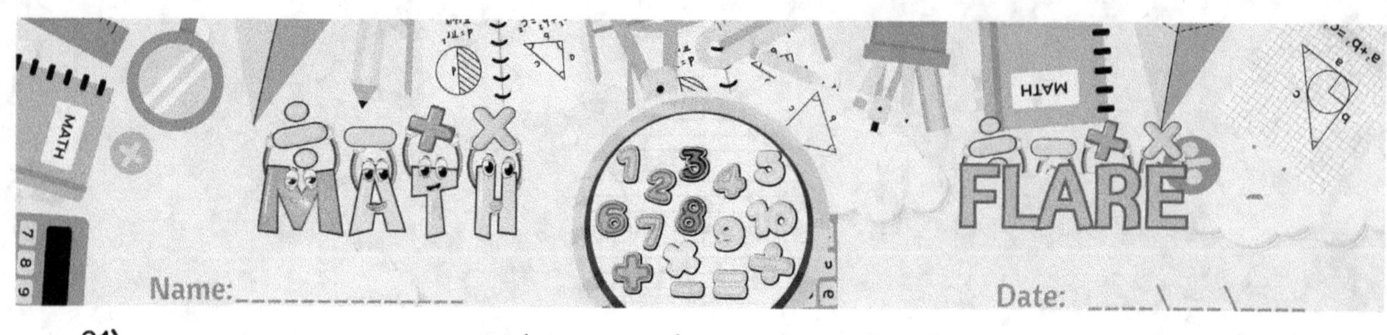

21) _________________ 2 thousands + 8 hundreds + 4 ones + 3 tenths

22) _________________ 7 hundreds + 9 tens + 4 ones + 4 tenths + 9 hundredths

23) _________________ 2 ten thousands + 2 thousands + 8 hundreds + 2 tens

24) _________________ 6 thousands + 7 hundreds + 7 tens + 8 ones

25) _________________ 5 thousands + 1 hundred + 3 tens + 2 ones + 4 tenths

26) _________________ 7 tens + 7 ones + 7 tenths + 9 hundredths

27) _________________ 3 hundreds + 4 tens + 8 ones + 3 tenths + 4 hundredths

28) _________________ 6 ten thousands + 5 thousands + 4 hundreds + 4 tens + 6 ones

29) _________________ 7 ten thousands + 6 thousands + 7 tens

30) _________________ 2 ten thousands + 2 thousands + 8 hundreds + 8 tens + 8 ones

31) _________________ 8 thousands + 8 ones + 3 tenths

32) _________________ 3 tens + 5 ones + 8 tenths + 6 hundredths + 6 thousandths

33) _________________ 9 tens + 1 one + 6 tenths + 3 hundredths

34) _________________ 9 hundreds + 1 ten + 9 ones + 3 tenths + 1 hundredth

35) _______________ 7 tens + 9 ones + 9 tenths + 7 hundredths + 6 thousandths

36) _______________ 2 thousands + 8 tens + 5 ones

37) _______________ 6 hundreds + 7 tens + 1 one + 1 tenth + 1 hundredth

38) _______________ 8 hundreds + 7 tens + 8 ones + 7 tenths + 9 hundredths

39) _______________ 3 tens + 2 ones + 8 tenths + 1 hundredth + 1 thousandth

40) _______________ 1 ten + 3 ones + 1 tenth + 2 hundredths

41) _______________ 1 ten + 5 ones + 6 tenths + 5 hundredths + 4 thousandths

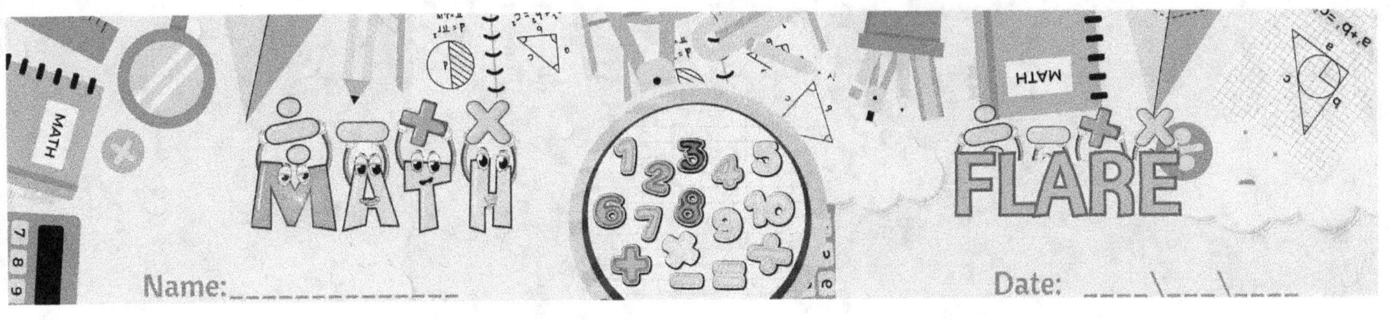

42) _________________ 4 tens + 1 one + 7 tenths + 4 hundredths + 7 thousandths

43) _________________ 7 ten thousands + 2 thousands + 3 hundreds + 7 tens + 7 ones

44) _________________ 4 tens + 3 ones + 2 tenths + 8 hundredths + 1 thousandth

45) _________________ 6 tens + 3 ones + 7 tenths + 4 thousandths

46) _________________ 3 ten thousands + 1 thousand + 2 hundreds + 9 tens + 4 ones

47) _________________ 7 ten thousands + 1 thousand + 8 hundreds + 5 tens + 9 ones

48) _________________ 8 tens + 8 ones + 2 tenths + 3 hundredths + 9 thousandths

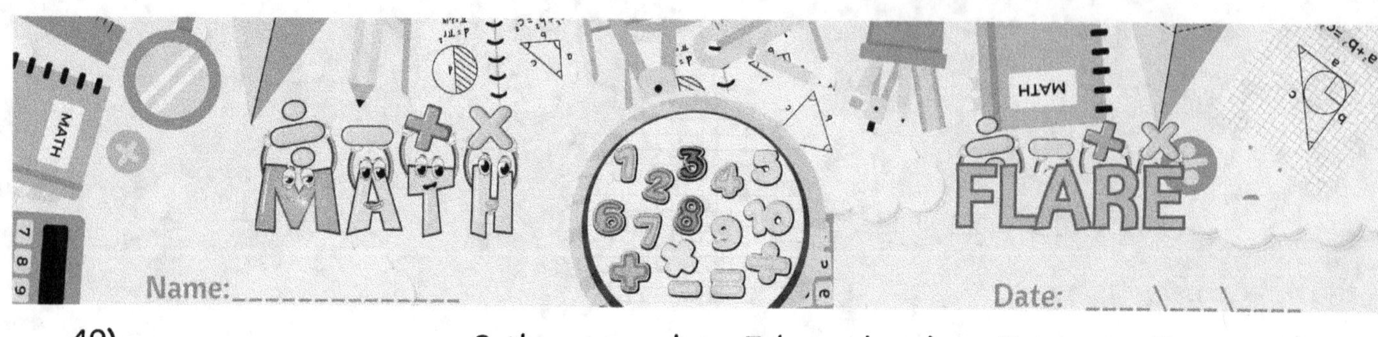

49) ________________ 9 thousands + 3 hundreds + 3 tens + 7 ones + 5 tenths

50) ________________ 1 ten thousand + 9 thousands + 5 ones

51) ________________ 1 ten thousand + 3 thousands + 3 hundreds + 7 tens + 6 ones

52) ________________ 6 hundreds + 2 tens + 2 ones + 8 tenths + 3 hundredths

53) ________________ 6 hundreds + 2 tens + 7 ones + 3 tenths + 7 hundredths

54) ________________ 9 hundreds + 3 tens + 1 one + 3 tenths + 9 hundredths

55) ________________ 8 ten thousands + 5 thousands + 1 hundred + 6 tens

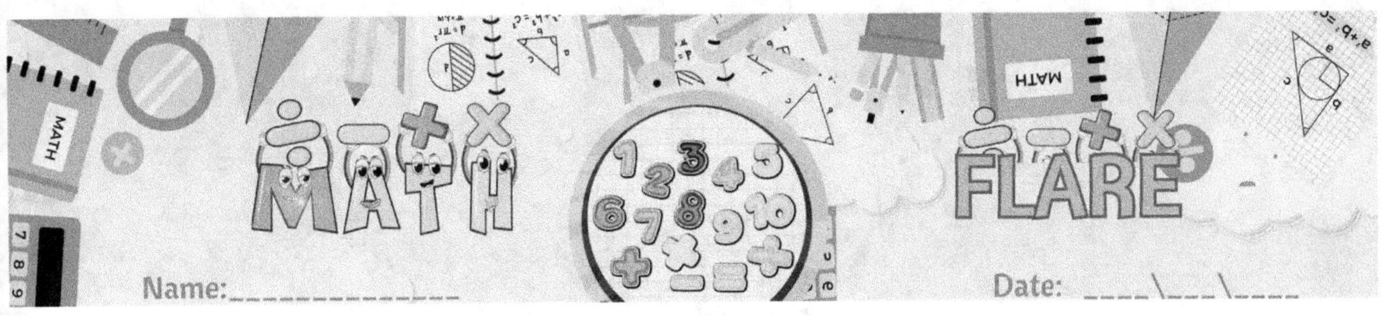

Name:_________________________   Date: ____________

56) _________________ 9 hundreds + 4 tens + 6 ones + 4 tenths + 3 hundredths

57) _________________ 5 thousands + 7 hundreds + 1 ten + 5 tenths

58) _________________ 4 thousands + 6 hundreds + 6 tens + 4 ones + 3 tenths

59) _________________ 9 thousands + 6 hundreds + 9 tens + 7 ones + 6 tenths

60) _________________ 8 thousands + 8 hundreds + 2 tens + 4 ones + 4 tenths

61) _________________ 4 hundreds + 3 ones + 9 tenths + 5 hundredths

62) _________________ 1 hundred + 8 tens + 2 ones + 3 tenths + 1 hundredth

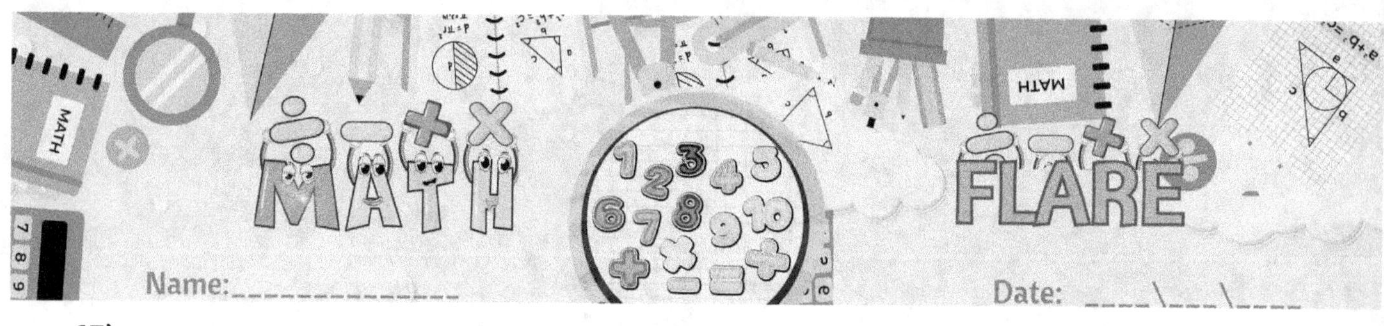

63) ___________________ 9 thousands + 3 hundreds + 1 ten + 5 tenths

64) ___________________ 7 tens + 9 ones + 6 tenths + 2 hundredths + 7 thousandths

65) ___________________ 8 tens + 5 ones + 6 tenths + 9 hundredths + 5 thousandths

66) ___________________ 2 tens + 5 ones + 3 tenths + 2 hundredths + 5 thousandths

67) ___________________ 4 ten thousands + 8 thousands + 8 tens + 3 ones

68) ___________________ 8 tens + 8 ones + 6 tenths + 4 hundredths + 3 thousandths

69) ___________________ 3 thousands + 8 hundreds + 1 ten + 8 tenths

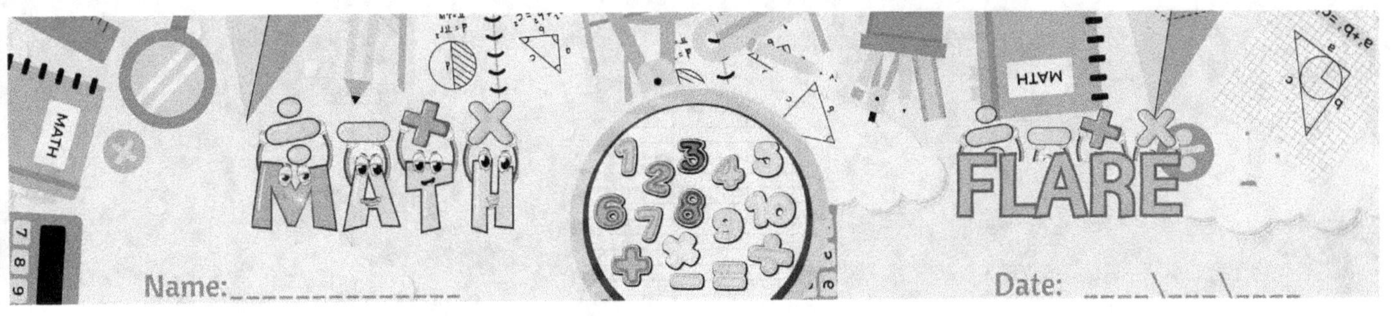

Place Value: Expanded Notation

Provide the expanded notation for each value.

1) 52,374   5 ten thousands + 2 thousands + 3 hundreds + 7 tens + 4 ones

2) 6,216.6

3) 1,884.5

4) 8,005.2

5) 2,639.2

6) 98.667

   88

7) 86,296 _______________________________

8) 170.72 _______________________________

9) 7,953.8 _______________________________

10) 14.076 _______________________________

11) 30.030 _______________________________

12) 15,931 _______________________________

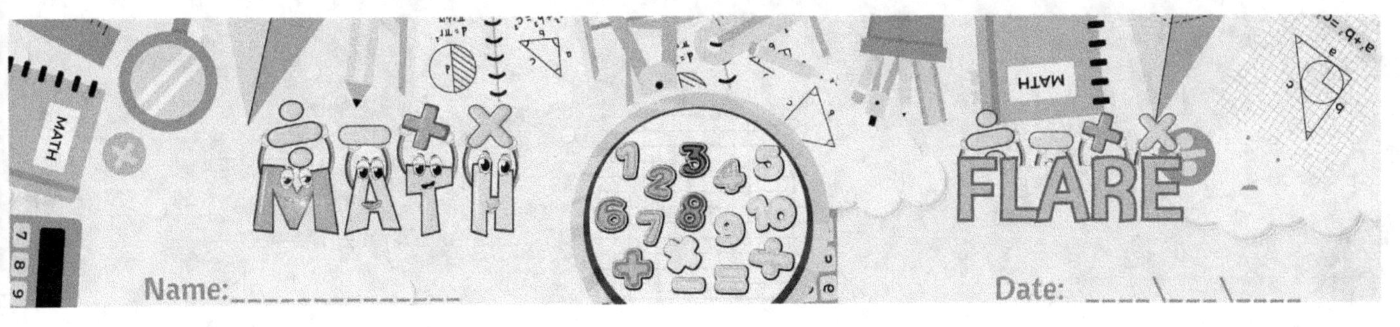

13) 4,659.4 _______________________________

____

14) 7,207.0 _______________________________

____

15) 67,065 _______________________________

____

16) 19.512 _______________________________

____

17) 2,779.9 _______________________________

____

18) 7,312.9 _______________________________

____

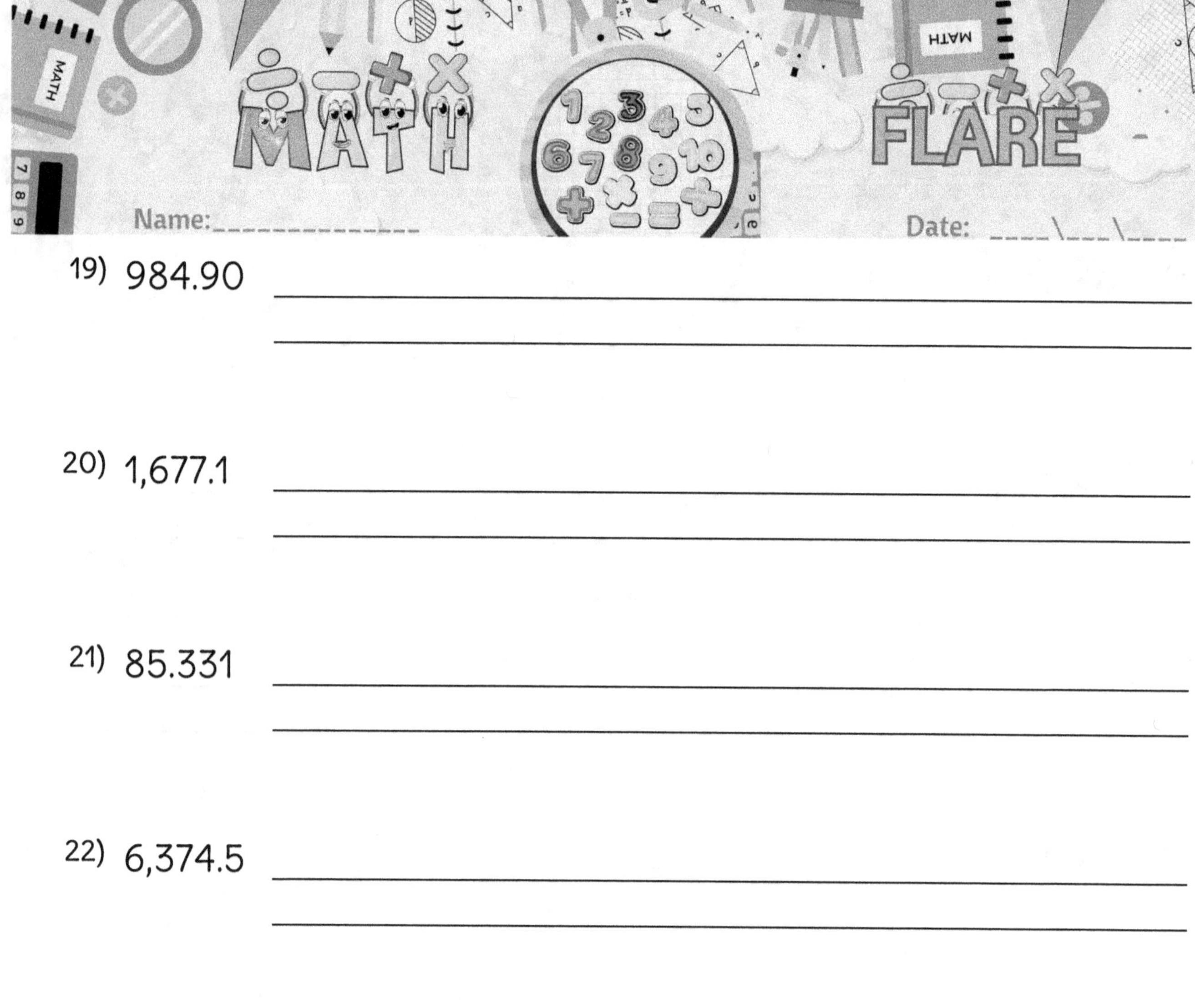

19) 984.90 ___________________________

20) 1,677.1 ___________________________

21) 85.331 ___________________________

22) 6,374.5 ___________________________

23) 3,046.8 ___________________________

24) 9,090.2 ___________________________

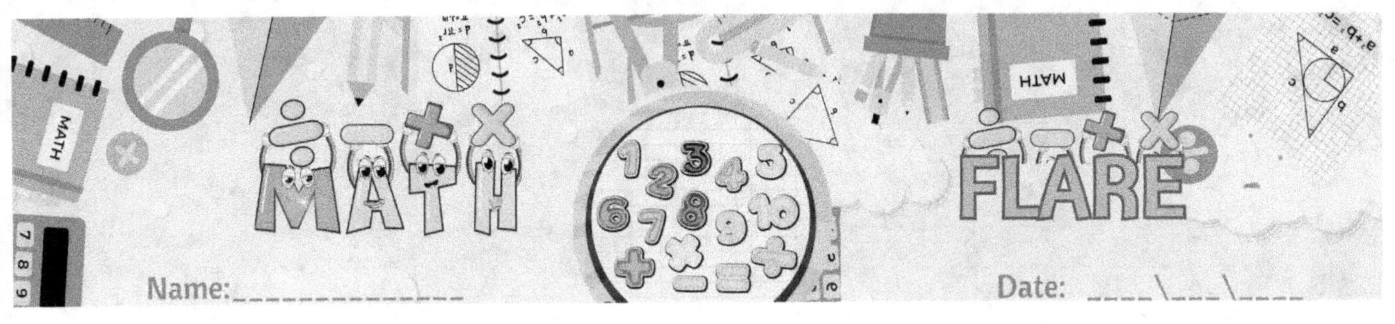

25) 44,566 __________________________

26) 72,724 __________________________

27) 974.22 __________________________

28) 4,864.1 __________________________

29) 92,749 __________________________

30) 57,585 __________________________

31) 48.379 ________________________
____

32) 83,210 ________________________
____

33) 8,321.5 ________________________
____

34) 60.131 ________________________
____

35) 51.001 ________________________
____

36) 56.838 ________________________
____

37) 94.530 _________________________

38) 82,230 _________________________

39) 4,634.5 _________________________

40) 944.71 _________________________

41) 98,864 _________________________

42) 87,571 _________________________

43) 77.566

____

____

44) 42,567

____

____

45) 769.46

____

____

46) 82.313

____

____

47) 93,800

____

____

48) 4,616.1

____

____

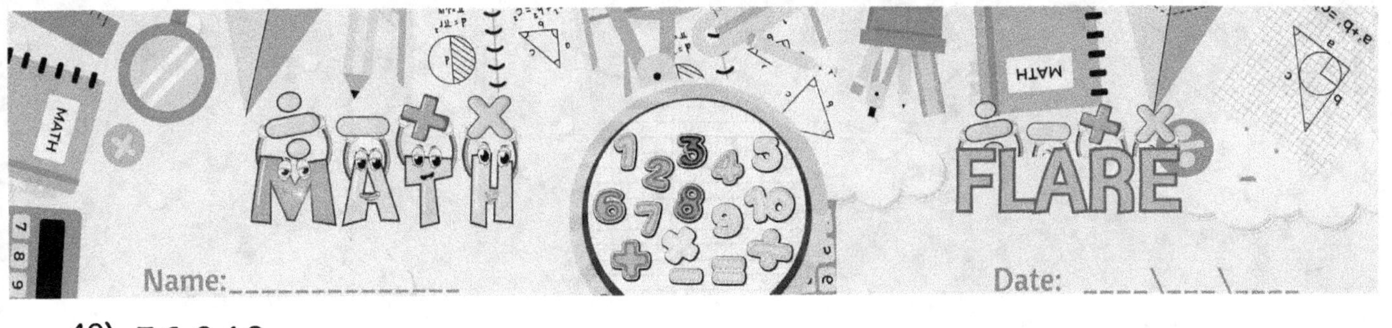

49) 36.040

50) 70.115

51) 6,789.6

52) 52.195

53) 4,959.2

54) 81,872

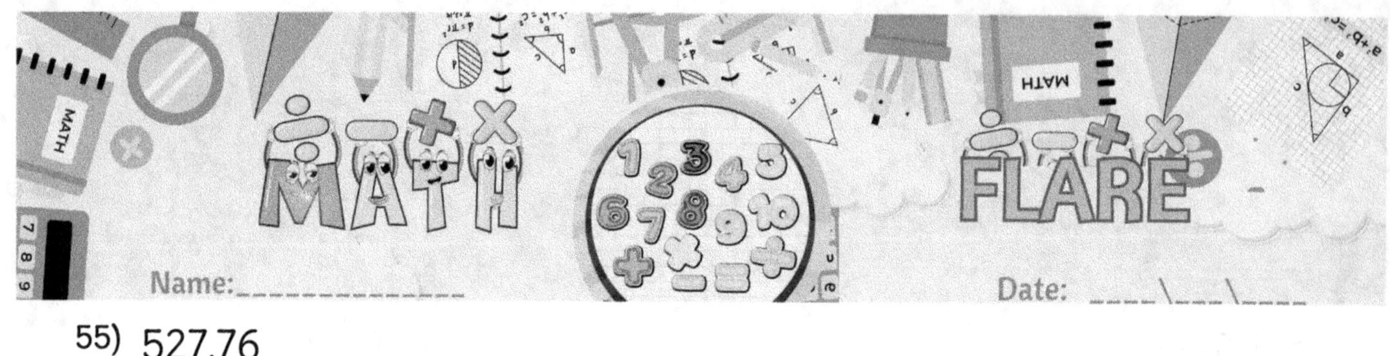

55) 527.76 _______________

56) 88.628 _______________

57) 41.698 _______________

58) 27,942 _______________

59) 4,548.6 _______________

60) 53,667 _______________

Chapter. 05

Fractions

Fractions represent parts of a whole. They consist of a numerator (the number on top) and a denominator (the number on the bottom).

For example:

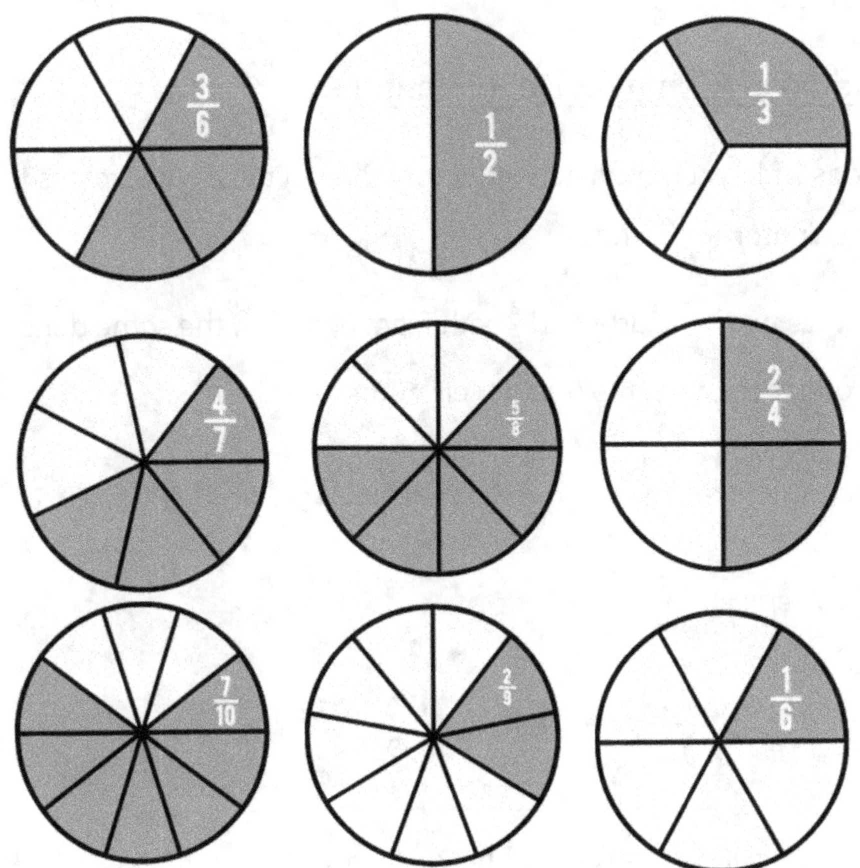

Comparing Fractions

When comparing fractions, we consider the size of their denominators. Generally, the larger the denominator, the smaller the fraction.

For example:

$$\frac{1}{3} \text{ is smaller than } \frac{1}{2} \text{ because the denominator 3 is larger than the denominator 2.}$$

If the denominators are the same, we can compare the numerators to determine which fraction is larger.

Let's solve a problem:

$$\frac{56}{60} \; \underline{<} \; \frac{57}{60}$$

Fractions Addition (Common Denominator)

To add fractions with a common denominator, we add their numerators together and keep the denominator the same.

For example: if we want to add $\frac{3}{5}$ and $\frac{2}{5}$ both fractions have the same denominator of 5. Therefore, to add them, we simply add their numerators:

$$\frac{3}{5} + \frac{2}{5} = \frac{3+2}{5} = \frac{5}{5}$$

Let's solve a problem:

$$\frac{1}{9} + \frac{7}{9} = \frac{1+7}{9} = \frac{8}{9}$$

Fractions Subtraction (Common Denominator)

To subtract fractions with a common denominator, we find the difference between their numerators and keep the denominator the same.

For example:

$$\frac{3}{5} - \frac{2}{5} = \frac{3-2}{5} = \frac{1}{5}$$

Let's solve a problem:

$$\frac{5}{8} - \frac{2}{8} = \frac{5-2}{8} = \frac{3}{8}$$

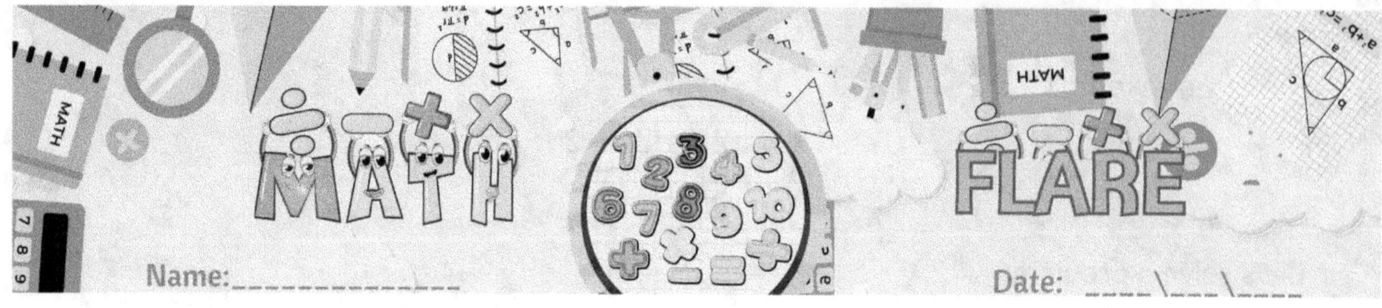

Fraction Identification

Identify fractions of each set of boxes.

1) $=\dfrac{2}{3}$ ___________________________

2) $=$ ___________________________

3) $=$ ___________________________

4) $=$ ___________________________

5) $=$ ___________________________

6) $=$ ___________________________

7) $=$ ___________________________

8) $=$ ___________________________

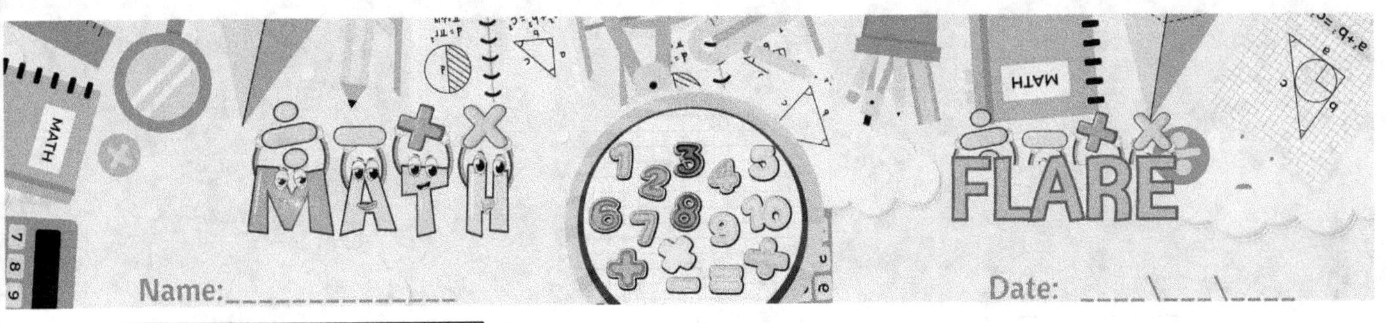

9)  =

____

10) =

____

11) =

____

12) =

____

13)  =

____

14) =

____

15) =

____

16) =

____

17) =

____

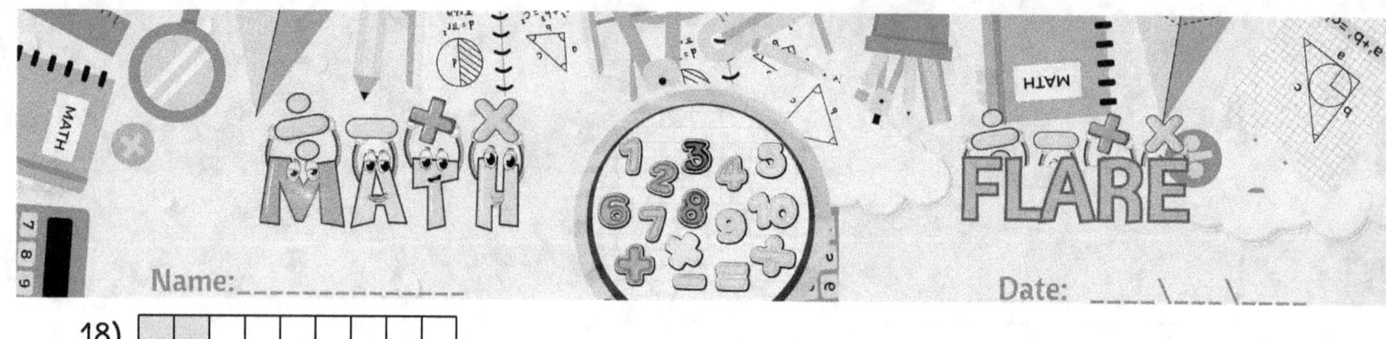

Name:______________________ Date: ________________

18) [bar] = ______________________

19) [bar] = ______________________

20) [bar] = ______________________

21) [bar] = ______________________

22) [bar] = ______________________

23) [bar] = ______________________

24) [bar] = ______________________

25) [bar] = ______________________

26) [bar] = ______________________

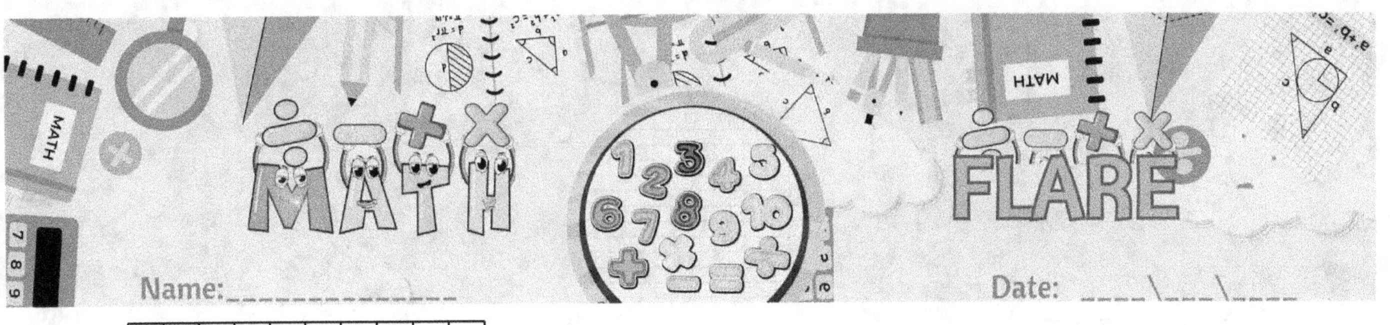

27) = _______________________________

28) = _______________________________

29) = _______________________________

30) = _______________________________

31) = _______________________________

32) = _______________________________

33) = _______________________________

34) = _______________________________

35) = _______________________________

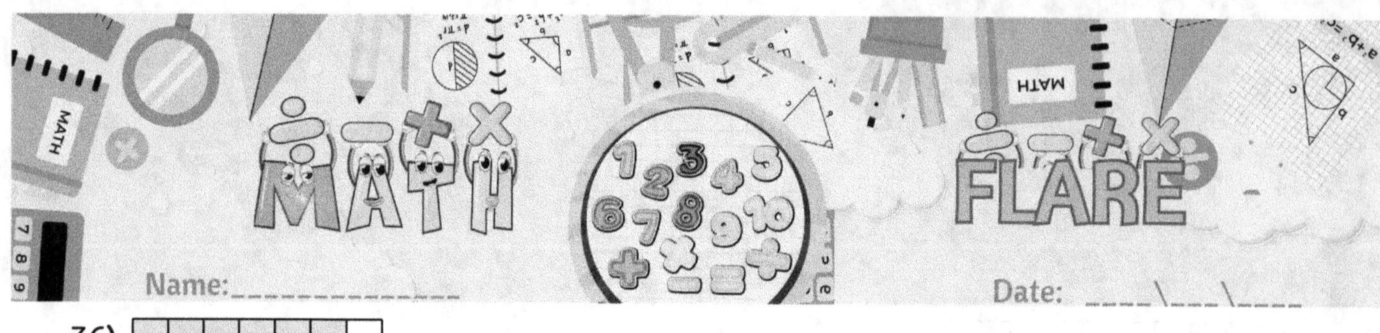

36) 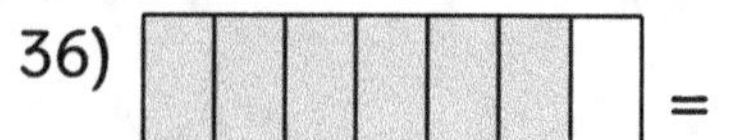 = ______________________________

37) = ______________________________

38) = ______________________________

39) = ______________________________

40) = ______________________________

41) = ______________________________

42) = ______________________________

43) = ______________________________

44) = ______________________________

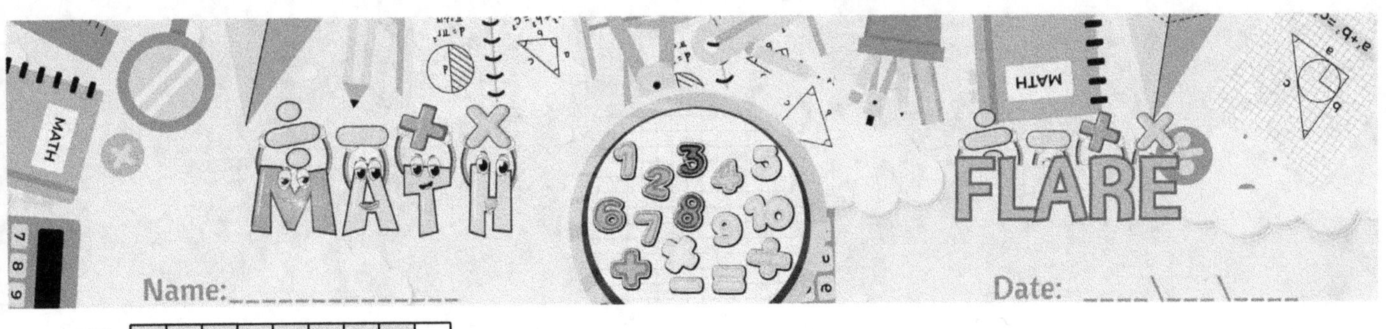

45) 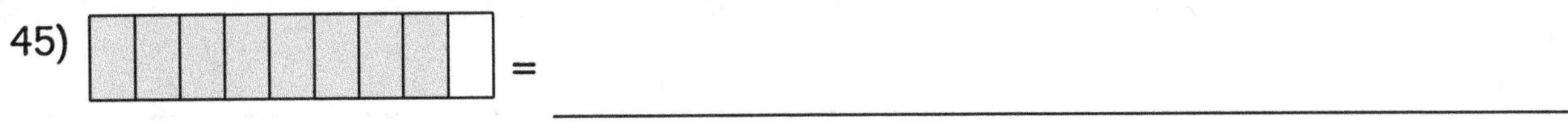 = _______________

46) = _______________

47) = _______________

48) = _______________

49) = _______________

50) = _______________

51) = _______________

52) = _______________

53)  = _______________

54) = _______________________

55) = _______________________

56) = _______________________

57) = _______________________

58) = _______________________

59) = _______________________

60) = _______________________

61) = _______________________

62) = _______________________

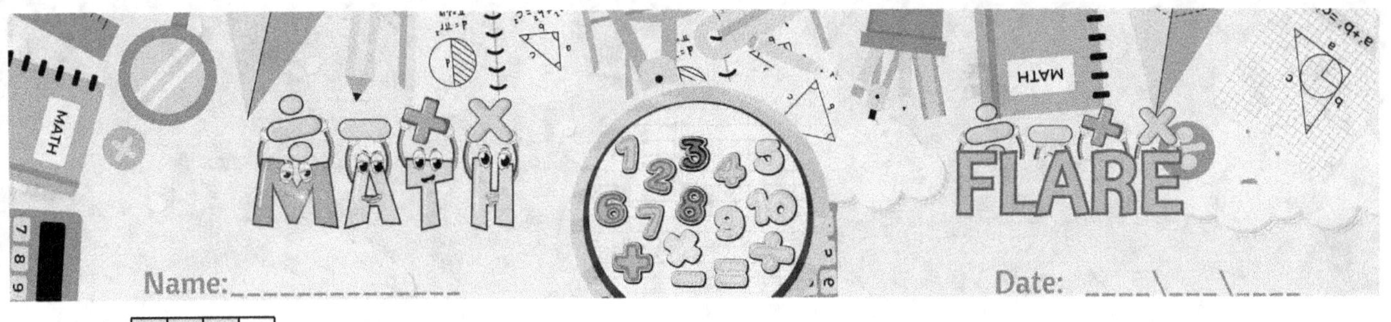

63) 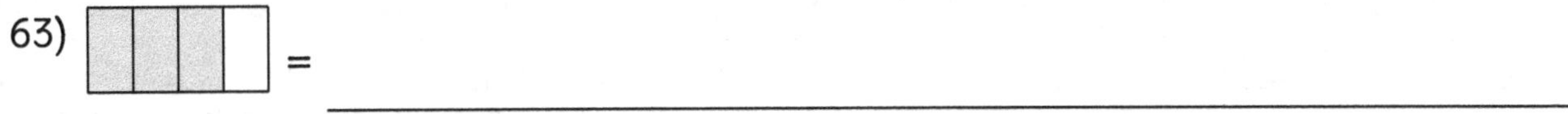 = _______________

64) = _______________

65) = _______________

66) = _______________

67) = _______________

68) = _______________

69) = _______________

70) = _______________

71) = _______________

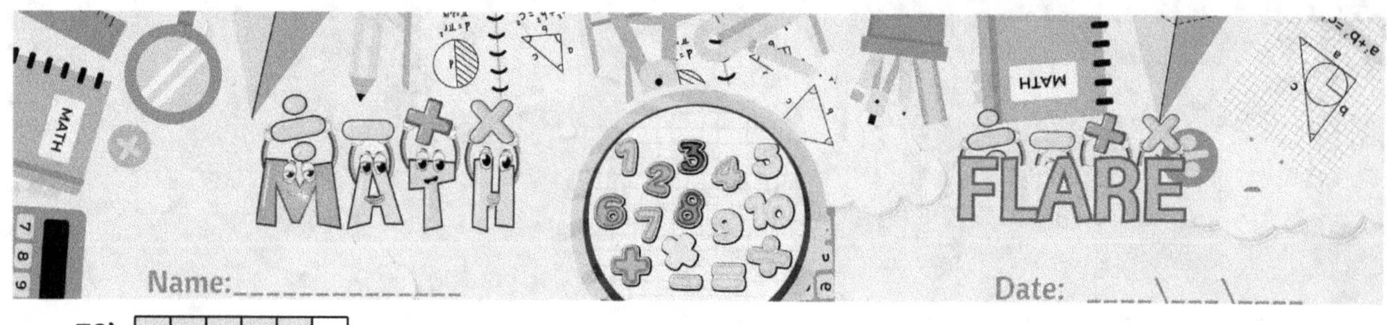

72) = _______________________________

73) = _______________________________

74) = _______________________________

75) = _______________________________

76) = _______________________________

77) = _______________________________

78) = _______________________________

79) = _______________________________

80) = _______________________________

Compare the Fractions

Compare the fractions. Put the signs < , >, or =

1) $\dfrac{56}{60}$ < $\dfrac{57}{60}$

2) $\dfrac{32}{13}$ __ $\dfrac{22}{13}$

3) $\dfrac{8}{23}$ __ $\dfrac{1}{23}$

4) $\dfrac{23}{10}$ __ $\dfrac{19}{10}$

5) $\dfrac{42}{19}$ __ $\dfrac{18}{19}$

6) $\dfrac{11}{25}$ __ $\dfrac{22}{25}$

7) $\dfrac{1}{4}$ __ $\dfrac{1}{4}$

8) $\dfrac{11}{18}$ __ $\dfrac{50}{18}$

9) $\dfrac{6}{24}$ __ $\dfrac{9}{24}$

10) $\dfrac{42}{54}$ __ $\dfrac{47}{54}$

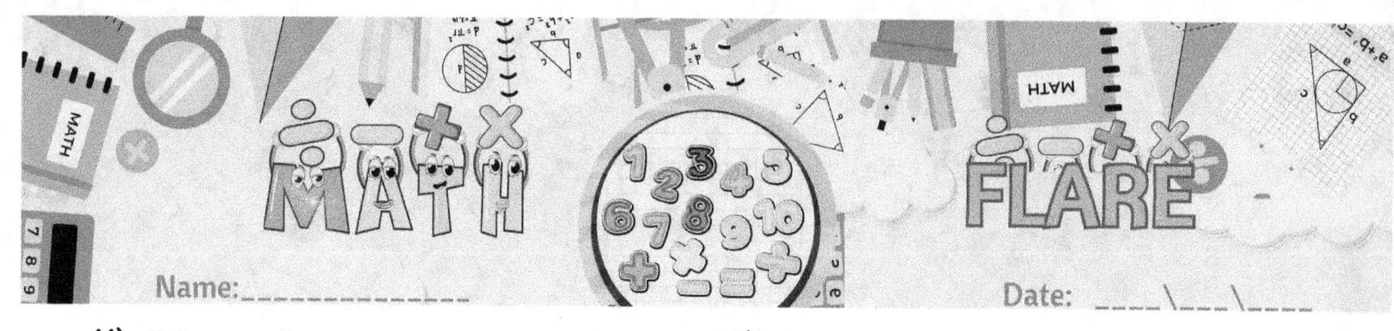

11) $\dfrac{54}{57}$ ___ $\dfrac{8}{57}$

12) $\dfrac{2}{7}$ ___ $\dfrac{5}{7}$

13) $\dfrac{54}{138}$ ___ $\dfrac{183}{138}$

14) $\dfrac{21}{25}$ ___ $\dfrac{13}{25}$

15) $\dfrac{42}{78}$ ___ $\dfrac{30}{78}$

16) $\dfrac{13}{21}$ ___ $\dfrac{13}{21}$

17) $\dfrac{37}{14}$ ___ $\dfrac{9}{14}$

18) $\dfrac{13}{24}$ ___ $\dfrac{7}{24}$

19) $\dfrac{13}{20}$ ___ $\dfrac{18}{20}$

20) $\dfrac{24}{16}$ ___ $\dfrac{25}{16}$

21) $\dfrac{12}{15}$ ___ $\dfrac{11}{15}$

22) $\dfrac{11}{10}$ ___ $\dfrac{19}{10}$

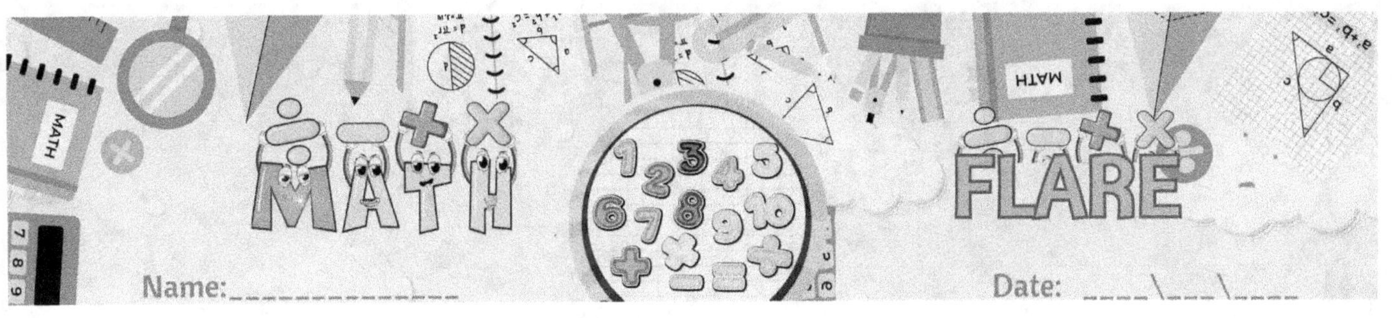

23) $\dfrac{6}{12}$ ___ $\dfrac{11}{12}$

24) $\dfrac{50}{18}$ ___ $\dfrac{9}{18}$

25) $\dfrac{84}{30}$ ___ $\dfrac{20}{30}$

26) $\dfrac{1}{4}$ ___ $\dfrac{9}{4}$

27) $\dfrac{9}{12}$ ___ $\dfrac{8}{12}$

28) $\dfrac{6}{18}$ ___ $\dfrac{11}{18}$

29) $\dfrac{15}{25}$ ___ $\dfrac{5}{25}$

30) $\dfrac{40}{17}$ ___ $\dfrac{6}{17}$

31) $\dfrac{26}{11}$ ___ $\dfrac{12}{11}$

32) $\dfrac{10}{8}$ ___ $\dfrac{5}{8}$

33) $\dfrac{2}{22}$ ___ $\dfrac{11}{22}$

34) $\dfrac{1}{2}$ ___ $\dfrac{1}{2}$

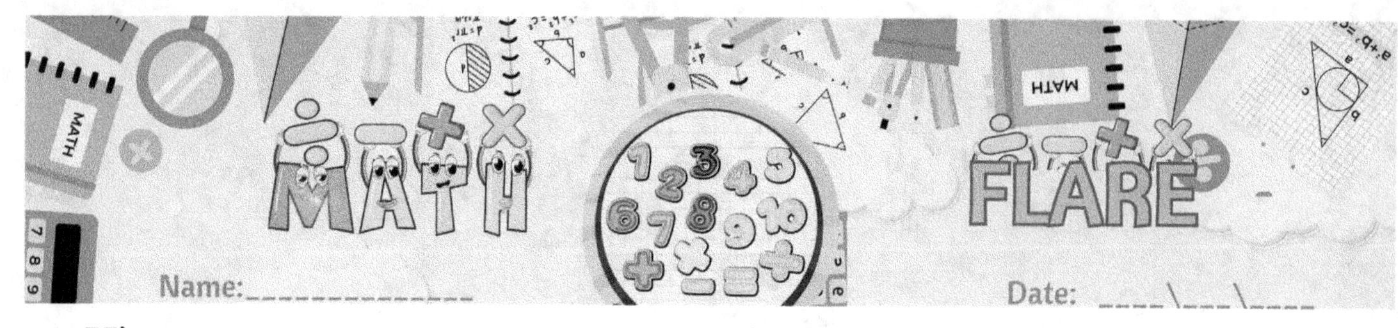

35) $\dfrac{21}{42}$ ___ $\dfrac{112}{42}$

36) $\dfrac{9}{10}$ ___ $\dfrac{1}{10}$

37) $\dfrac{5}{2}$ ___ $\dfrac{3}{2}$

38) $\dfrac{15}{20}$ ___ $\dfrac{9}{20}$

39) $\dfrac{52}{18}$ ___ $\dfrac{16}{18}$

40) $\dfrac{19}{17}$ ___ $\dfrac{10}{17}$

41) $\dfrac{10}{15}$ ___ $\dfrac{13}{15}$

42) $\dfrac{6}{9}$ ___ $\dfrac{6}{9}$

43) $\dfrac{20}{120}$ ___ $\dfrac{283}{120}$

44) $\dfrac{32}{38}$ ___ $\dfrac{83}{38}$

45) $\dfrac{29}{25}$ ___ $\dfrac{6}{25}$

46) $\dfrac{3}{15}$ ___ $\dfrac{12}{15}$

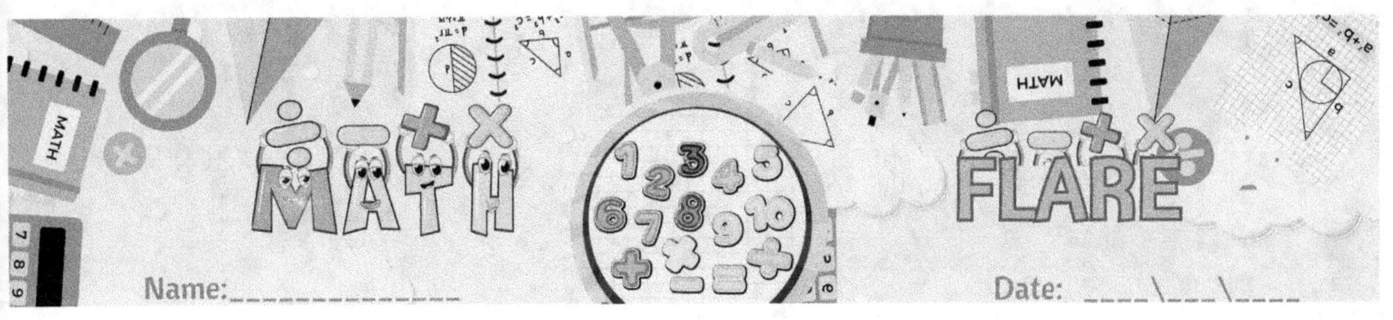

47) $\dfrac{10}{30}$ ___ $\dfrac{28}{30}$

48) $\dfrac{38}{20}$ ___ $\dfrac{18}{20}$

49) $\dfrac{8}{15}$ ___ $\dfrac{19}{15}$

50) $\dfrac{15}{7}$ ___ $\dfrac{19}{7}$

51) $\dfrac{60}{21}$ ___ $\dfrac{12}{21}$

52) $\dfrac{26}{46}$ ___ $\dfrac{75}{46}$

53) $\dfrac{8}{11}$ ___ $\dfrac{25}{11}$

54) $\dfrac{12}{8}$ ___ $\dfrac{3}{8}$

55) $\dfrac{47}{30}$ ___ $\dfrac{21}{30}$

56) $\dfrac{45}{65}$ ___ $\dfrac{146}{65}$

57) $\dfrac{20}{22}$ ___ $\dfrac{30}{22}$

58) $\dfrac{15}{16}$ ___ $\dfrac{29}{16}$

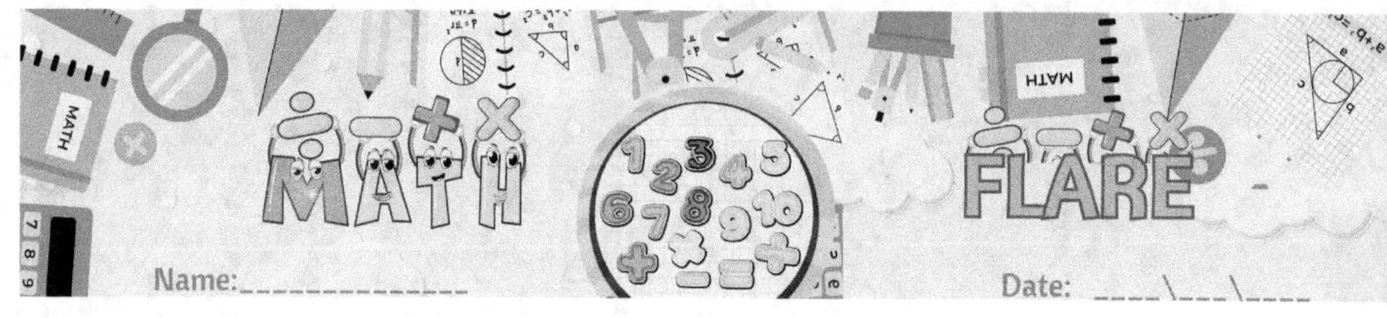

Fractions Addition: Common Denominator

Find the sum.

1) $\dfrac{1}{9} + \dfrac{7}{9} =$ $\dfrac{1+7}{9} = \dfrac{8}{9}$

2) $\dfrac{5}{10} + \dfrac{2}{10} =$ _____________

3) $\dfrac{1}{5} + \dfrac{3}{5} =$ _____________

4) $\dfrac{2}{7} + \dfrac{4}{7} =$ _____________

5) $\dfrac{2}{9} + \dfrac{1}{9} =$ _____________

6) $\dfrac{2}{4} + \dfrac{1}{4} =$ _____________

7) $\dfrac{2}{5} + \dfrac{1}{5} =$ _____________

8) $\dfrac{1}{8} + \dfrac{5}{8} =$ _____________

9) $\dfrac{1}{3} + \dfrac{1}{3} =$ _____________

10) $\dfrac{1}{11} + \dfrac{4}{11} =$ _____________

11) $\dfrac{1}{2} + \dfrac{1}{2} =$ _____________

12) $\dfrac{1}{6} + \dfrac{3}{6} =$ _____________

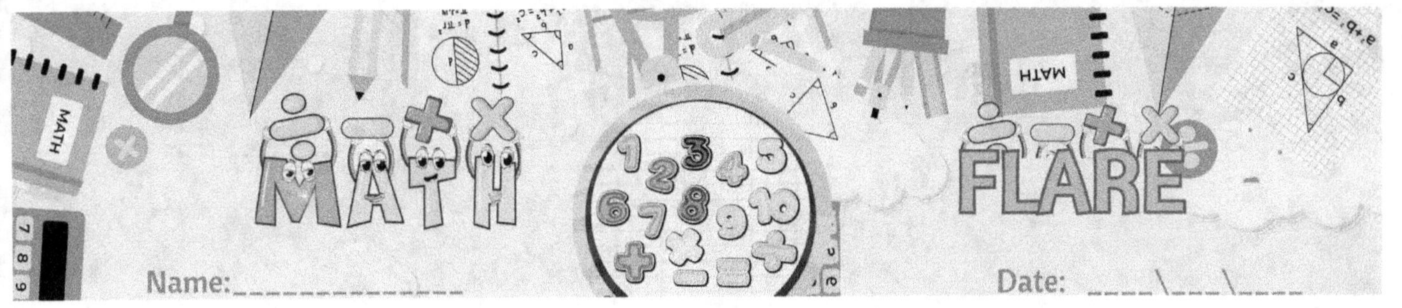

13) $\dfrac{1}{12} + \dfrac{7}{12} =$ _______________

14) $\dfrac{2}{10} + \dfrac{1}{10} =$ _______________

15) $\dfrac{1}{7} + \dfrac{5}{7} =$ _______________

16) $\dfrac{1}{10} + \dfrac{7}{10} =$ _______________

17) $\dfrac{2}{9} + \dfrac{3}{9} =$ _______________

18) $\dfrac{3}{5} + \dfrac{1}{5} =$ _______________

19) $\dfrac{3}{11} + \dfrac{7}{11} =$ _______________

20) $\dfrac{2}{6} + \dfrac{3}{6} =$ _______________

21) $\dfrac{1}{12} + \dfrac{10}{12} =$ _______________

22) $\dfrac{1}{4} + \dfrac{1}{4} =$ _______________

23) $\dfrac{1}{8} + \dfrac{4}{8} =$ _______________

24) $\dfrac{1}{5} + \dfrac{1}{5} =$ _______________

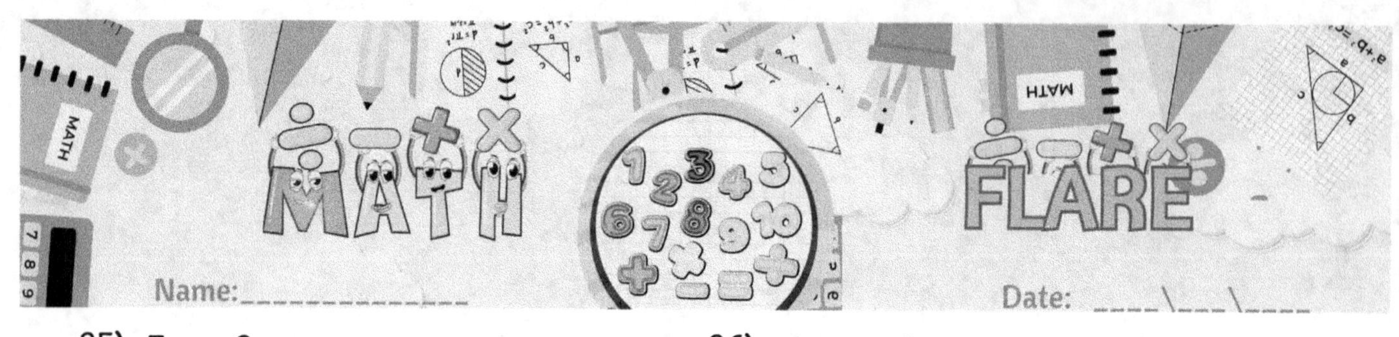

25) $\dfrac{3}{6} + \dfrac{2}{6} =$ _______________

26) $\dfrac{1}{10} + \dfrac{6}{10} =$ _______________

27) $\dfrac{1}{7} + \dfrac{1}{7} =$ _______________

28) $\dfrac{8}{12} + \dfrac{1}{12} =$ _______________

29) $\dfrac{3}{11} + \dfrac{2}{11} =$ _______________

30) $\dfrac{1}{9} + \dfrac{4}{9} =$ _______________

31) $\dfrac{5}{8} + \dfrac{2}{8} =$ _______________

32) $\dfrac{1}{9} + \dfrac{6}{9} =$ _______________

33) $\dfrac{4}{12} + \dfrac{6}{12} =$ _______________

34) $\dfrac{4}{11} + \dfrac{1}{11} =$ _______________

35) $\dfrac{1}{7} + \dfrac{2}{7} =$ _______________

36) $\dfrac{1}{5} + \dfrac{2}{5} =$ _______________

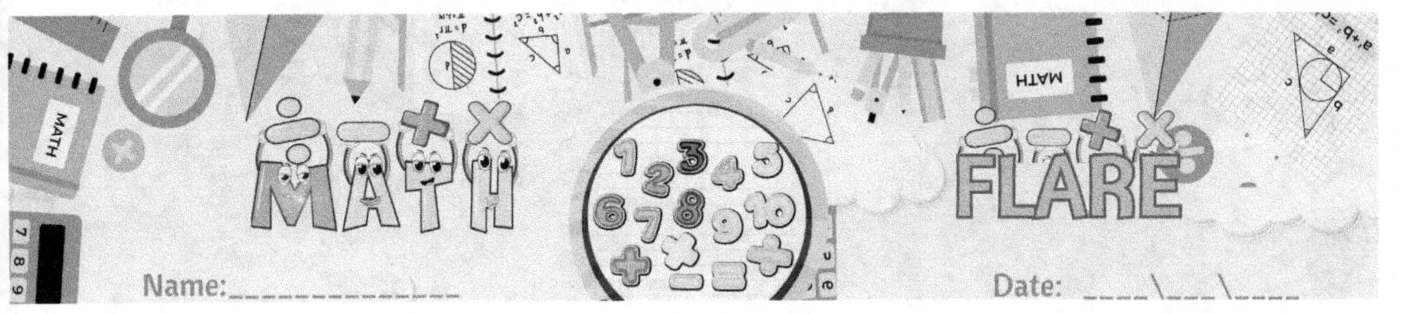

37) $\dfrac{4}{10} + \dfrac{1}{10} =$ _____________

38) $\dfrac{7}{10} + \dfrac{1}{10} =$ _____________

39) $\dfrac{5}{8} + \dfrac{1}{8} =$ _____________

40) $\dfrac{3}{9} + \dfrac{5}{9} =$ _____________

41) $\dfrac{2}{6} + \dfrac{2}{6} =$ _____________

42) $\dfrac{4}{11} + \dfrac{5}{11} =$ _____________

43) $\dfrac{5}{12} + \dfrac{2}{12} =$ _____________

44) $\dfrac{1}{4} + \dfrac{2}{4} =$ _____________

45) $\dfrac{3}{7} + \dfrac{3}{7} =$ _____________

46) $\dfrac{2}{9} + \dfrac{5}{9} =$ _____________

47) $\dfrac{1}{12} + \dfrac{5}{12} =$ _____________

48) $\dfrac{2}{7} + \dfrac{3}{7} =$ _____________

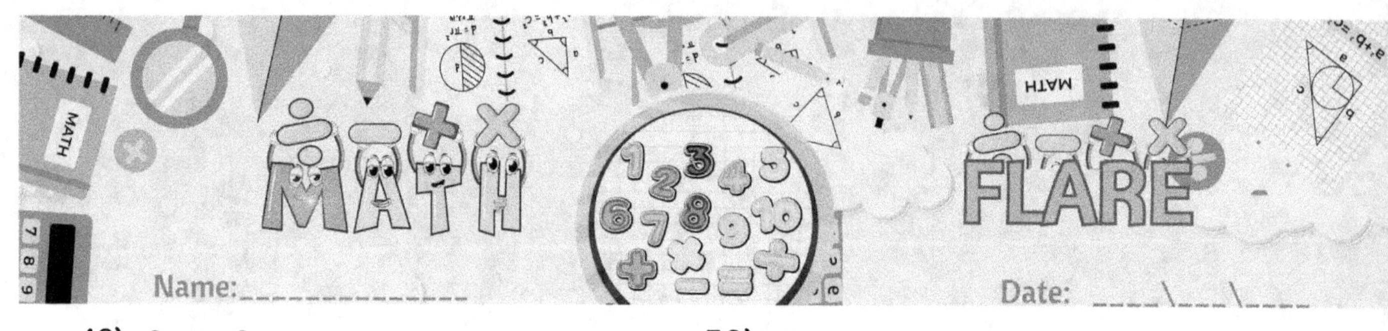

49) $\dfrac{2}{8} + \dfrac{2}{8} =$ _______________

50) $\dfrac{5}{11} + \dfrac{1}{11} =$ _______________

51) $\dfrac{2}{10} + \dfrac{6}{10} =$ _______________

52) $\dfrac{1}{6} + \dfrac{4}{6} =$ _______________

53) $\dfrac{7}{10} + \dfrac{2}{10} =$ _______________

54) $\dfrac{3}{9} + \dfrac{2}{9} =$ _______________

55) $\dfrac{4}{6} + \dfrac{1}{6} =$ _______________

56) $\dfrac{7}{12} + \dfrac{3}{12} =$ _______________

57) $\dfrac{4}{11} + \dfrac{3}{11} =$ _______________

58) $\dfrac{3}{8} + \dfrac{3}{8} =$ _______________

59) $\dfrac{1}{8} + \dfrac{2}{8} =$ _______________

60) $\dfrac{1}{6} + \dfrac{1}{6} =$ _______________

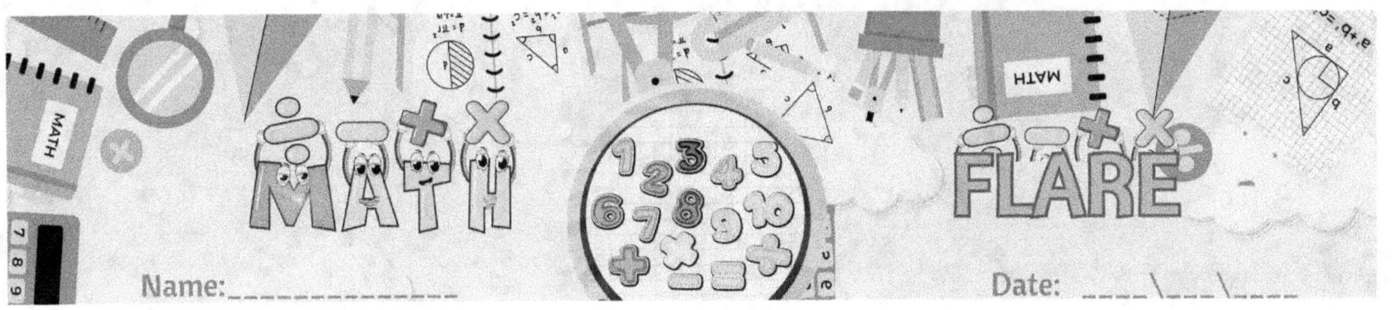

61) $\dfrac{2}{11} + \dfrac{3}{11}$ = _______________

62) $\dfrac{2}{10} + \dfrac{2}{10}$ = _______________

63) $\dfrac{4}{7} + \dfrac{1}{7}$ = _______________

64) $\dfrac{1}{9} + \dfrac{5}{9}$ = _______________

65) $\dfrac{7}{12} + \dfrac{1}{12}$ = _______________

66) $\dfrac{1}{9} + \dfrac{1}{9}$ = _______________

67) $\dfrac{3}{12} + \dfrac{2}{12}$ = _______________

68) $\dfrac{2}{8} + \dfrac{3}{8}$ = _______________

69) $\dfrac{3}{7} + \dfrac{2}{7}$ = _______________

70) $\dfrac{1}{10} + \dfrac{1}{10}$ = _______________

71) $\dfrac{3}{8} + \dfrac{1}{8}$ = _______________

72) $\dfrac{3}{6} + \dfrac{1}{6}$ = _______________

73) $\dfrac{3}{9} + \dfrac{4}{9} =$ _______________

74) $\dfrac{2}{7} + \dfrac{2}{7} =$ _______________

75) $\dfrac{3}{7} + \dfrac{1}{7} =$ _______________

76) $\dfrac{1}{9} + \dfrac{3}{9} =$ _______________

77) $\dfrac{3}{10} + \dfrac{3}{10} =$ _______________

78) $\dfrac{2}{8} + \dfrac{5}{8} =$ _______________

79) $\dfrac{2}{11} + \dfrac{4}{11} =$ _______________

80) $\dfrac{5}{12} + \dfrac{3}{12} =$ _______________

81) $\dfrac{7}{9} + \dfrac{1}{9} =$ _______________

82) $\dfrac{2}{11} + \dfrac{1}{11} =$ _______________

83) $\dfrac{1}{6} + \dfrac{2}{6} =$ _______________

84) $\dfrac{4}{8} + \dfrac{2}{8} =$ _______________

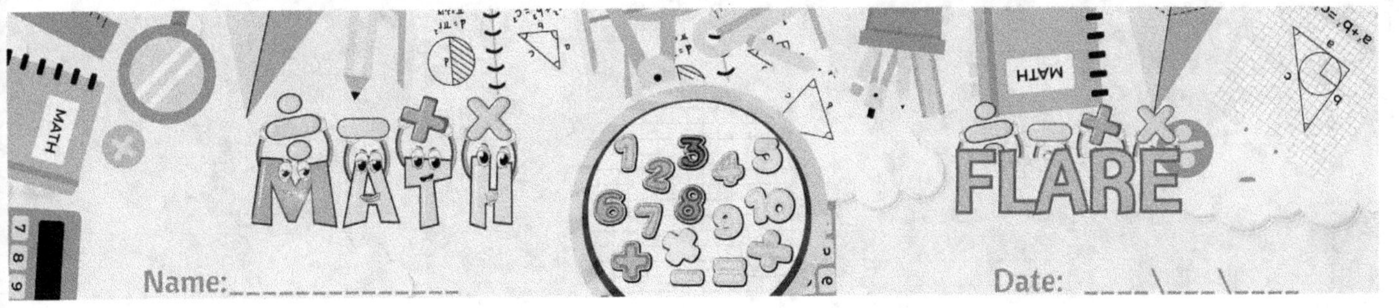

Name: _______________   Date: ____________

85) $\dfrac{2}{5} + \dfrac{2}{5} =$ _______________

86) $\dfrac{3}{10} + \dfrac{2}{10} =$ _______________

87) $\dfrac{1}{7} + \dfrac{3}{7} =$ _______________

88) $\dfrac{1}{12} + \dfrac{9}{12} =$ _______________

89) $\dfrac{2}{8} + \dfrac{4}{8} =$ _______________

90) $\dfrac{8}{11} + \dfrac{2}{11} =$ _______________

91) $\dfrac{2}{11} + \dfrac{5}{11} =$ _______________

92) $\dfrac{2}{12} + \dfrac{7}{12} =$ _______________

93) $\dfrac{1}{10} + \dfrac{4}{10} =$ _______________

94) $\dfrac{5}{7} + \dfrac{1}{7} =$ _______________

95) $\dfrac{1}{9} + \dfrac{2}{9} =$ _______________

96) $\dfrac{5}{10} + \dfrac{3}{10} =$ _______________

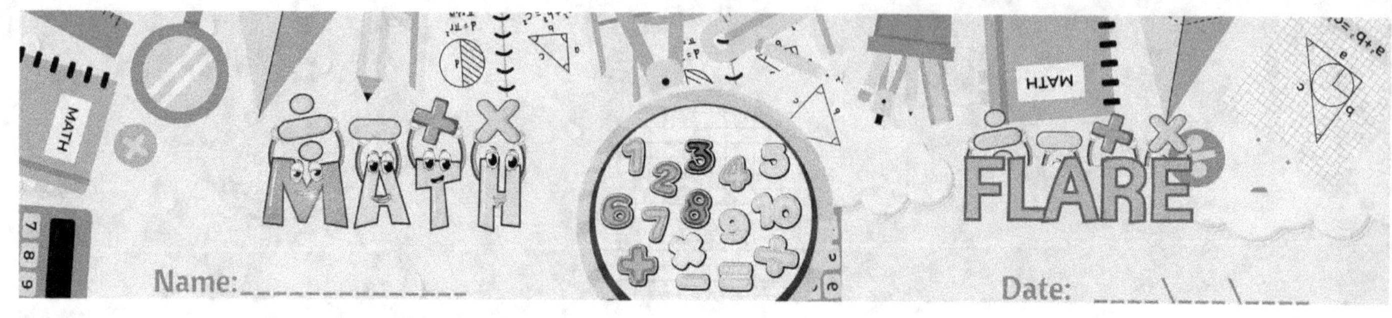

Fractions Subtraction - Common Denominator

Find the difference.

1) $\dfrac{5}{8} - \dfrac{2}{8} = \dfrac{5-2}{8} = \dfrac{3}{8}$

2) $\dfrac{4}{5} - \dfrac{1}{5} = $ ___________

3) $\dfrac{3}{6} - \dfrac{2}{6} = $ ___________

4) $\dfrac{9}{12} - \dfrac{4}{12} = $ ___________

5) $\dfrac{2}{3} - \dfrac{1}{3} = $ ___________

6) $\dfrac{8}{12} - \dfrac{7}{12} = $ ___________

7) $\dfrac{4}{8} - \dfrac{3}{8} = $ ___________

8) $\dfrac{5}{9} - \dfrac{3}{9} = $ ___________

9) $\dfrac{6}{10} - \dfrac{3}{10} = $ ___________

10) $\dfrac{3}{4} - \dfrac{1}{4} = $ ___________

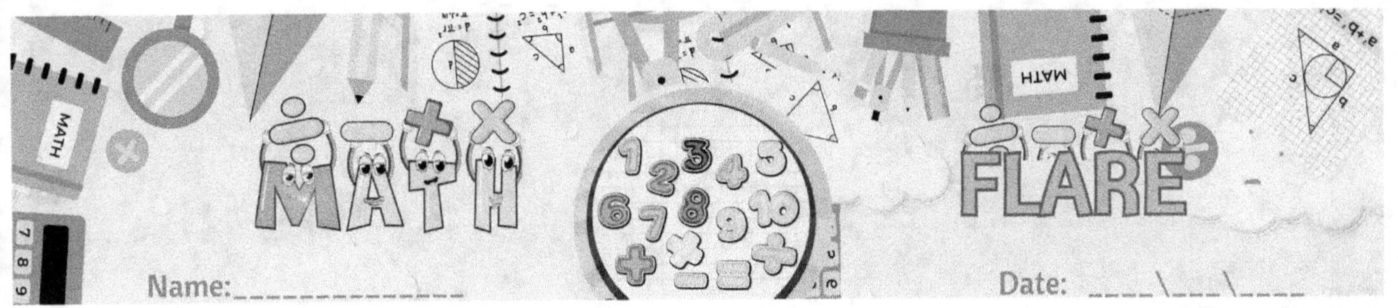

11) $\dfrac{2}{5} - \dfrac{1}{5} =$ _____________

12) $\dfrac{10}{11} - \dfrac{7}{11} =$ _____________

13) $\dfrac{6}{7} - \dfrac{3}{7} =$ _____________

14) $\dfrac{5}{6} - \dfrac{4}{6} =$ _____________

15) $\dfrac{6}{8} - \dfrac{4}{8} =$ _____________

16) $\dfrac{5}{6} - \dfrac{3}{6} =$ _____________

17) $\dfrac{5}{7} - \dfrac{1}{7} =$ _____________

18) $\dfrac{8}{10} - \dfrac{5}{10} =$ _____________

19) $\dfrac{7}{9} - \dfrac{4}{9} =$ _____________

20) $\dfrac{6}{12} - \dfrac{1}{12} =$ _____________

21) $\dfrac{2}{4} - \dfrac{1}{4} =$ _____________

22) $\dfrac{7}{12} - \dfrac{5}{12} =$ _____________

23) $\dfrac{8}{10} - \dfrac{6}{10} =$ _____________

24) $\dfrac{2}{8} - \dfrac{1}{8} =$ _____________

25) $\dfrac{6}{7} - \dfrac{2}{7} =$ _____________

26) $\dfrac{8}{11} - \dfrac{7}{11} =$ _____________

27) $\dfrac{4}{5} - \dfrac{2}{5} =$ _____________

28) $\dfrac{8}{9} - \dfrac{7}{9} =$ _____________

29) $\dfrac{5}{7} - \dfrac{2}{7} =$ _____________

30) $\dfrac{11}{12} - \dfrac{10}{12} =$ _____________

31) $\dfrac{3}{4} - \dfrac{2}{4} =$ _____________

32) $\dfrac{10}{11} - \dfrac{4}{11} =$ _____________

33) $\dfrac{7}{9} - \dfrac{6}{9} =$ _____________

34) $\dfrac{5}{10} - \dfrac{2}{10} =$ _____________

35) $\dfrac{6}{8} - \dfrac{5}{8} =$ _____________

36) $\dfrac{4}{6} - \dfrac{3}{6} =$ _____________

37) $\dfrac{4}{9} - \dfrac{3}{9} =$ _____________

38) $\dfrac{11}{12} - \dfrac{4}{12} =$ _____________

39) $\dfrac{4}{5} - \dfrac{3}{5} =$ _____________

40) $\dfrac{9}{10} - \dfrac{6}{10} =$ _____________

41) $\dfrac{3}{7} - \dfrac{2}{7} =$ _____________

42) $\dfrac{9}{11} - \dfrac{8}{11} =$ _____________

43) $\dfrac{5}{6} - \dfrac{2}{6} =$ _____________

44) $\dfrac{9}{10} - \dfrac{8}{10} =$ _____________

45) $\dfrac{5}{7} - \dfrac{4}{7} =$ _____________

46) $\dfrac{10}{11} - \dfrac{9}{11} =$ _____________

Name:______________   Date: ____________

47) $\dfrac{8}{9} - \dfrac{2}{9} =$ _______________

48) $\dfrac{10}{12} - \dfrac{6}{12} =$ _______________

49) $\dfrac{8}{10} - \dfrac{4}{10} =$ _______________

50) $\dfrac{6}{7} - \dfrac{5}{7} =$ _______________

51) $\dfrac{8}{12} - \dfrac{4}{12} =$ _______________

52) $\dfrac{8}{11} - \dfrac{2}{11} =$ _______________

53) $\dfrac{5}{8} - \dfrac{1}{8} =$ _______________

54) $\dfrac{10}{11} - \dfrac{2}{11} =$ _______________

55) $\dfrac{6}{9} - \dfrac{5}{9} =$ _______________

56) $\dfrac{4}{7} - \dfrac{3}{7} =$ _______________

57) $\dfrac{10}{12} - \dfrac{9}{12} =$ _______________

58) $\dfrac{7}{8} - \dfrac{5}{8} =$ _______________

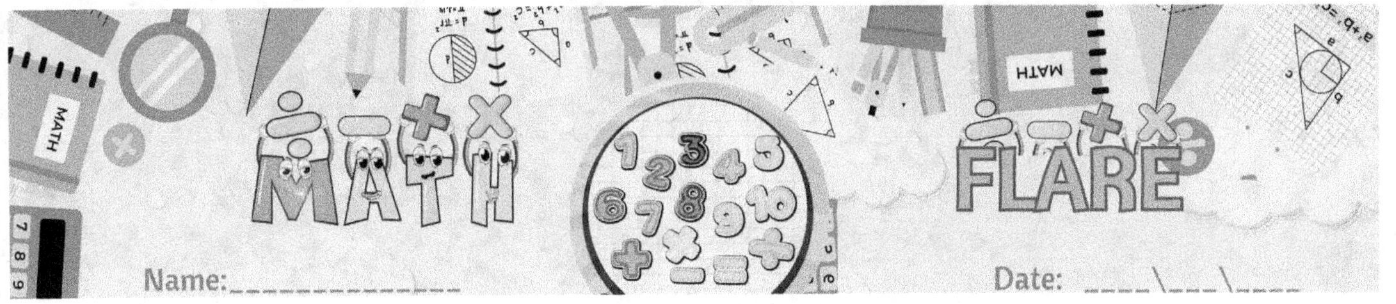

59) $\dfrac{7}{10} - \dfrac{4}{10} =$ _______________

60) $\dfrac{10}{12} - \dfrac{7}{12} =$ _______________

61) $\dfrac{6}{10} - \dfrac{2}{10} =$ _______________

62) $\dfrac{3}{5} - \dfrac{1}{5} =$ _______________

63) $\dfrac{4}{12} - \dfrac{2}{12} =$ _______________

64) $\dfrac{7}{8} - \dfrac{4}{8} =$ _______________

65) $\dfrac{8}{9} - \dfrac{5}{9} =$ _______________

66) $\dfrac{9}{10} - \dfrac{5}{10} =$ _______________

67) $\dfrac{6}{11} - \dfrac{3}{11} =$ _______________

68) $\dfrac{11}{12} - \dfrac{9}{12} =$ _______________

69) $\dfrac{5}{10} - \dfrac{3}{10} =$ _______________

70) $\dfrac{5}{7} - \dfrac{3}{7} =$ _______________

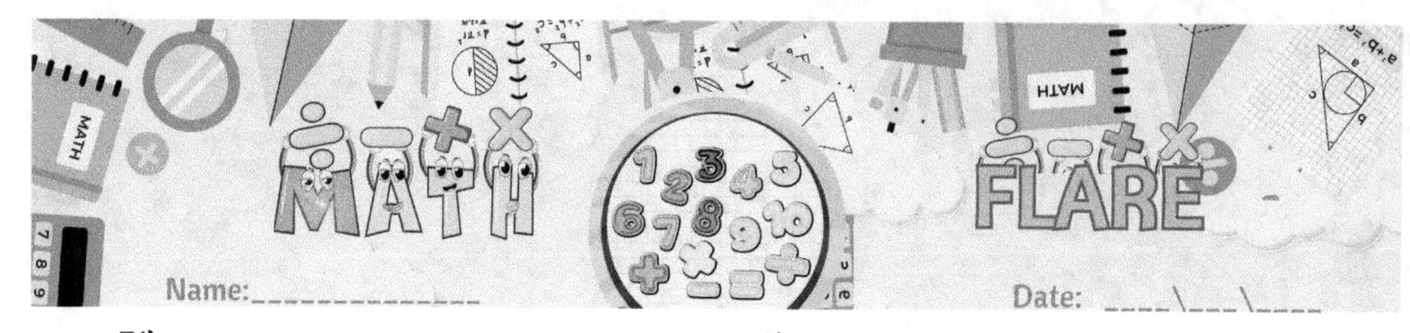

71) $\dfrac{11}{12} - \dfrac{7}{12} =$ _______________

72) $\dfrac{9}{10} - \dfrac{3}{10} =$ _______________

73) $\dfrac{7}{11} - \dfrac{5}{11} =$ _______________

74) $\dfrac{7}{8} - \dfrac{3}{8} =$ _______________

75) $\dfrac{6}{7} - \dfrac{4}{7} =$ _______________

76) $\dfrac{8}{10} - \dfrac{1}{10} =$ _______________

77) $\dfrac{7}{8} - \dfrac{6}{8} =$ _______________

78) $\dfrac{5}{9} - \dfrac{1}{9} =$ _______________

79) $\dfrac{5}{6} - \dfrac{1}{6} =$ _______________

80) $\dfrac{6}{11} - \dfrac{1}{11} =$ _______________

81) $\dfrac{7}{12} - \dfrac{4}{12} =$ _______________

82) $\dfrac{6}{10} - \dfrac{1}{10} =$ _______________

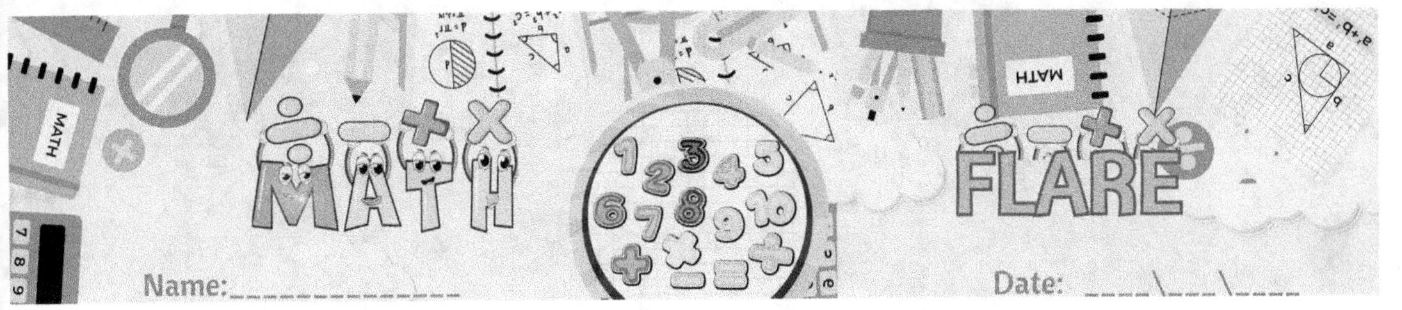

83) $\dfrac{4}{11} - \dfrac{3}{11} =$ _______________

84) $\dfrac{8}{10} - \dfrac{3}{10} =$ _______________

85) $\dfrac{4}{12} - \dfrac{3}{12} =$ _______________

86) $\dfrac{5}{12} - \dfrac{3}{12} =$ _______________

87) $\dfrac{3}{8} - \dfrac{1}{8} =$ _______________

88) $\dfrac{8}{9} - \dfrac{6}{9} =$ _______________

89) $\dfrac{11}{12} - \dfrac{5}{12} =$ _______________

90) $\dfrac{6}{12} - \dfrac{3}{12} =$ _______________

91) $\dfrac{7}{11} - \dfrac{1}{11} =$ _______________

92) $\dfrac{4}{6} - \dfrac{2}{6} =$ _______________

93) $\dfrac{7}{11} - \dfrac{6}{11} =$ _______________

94) $\dfrac{3}{12} - \dfrac{2}{12} =$ _______________

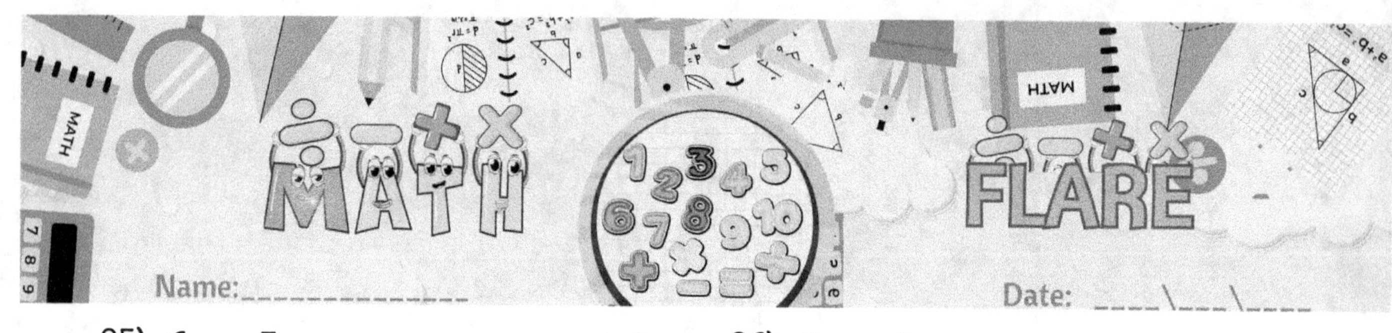

95) $\dfrac{6}{9} - \dfrac{3}{9} =$ _______________

96) $\dfrac{6}{9} - \dfrac{1}{9} =$ _______________

97) $\dfrac{5}{8} - \dfrac{4}{8} =$ _______________

98) $\dfrac{7}{9} - \dfrac{3}{9} =$ _______________

99) $\dfrac{7}{12} - \dfrac{6}{12} =$ _______________

100) $\dfrac{6}{8} - \dfrac{1}{8} =$ _______________

101) $\dfrac{5}{10} - \dfrac{4}{10} =$ _______________

102) $\dfrac{9}{10} - \dfrac{7}{10} =$ _______________

103) $\dfrac{7}{10} - \dfrac{6}{10} =$ _______________

104) $\dfrac{3}{5} - \dfrac{2}{5} =$ _______________

Chapter. 06

Geometry

Area and Perimeter

The area of a shape represents the amount of space it occupies. The perimeter of a shape is the total distance around its outer edge.

Area of Rectangle

For a square, since all four sides are equal, we only need to know the length of one side to find its area. We can calculate the area of a square by multiplying the length of one side by itself (squared). So, if the length of one side of the square is 's', then the area (A) is given by:

$$A = s \times s$$

4 in

4 in

$$A = 4 \times 4$$
$$A = 16$$

Perimeter of Rectangle

For a square, since all four sides are equal, we can find the perimeter by adding up the lengths of all four sides. If 's' represents the length of one side, then the perimeter (P) is given by:

$$P = 4 \times s$$

$$P = 4 \times 4$$

$$P = 16$$

Area of Triangle:

The area of a triangle represents the amount of space enclosed within its three sides. The formula for calculating the area of a triangle depends on the type of triangle. For a general triangle, we use the formula:

$$A = \frac{1}{2} \times base \times height$$

Where:

- *A* represents the area of the triangle.

- The base is the length of any one side of the triangle.

- The height is the perpendicular distance from the base to the opposite vertex.

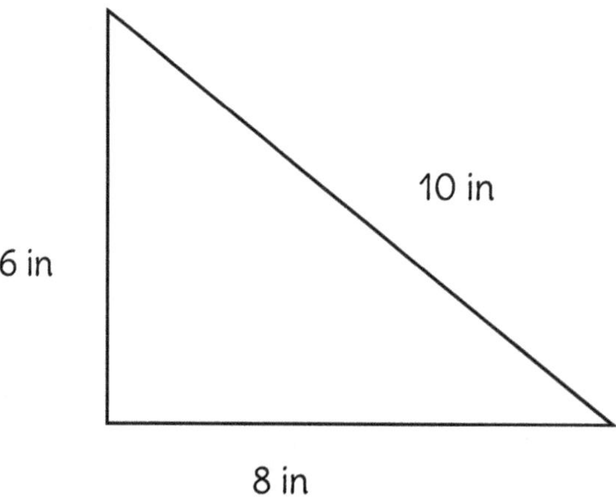

$$A = \frac{1}{2} \times \text{base} \times \text{height}$$

$$A = \frac{1}{2} \times 6 \times 8$$

$$A = \frac{1}{2} \times 48$$

$$A = 24$$

Perimeter of Triangle:

The perimeter of a triangle is the total length of its three sides. To find the perimeter, we simply add the lengths of all three sides together:

$$P = side1 + side2 + side3$$

$$P = 6 + 8 + 10$$

$$P = 24$$

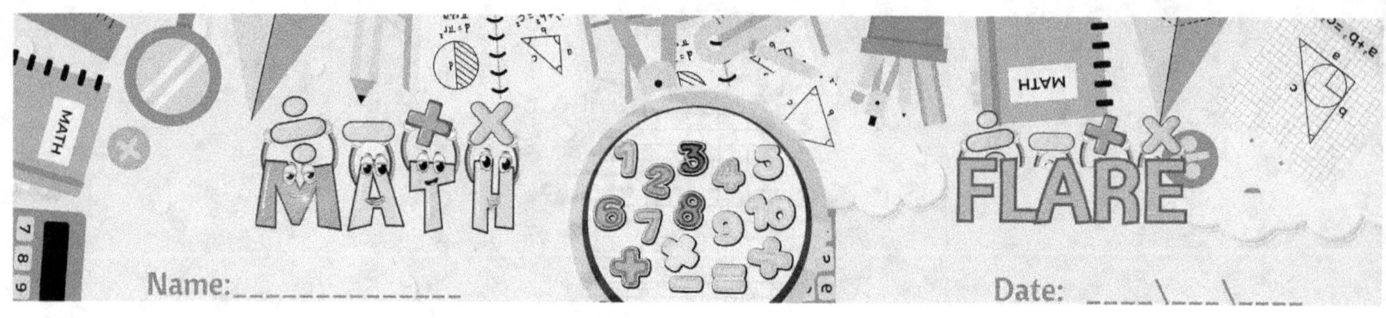

Area and Perimeter: Rectangles and Triangles

1)
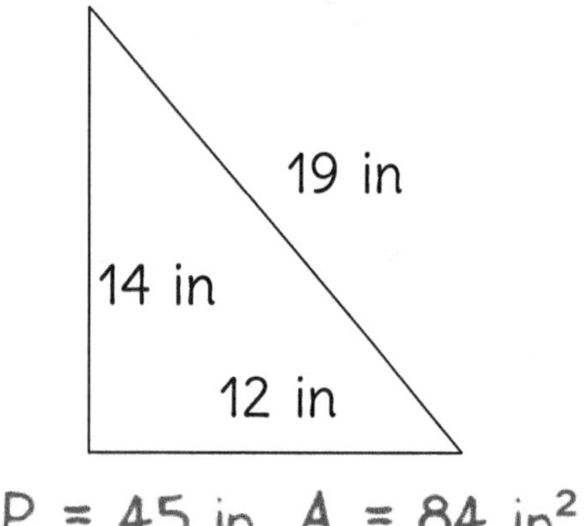

P = 45 in A = 84 in²

2)
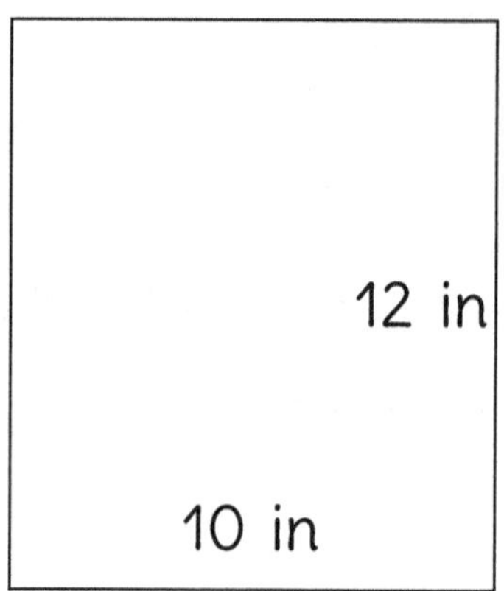

3)
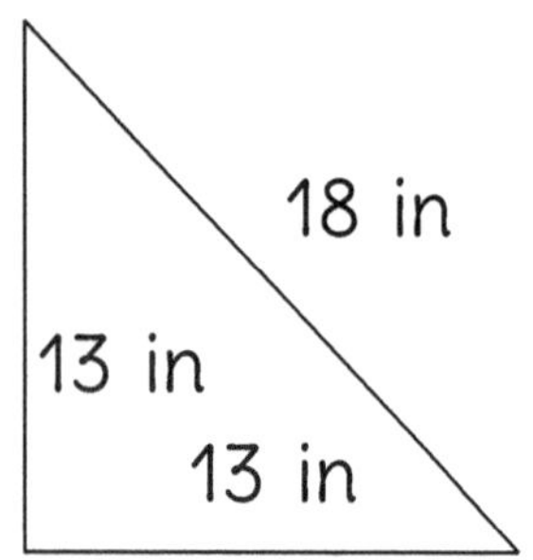

4)
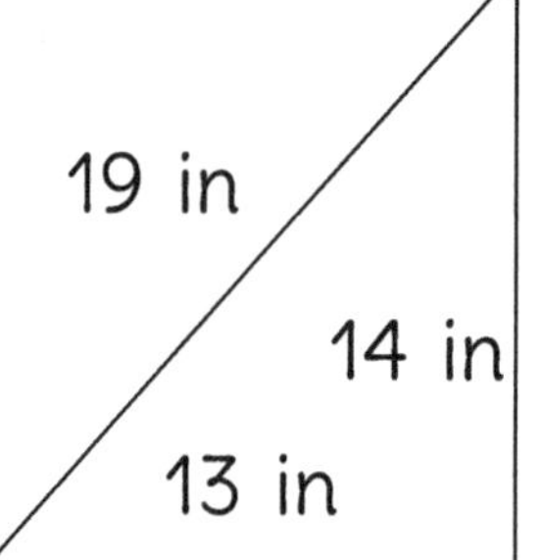

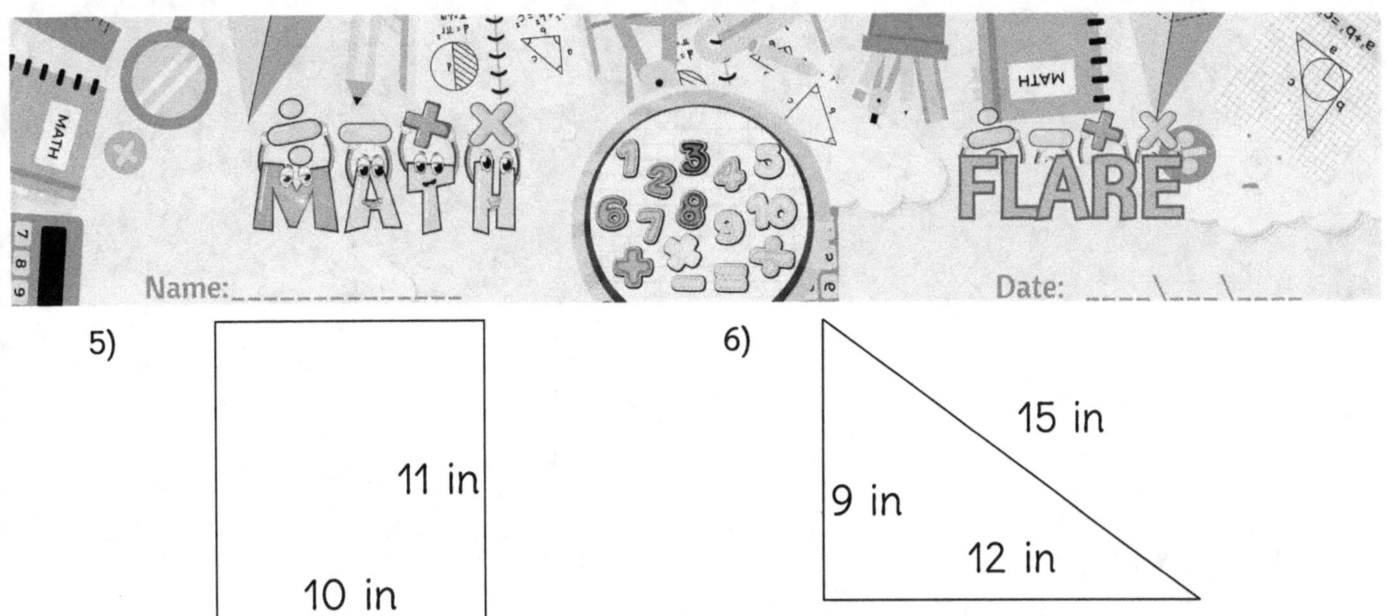

5)

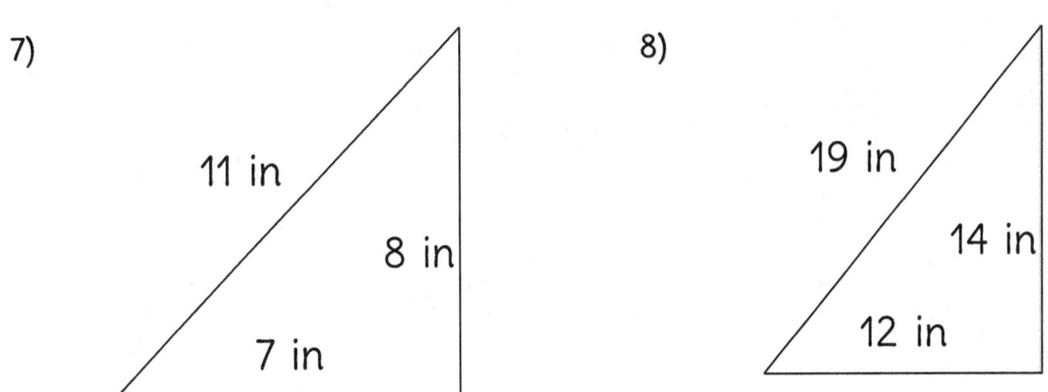

11 in

10 in

6)

15 in

9 in

12 in

7)

11 in

8 in

7 in

8)

19 in

14 in

12 in

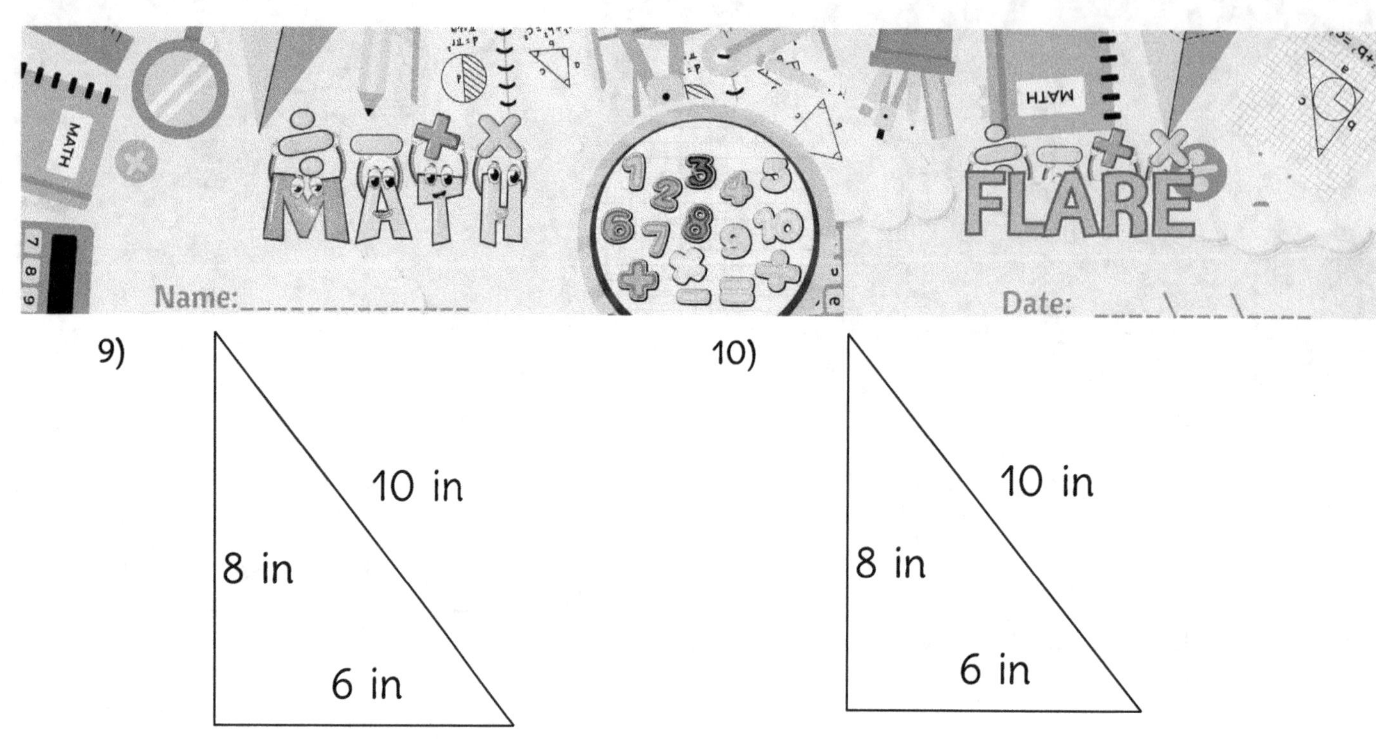

9)

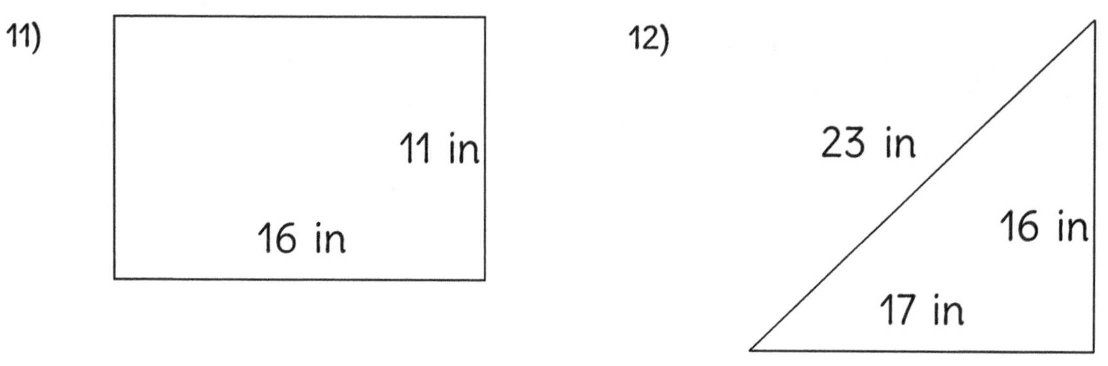

10)

10 in
8 in
6 in

11)

11 in
16 in

12)

23 in
16 in
17 in

13)
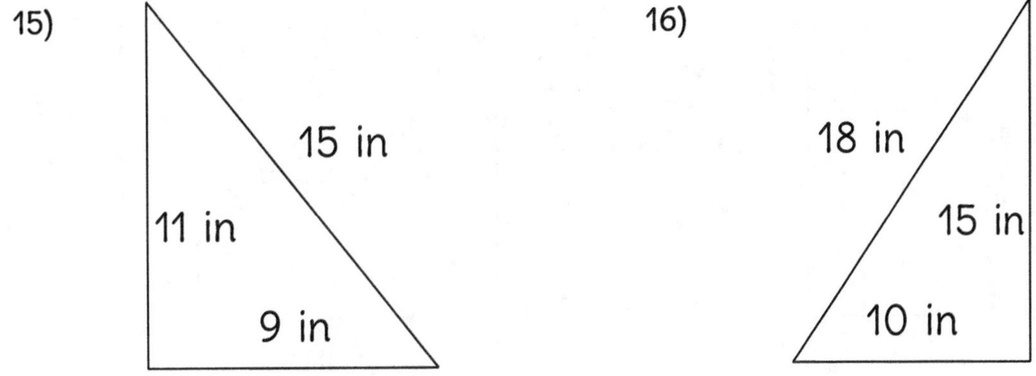

9 in

9 in

14)

8 in

9 in

15)

15 in

11 in

9 in

16)

18 in

15 in

10 in

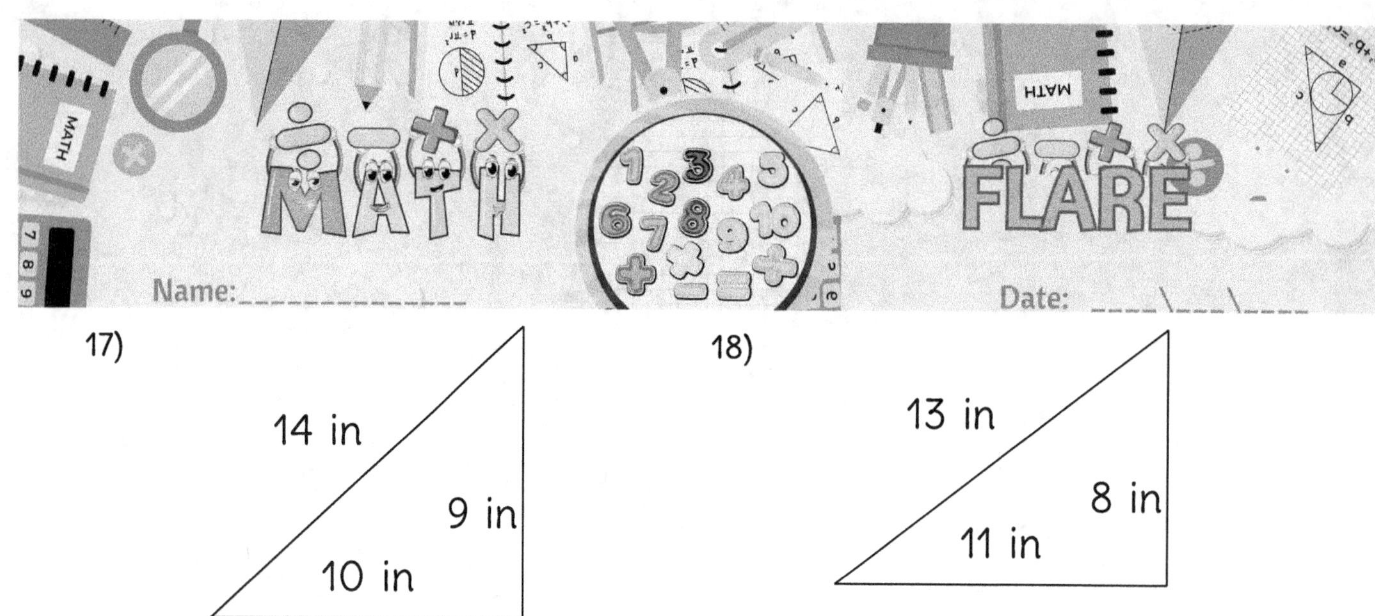

17)

14 in
9 in
10 in

18)

13 in
8 in
11 in

19)

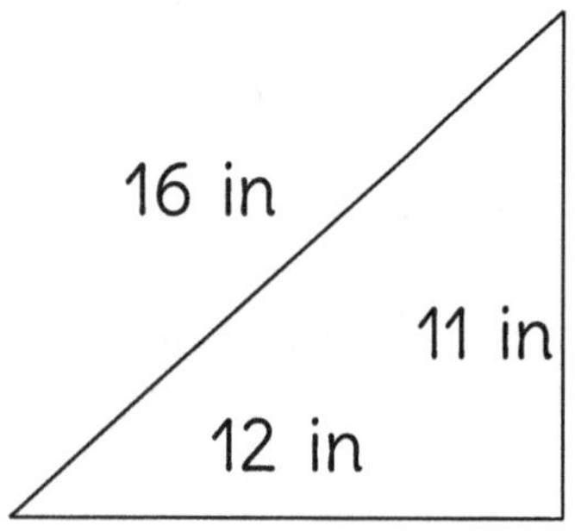

16 in
11 in
12 in

20)

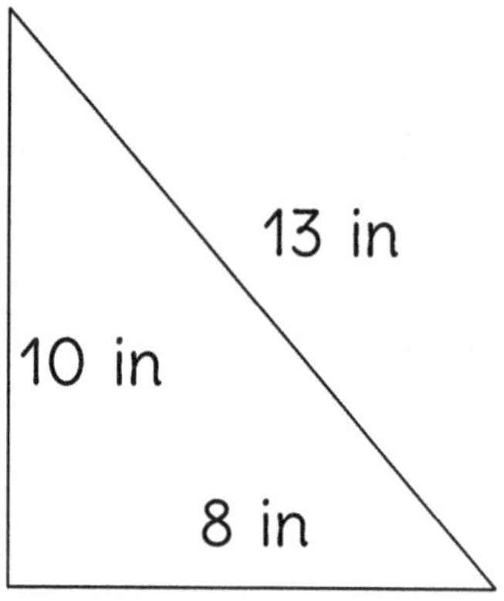

13 in
10 in
8 in

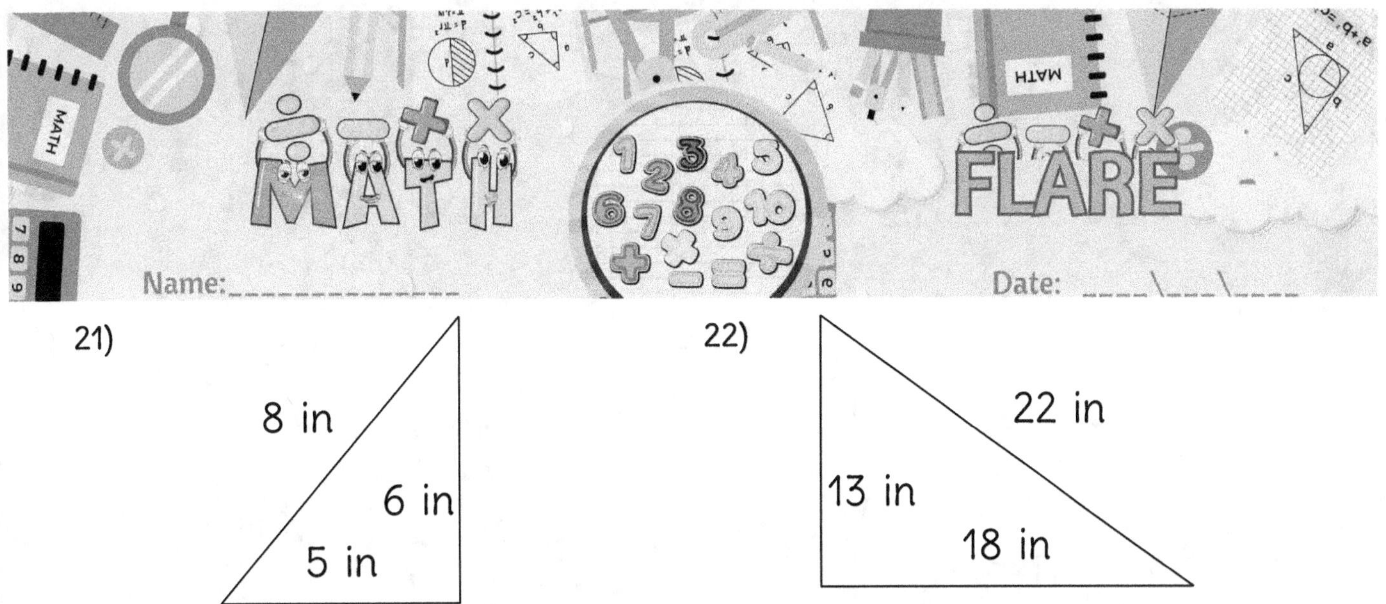

21)

8 in

6 in

5 in

22)

22 in

13 in

18 in

23)

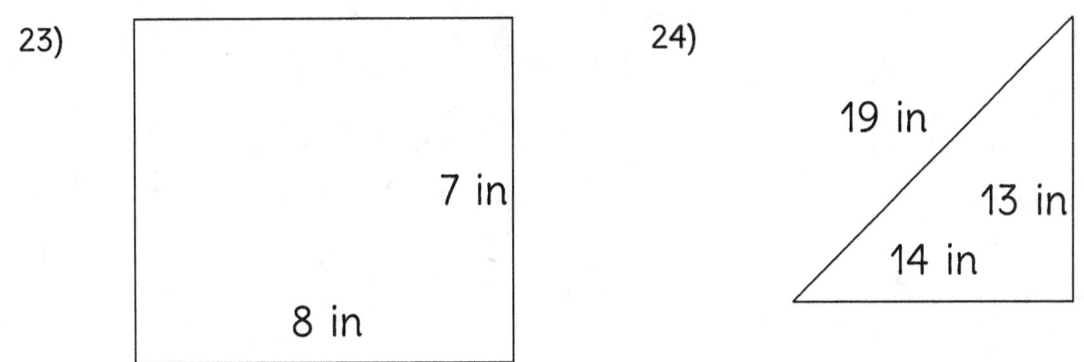

7 in

8 in

24)

19 in

13 in

14 in

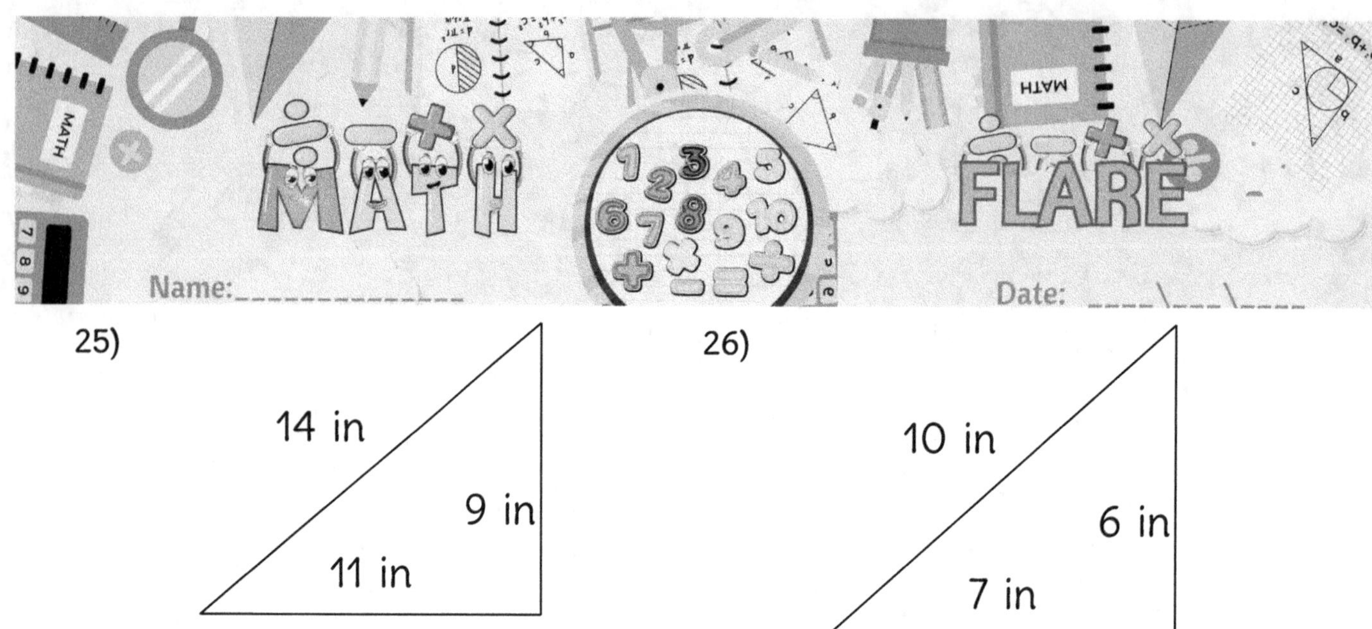

25)

14 in
9 in
11 in

26)

10 in
6 in
7 in

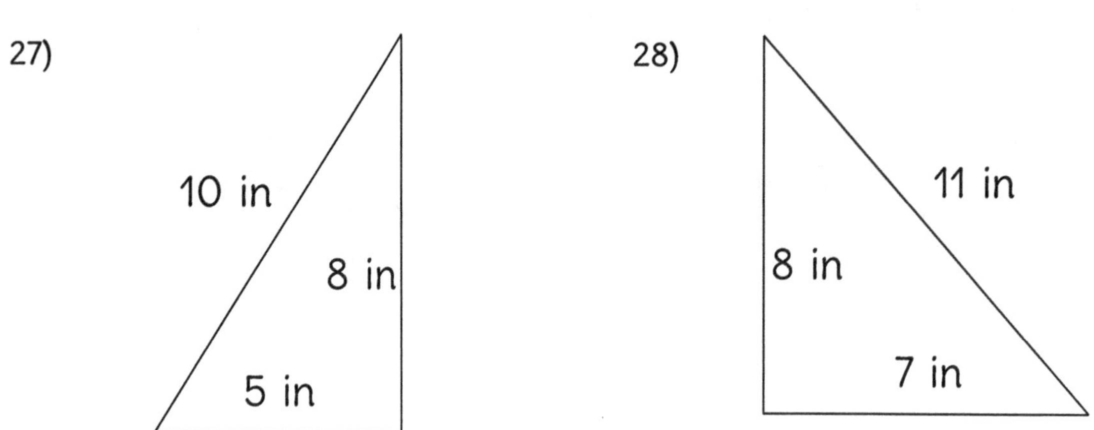

27)

10 in
8 in
5 in

28)

11 in
8 in
7 in

135

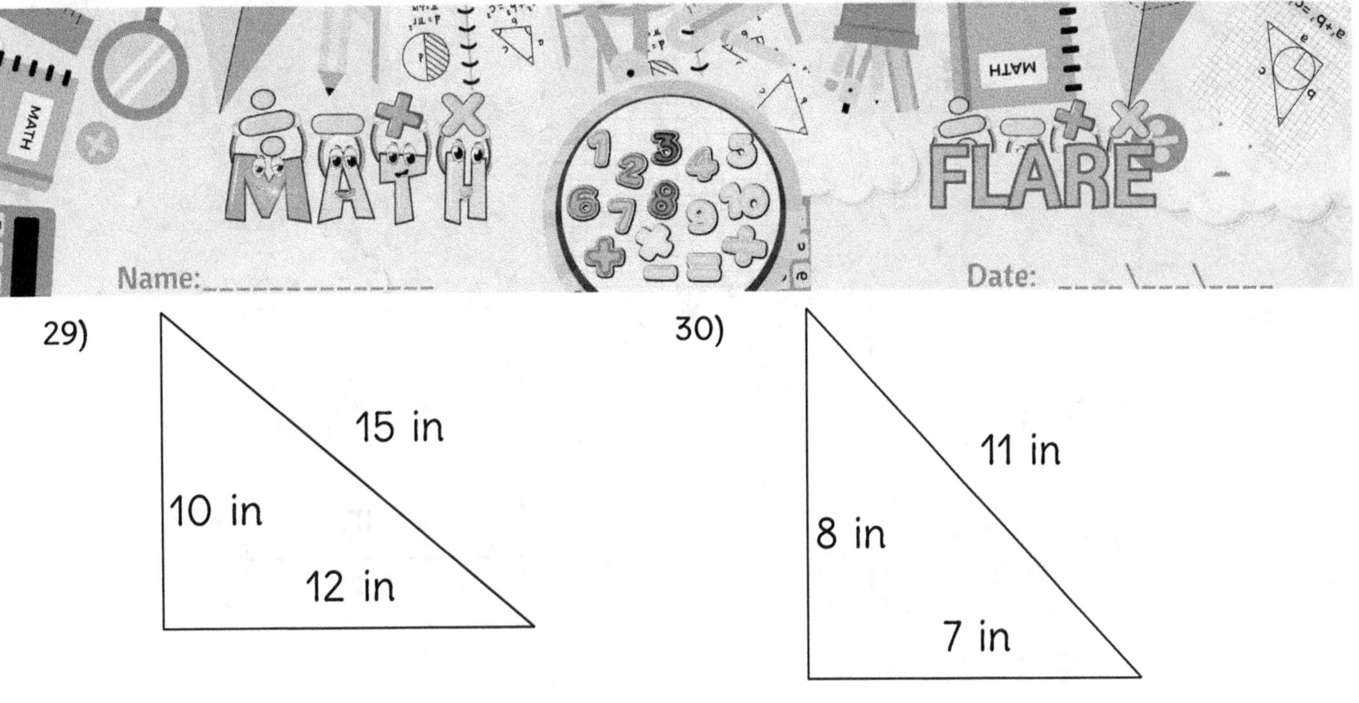

29)

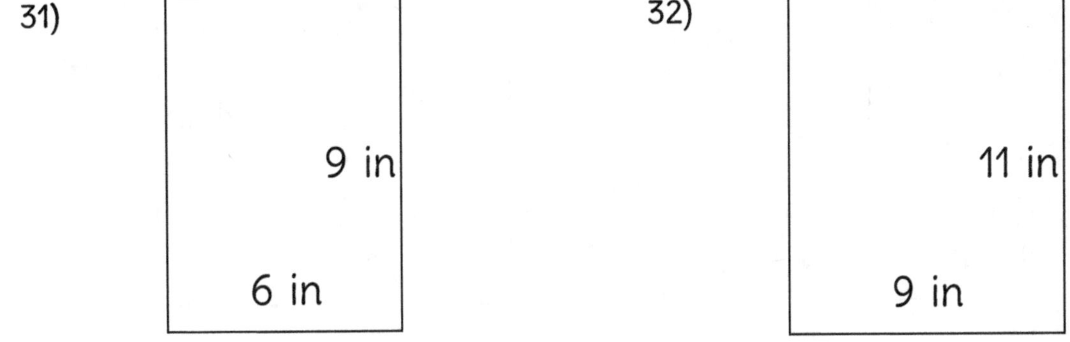

15 in

10 in

12 in

30)

11 in

8 in

7 in

31)

9 in

6 in

32)

11 in

9 in

Name: _________________ Date: ____________

33)

9 in
6 in
6 in

34)

12 in
13 in

35)

21 in
17 in
12 in

36)

14 in
13 in

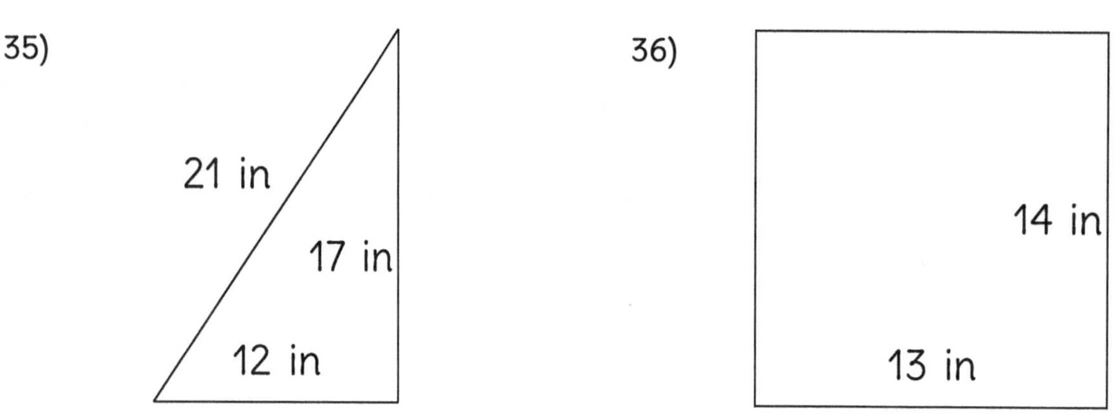

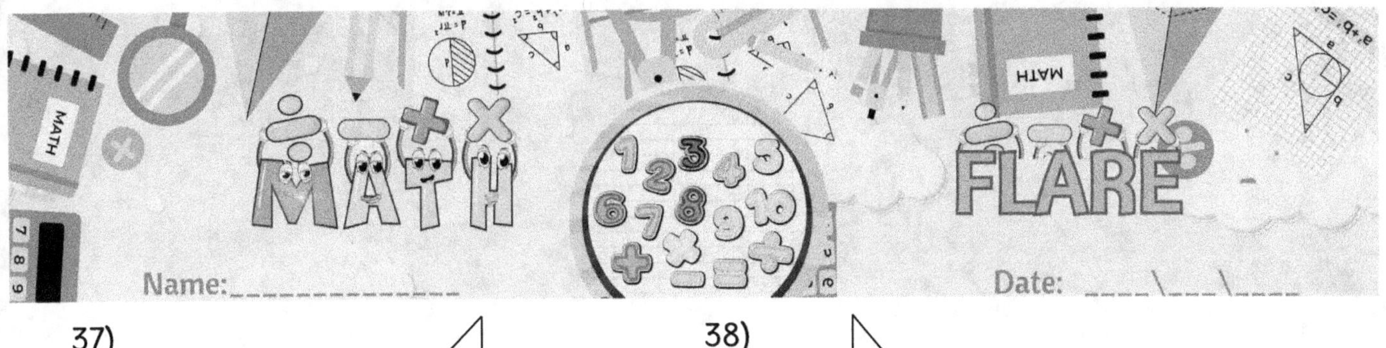

37)

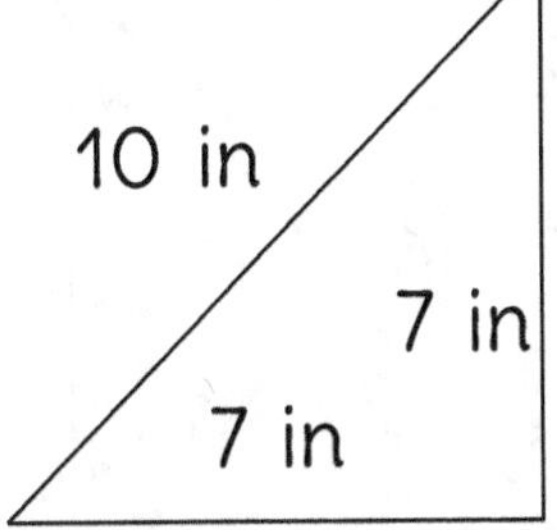

38)

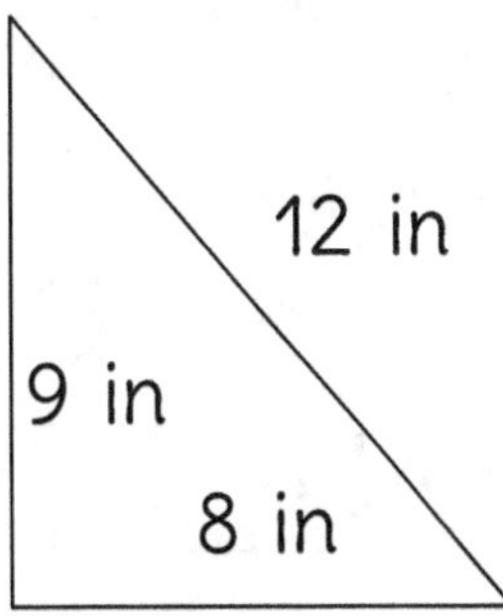

39)

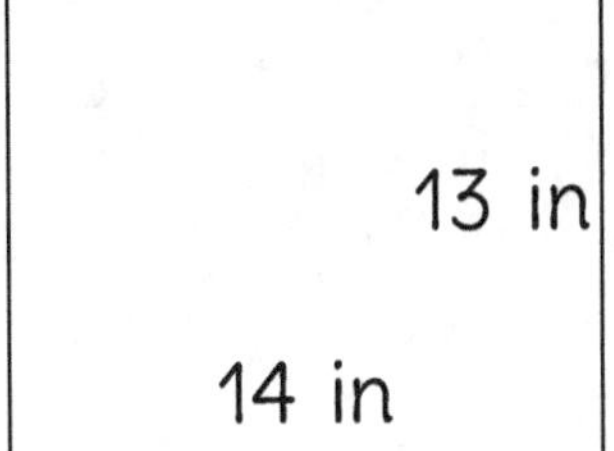

40)

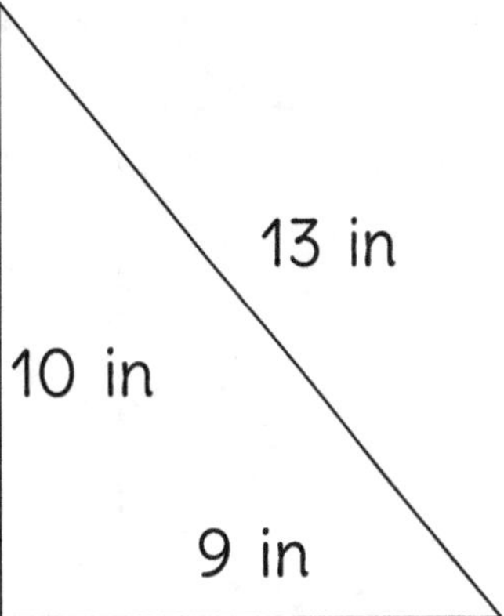

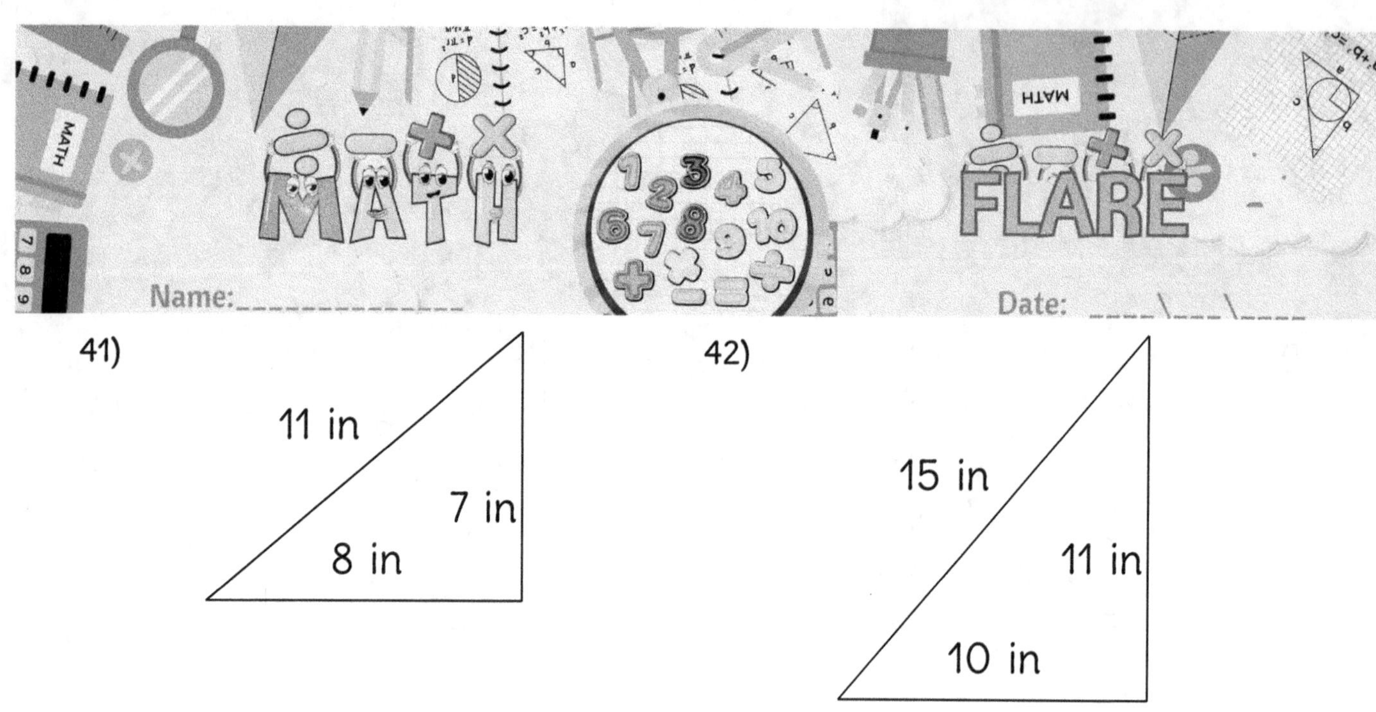

41)

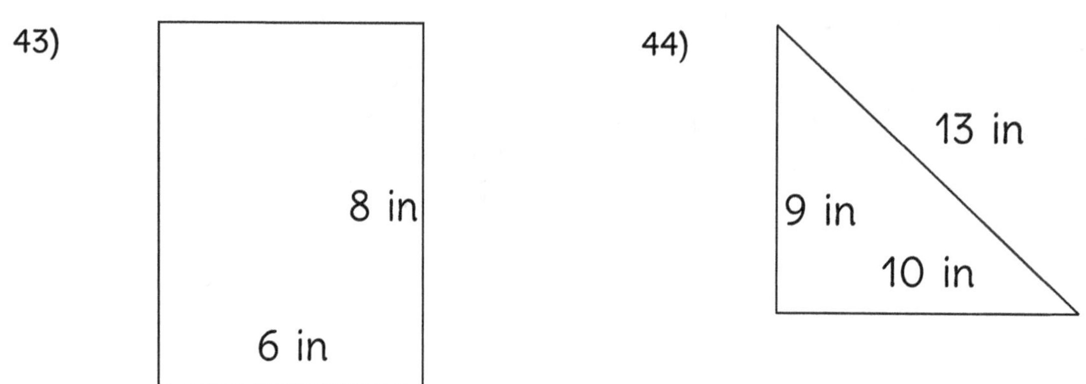

42)

43)

44)

Name:
Date:
MATH
FLARE

45)

10 in
7 in
8 in

46)

11 in
8 in
8 in

47)

19 in
13 in
13 in

48)

12 in
7 in
10 in

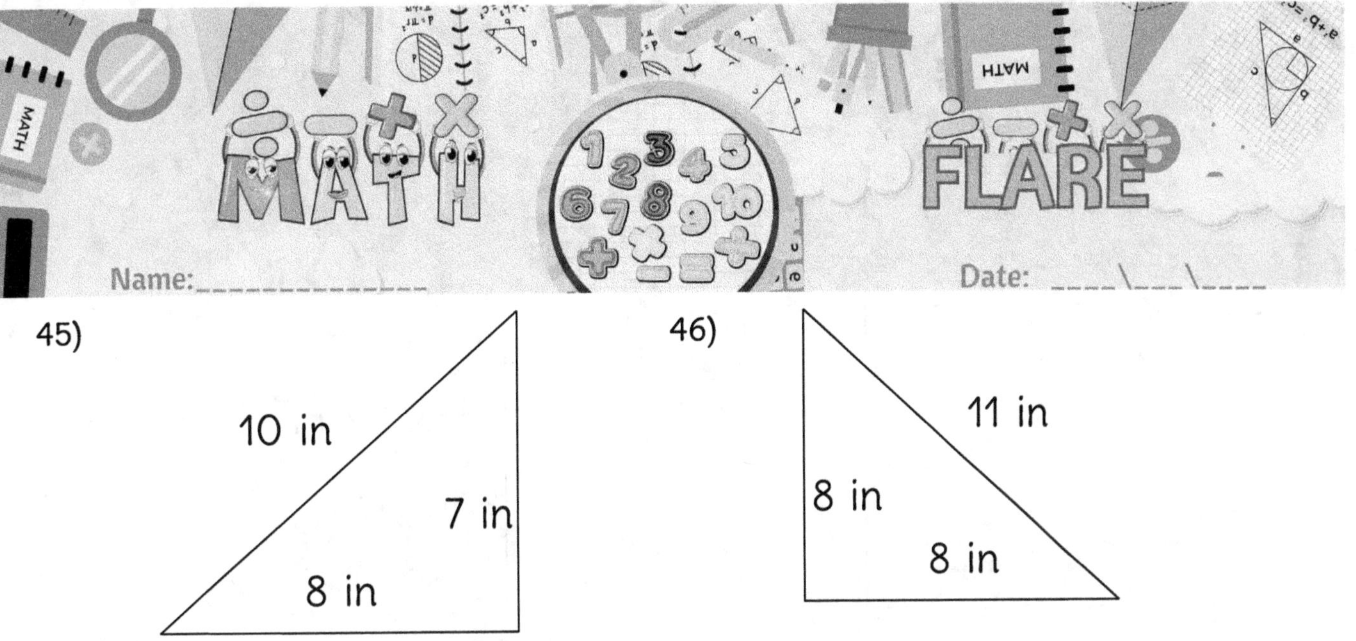

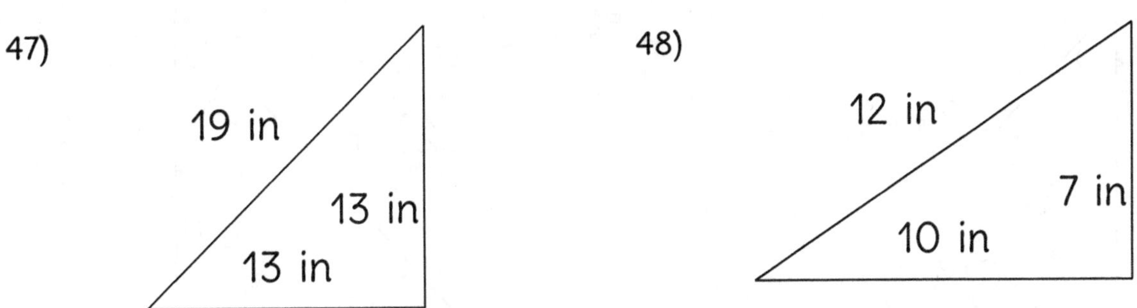

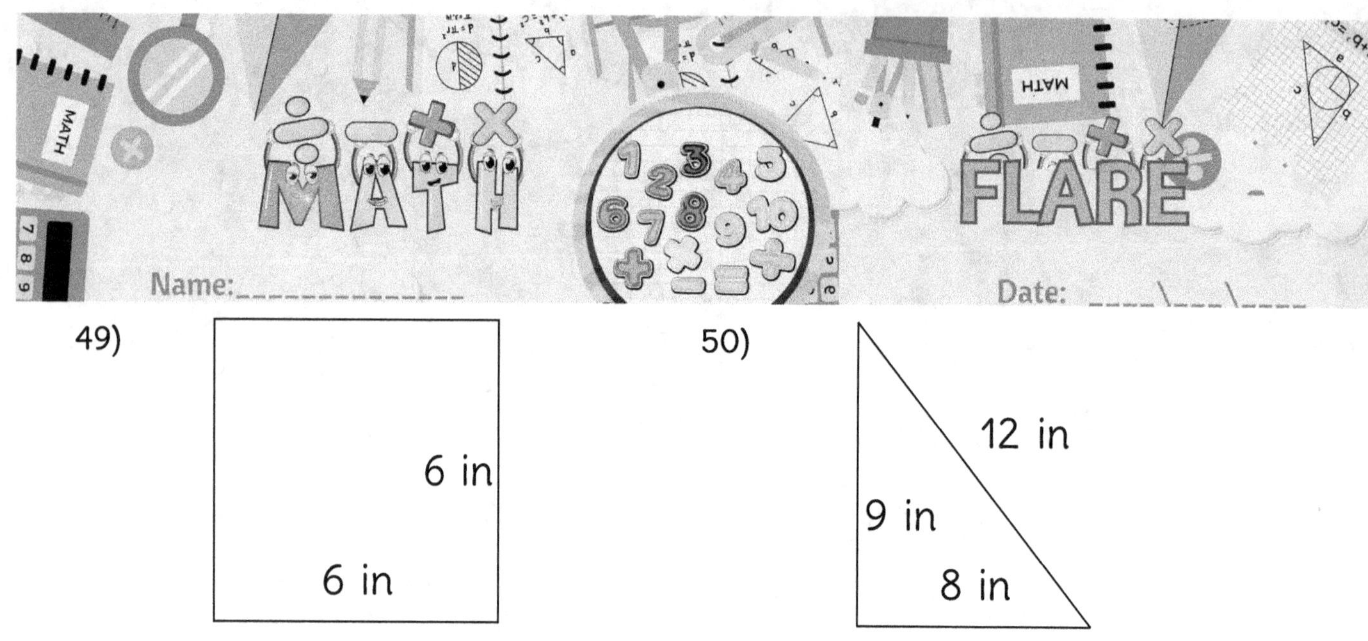

49)

50)

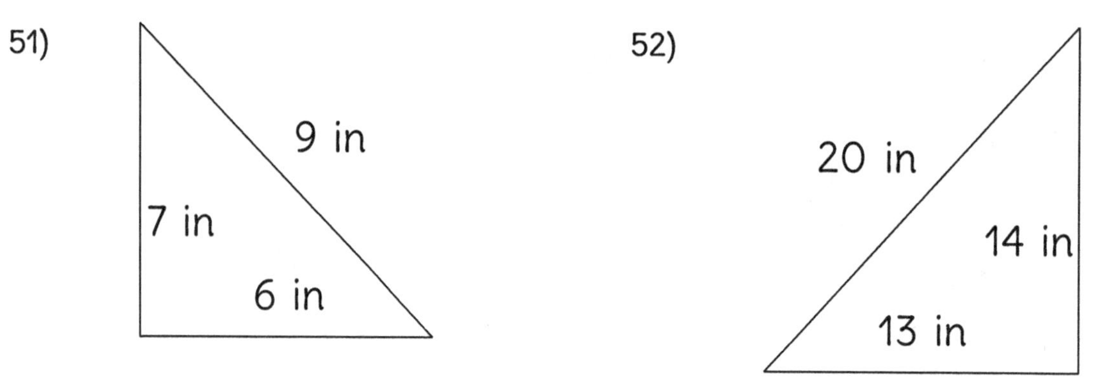

51)

52)

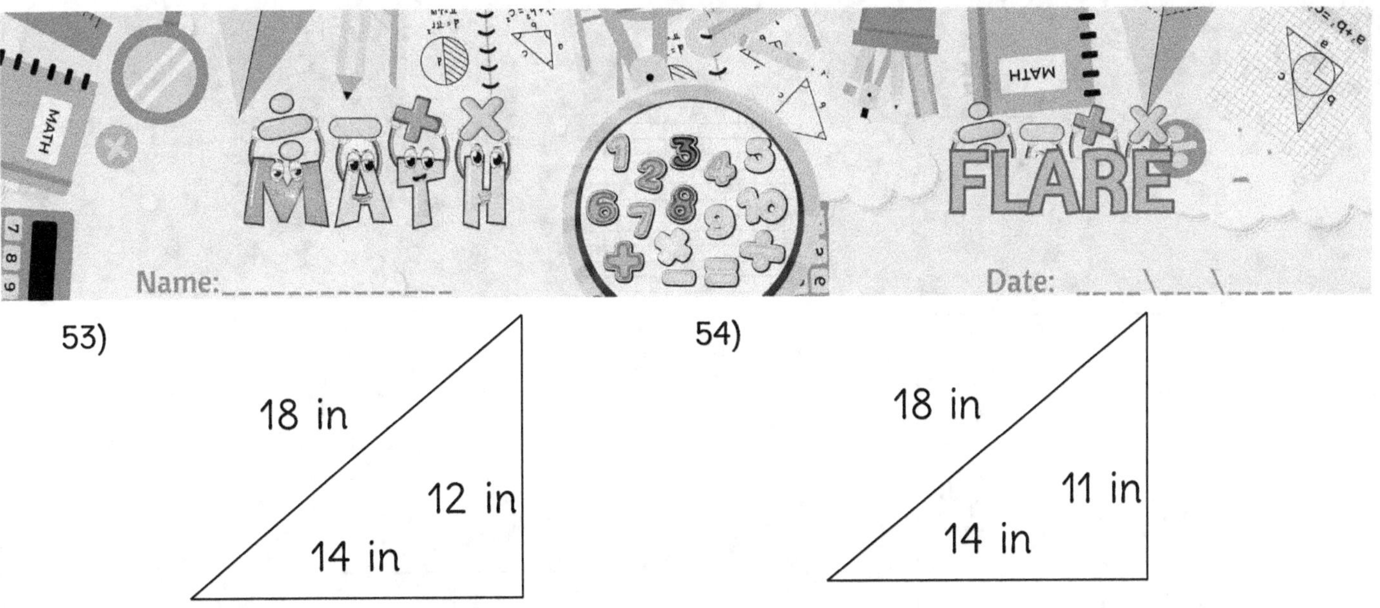

53)

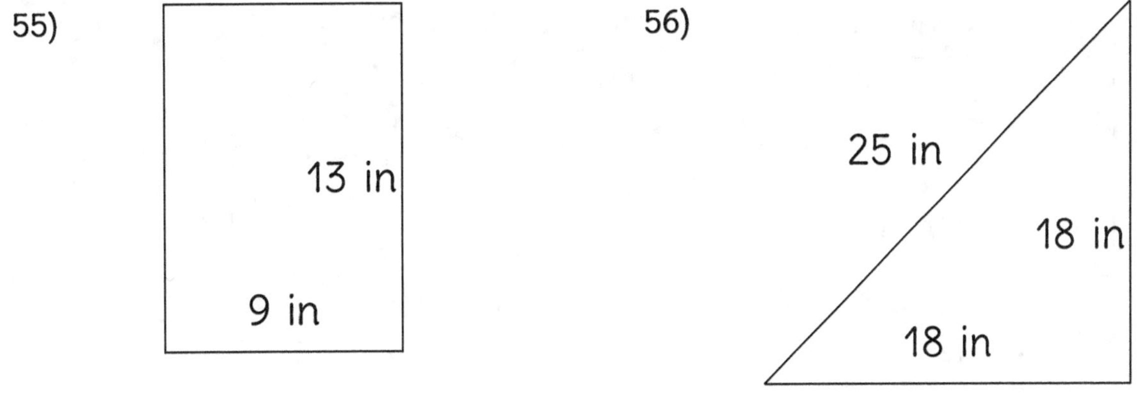

54)

18 in
11 in
14 in

55)

13 in

9 in

56)

25 in
18 in
18 in

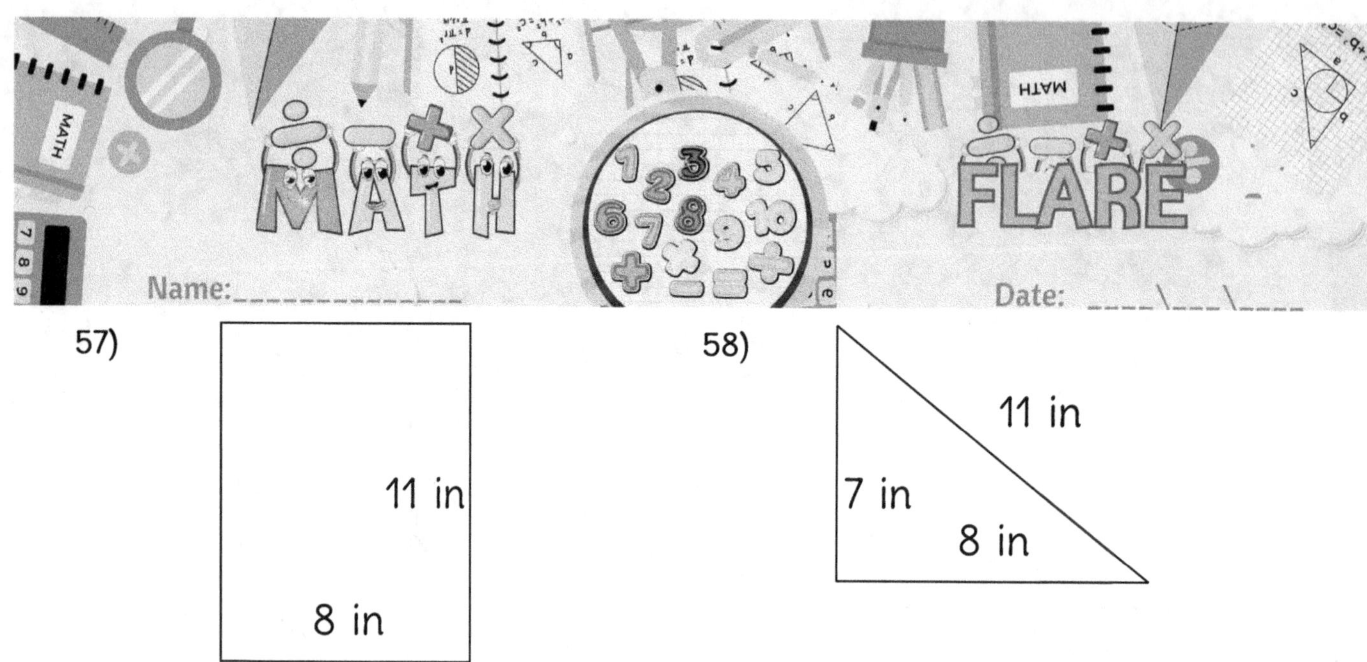

57)

58)

59)

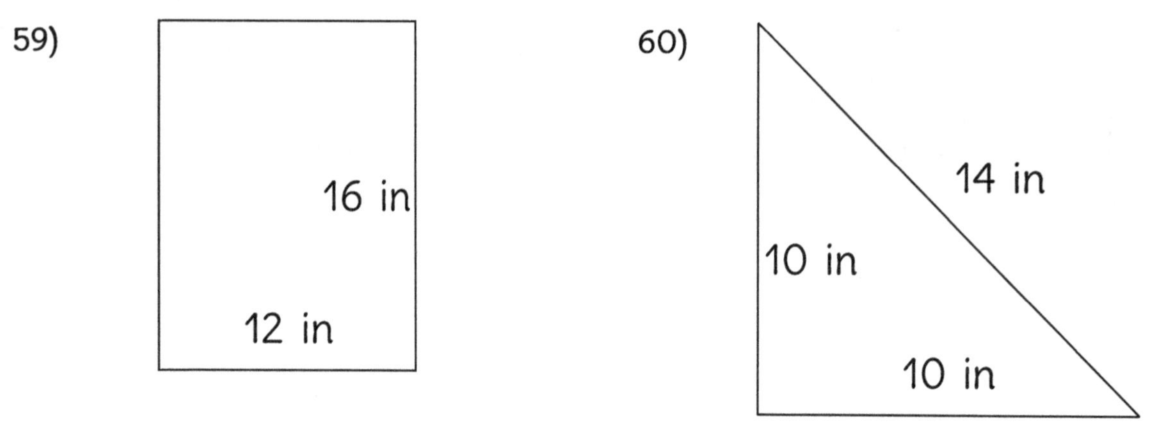

60)

143

MATH
FLARE
Name:
Date:

61)

9 in
7 in
6 in

62)

17 in
12 in
12 in

63)

15 in
13 in

64)

17 in
13 in

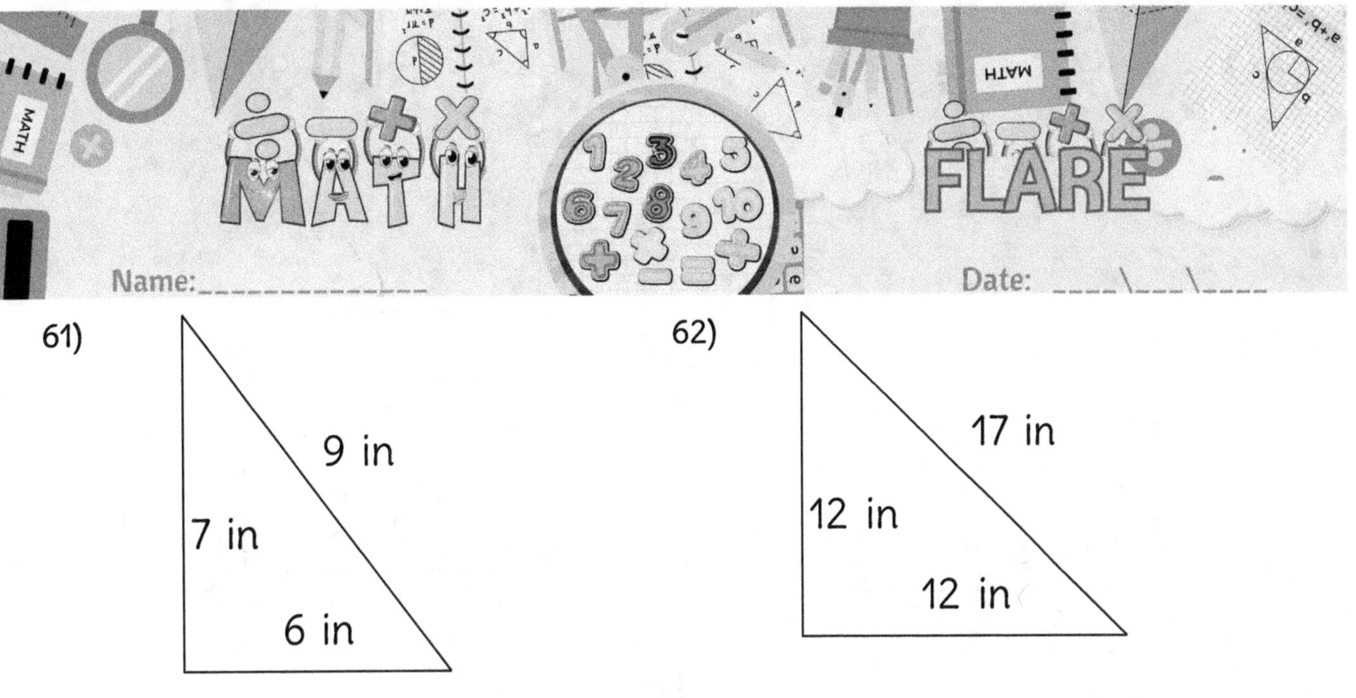

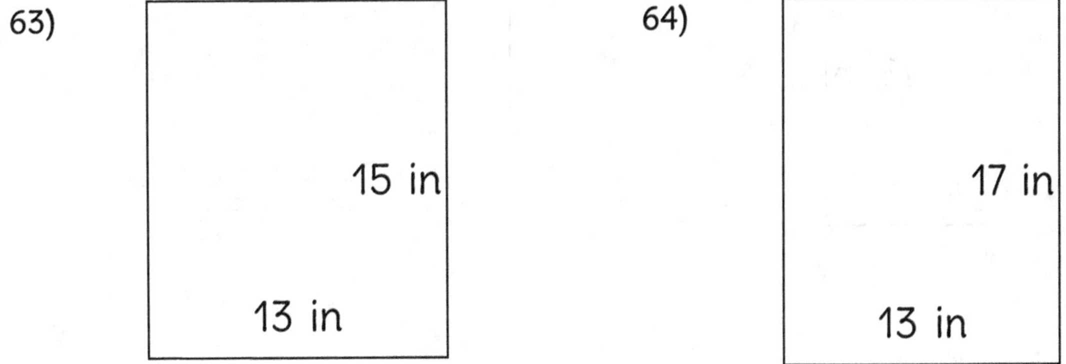

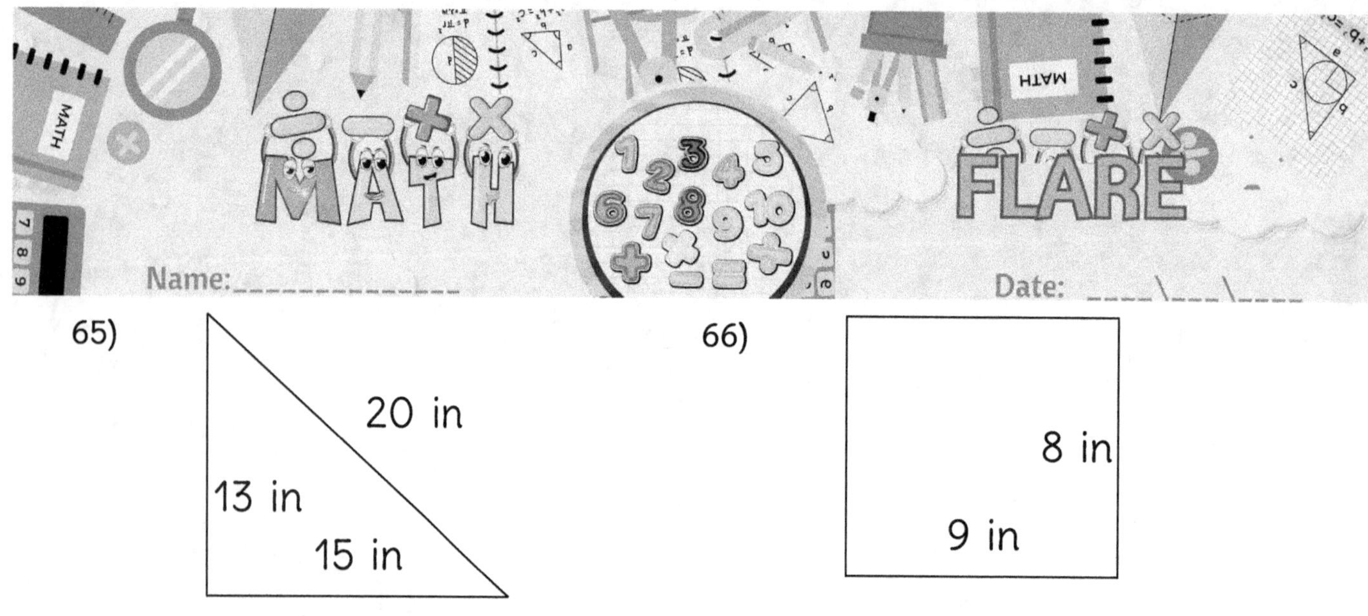

65)

20 in

13 in

15 in

66)

8 in

9 in

67)

13 in

13 in

68)

6 in

8 in

Name:
Date:
MATH
FLARE

69)

10 in
9 in

70)

13 in
10 in
10 in

71)

9 in
7 in

72)

16 in
11 in
11 in

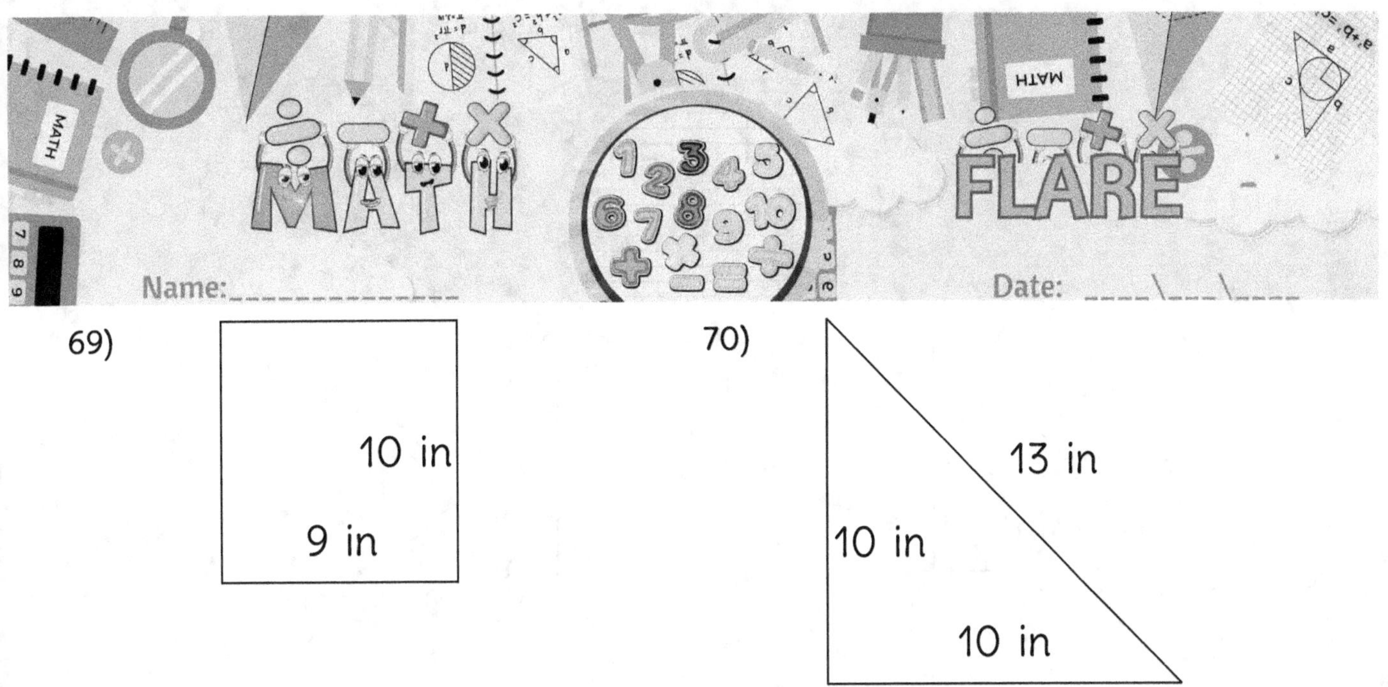

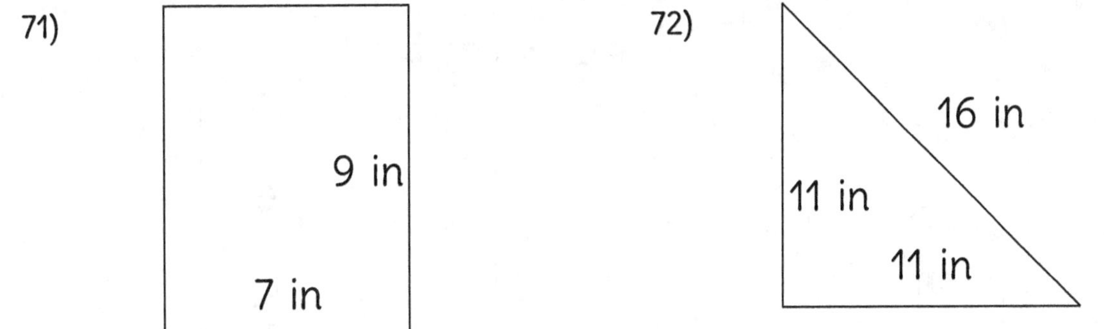

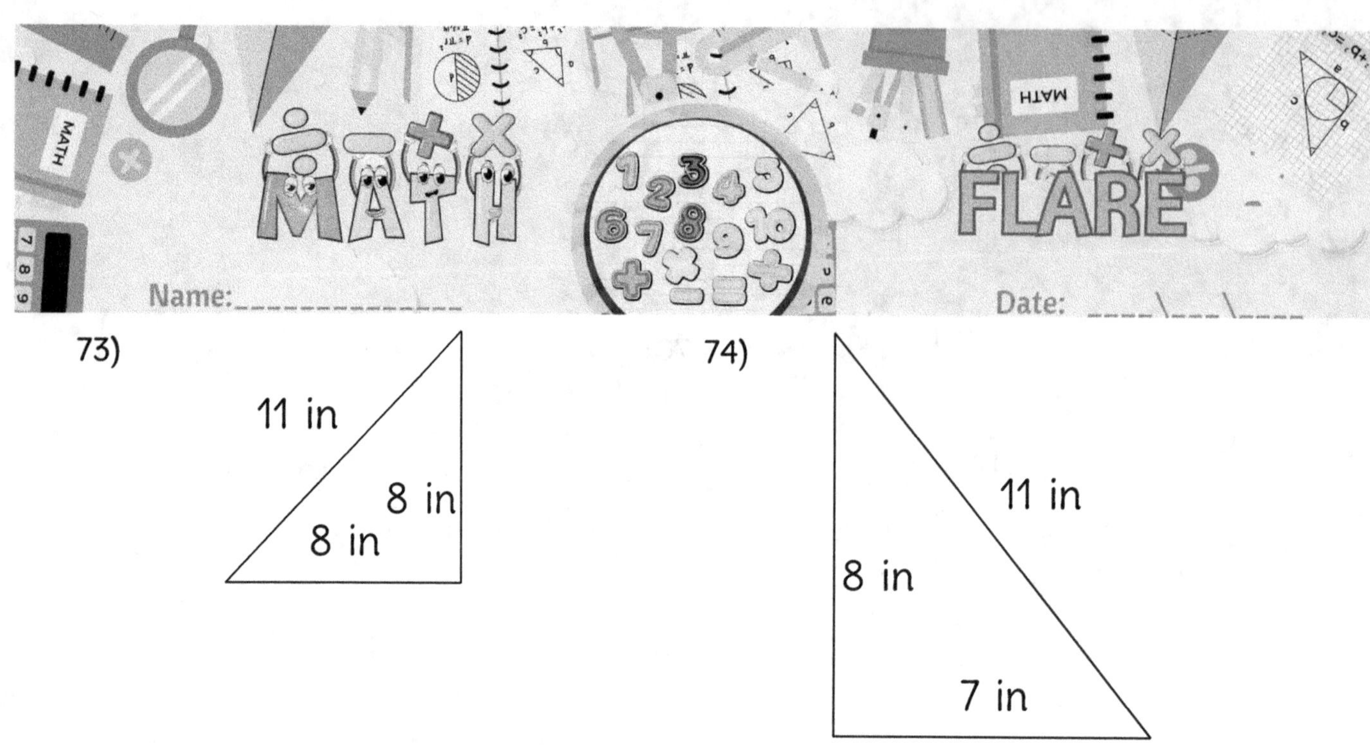

73)

11 in
8 in
8 in

74)

11 in
8 in
7 in

75)

22 in
13 in
18 in

76)

6 in
6 in

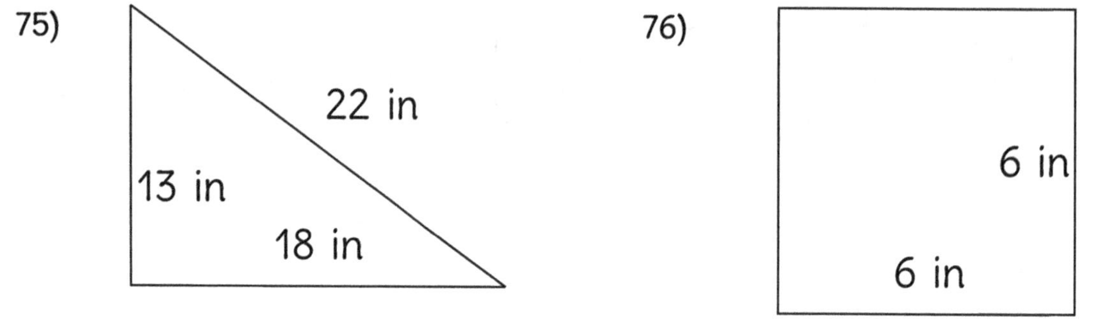

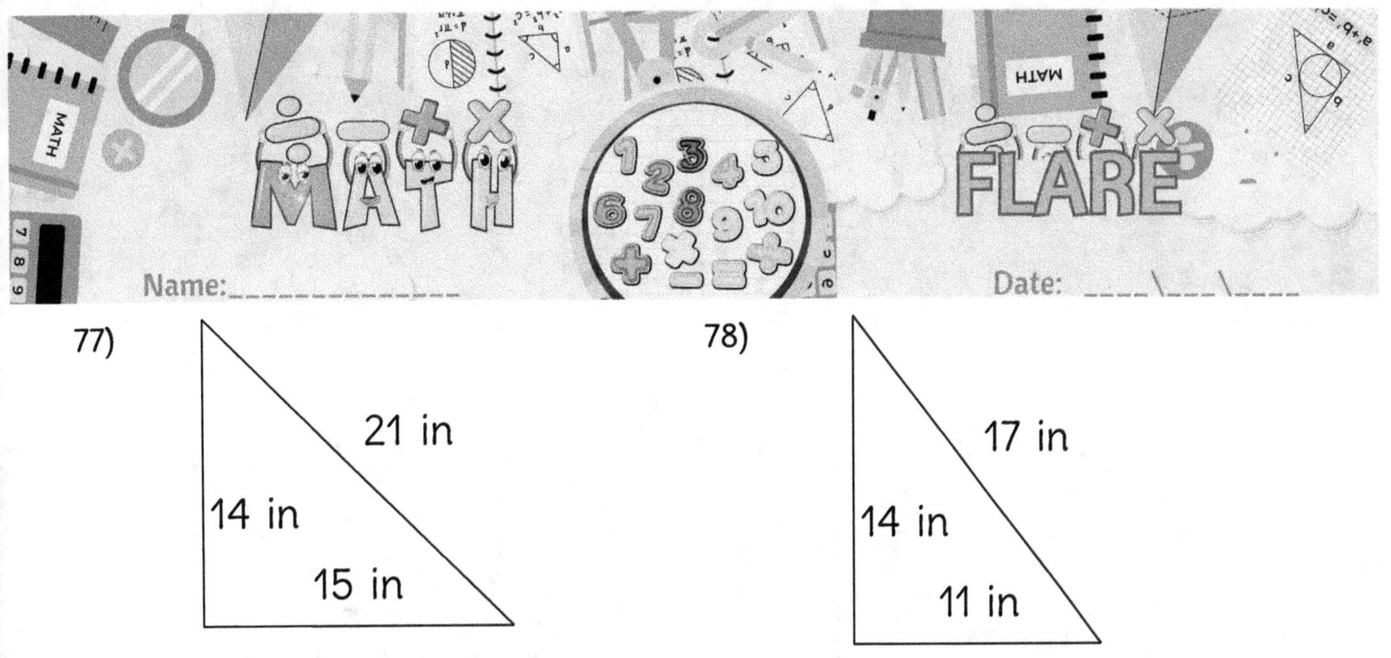

77)

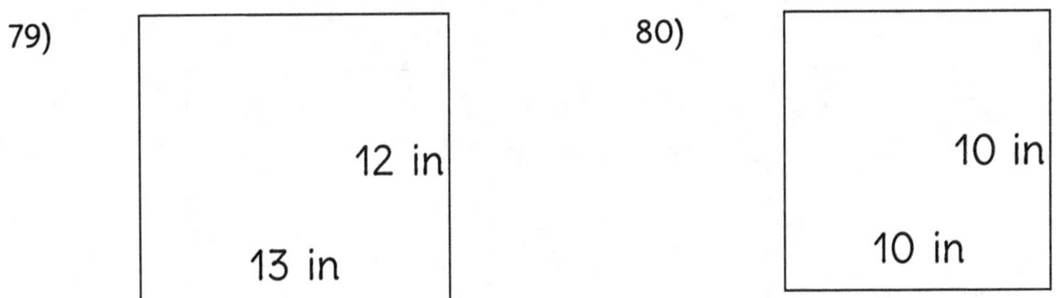

78)

21 in → 17 in
14 in
11 in

79)

12 in
13 in

80)

10 in
10 in

Name:
Date:
MATH
FLARE

81)

11 in
8 in
8 in

82)

13 in
9 in
10 in

83)

11 in
14 in

84)

16 in
15 in

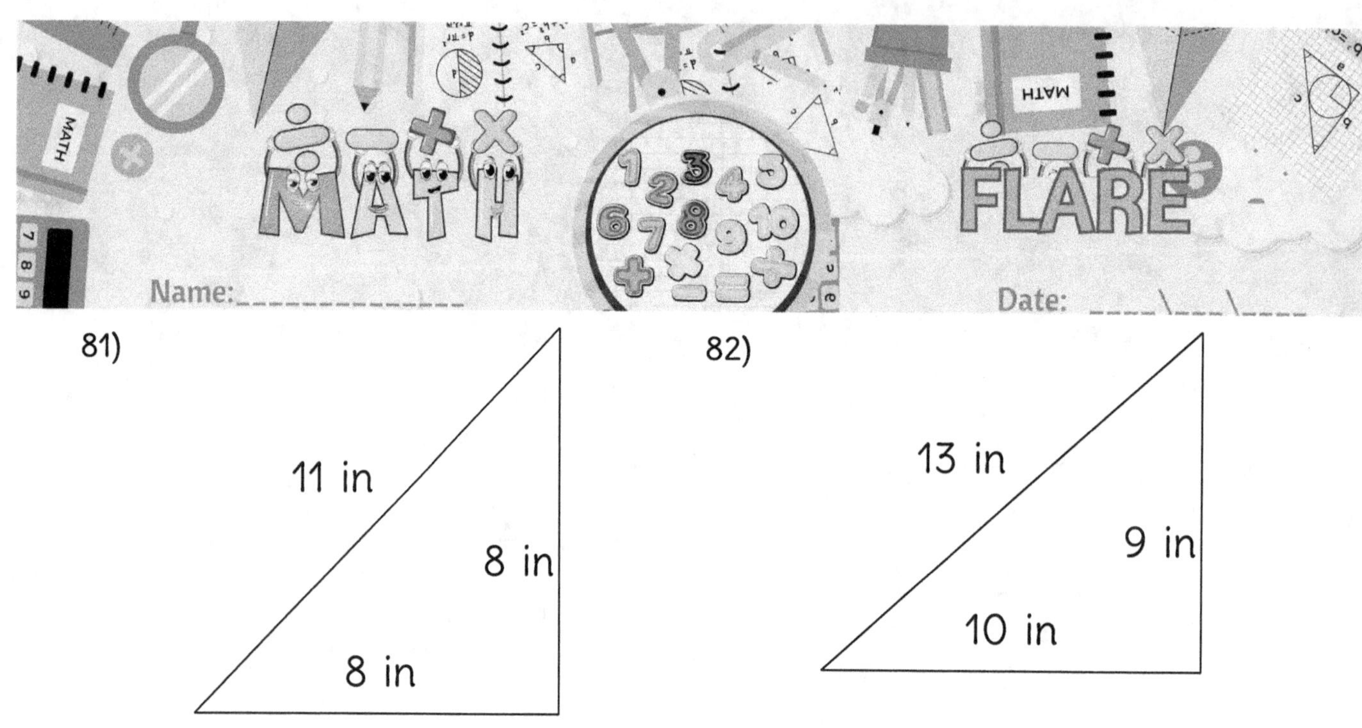

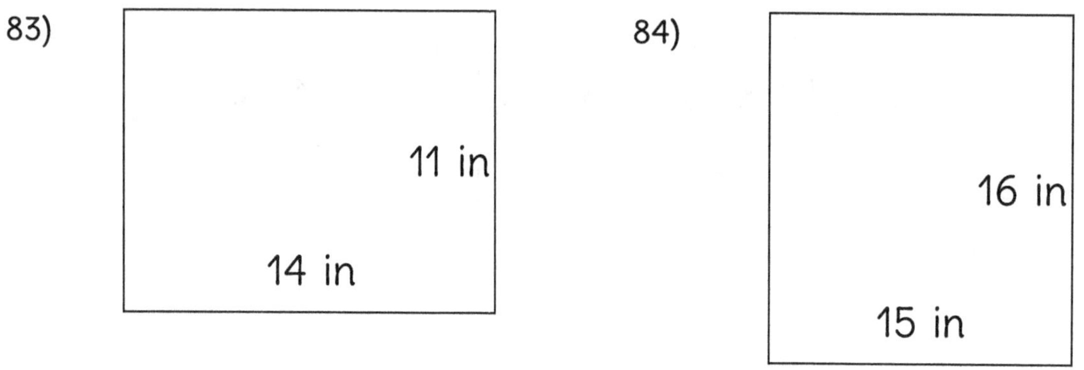

MATH
FLARE
Name:
Date:

85)

8 in
7 in

86)

9 in
6 in
7 in

87)

8 in
11 in

88)

13 in
8 in
10 in

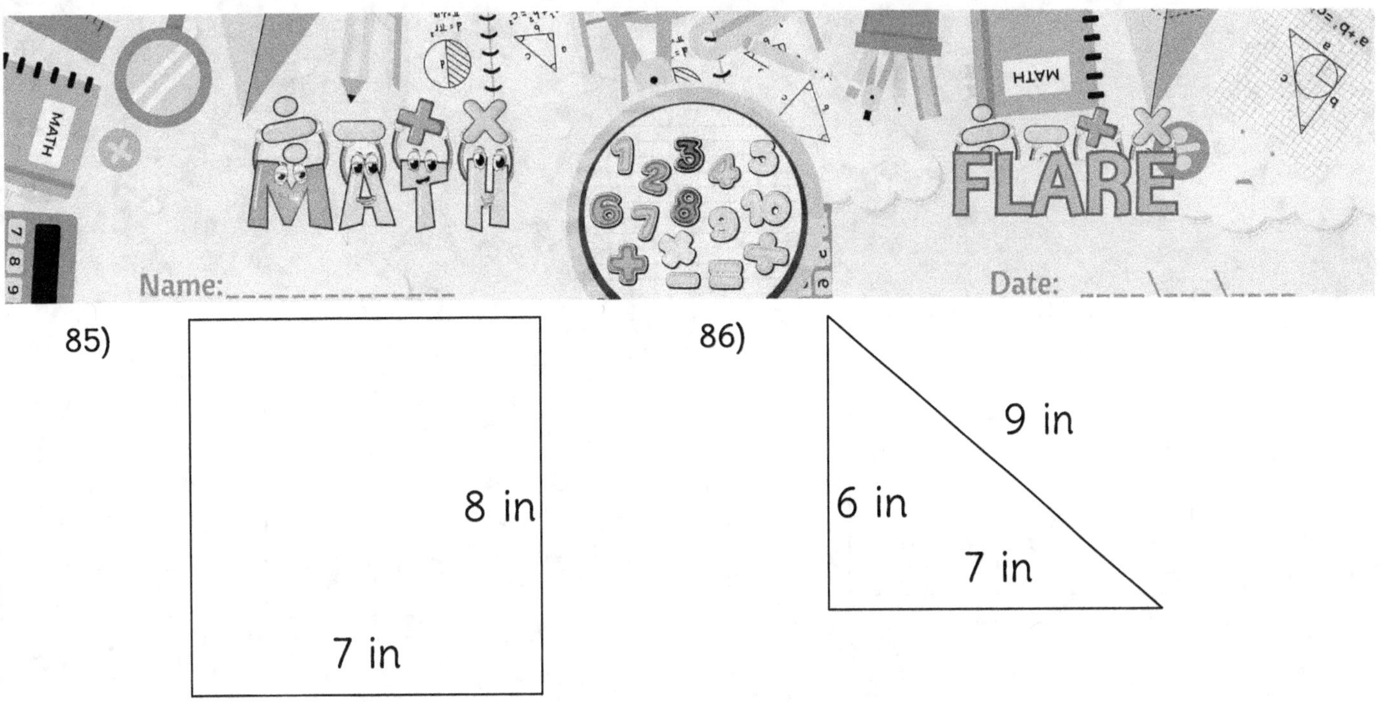

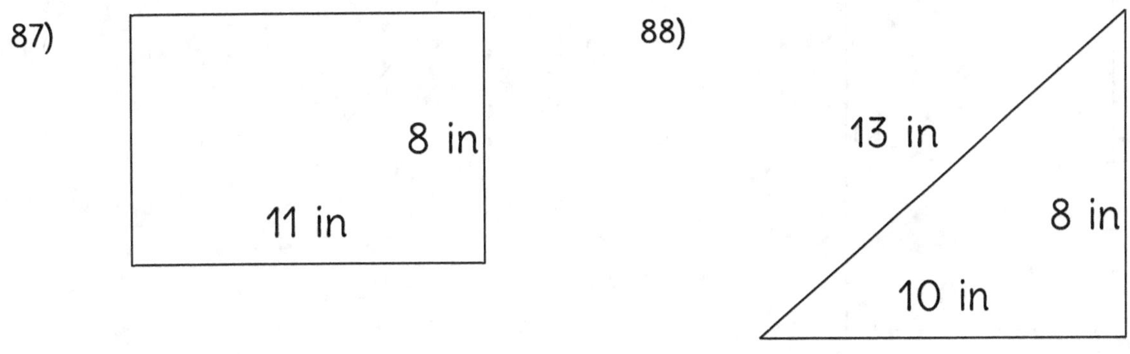

MATH
FLARE
Name:
Date:

89)

13 in
17 in

90)

8 in
7 in

91)

17 in
12 in

92)

21 in
16 in
12 in

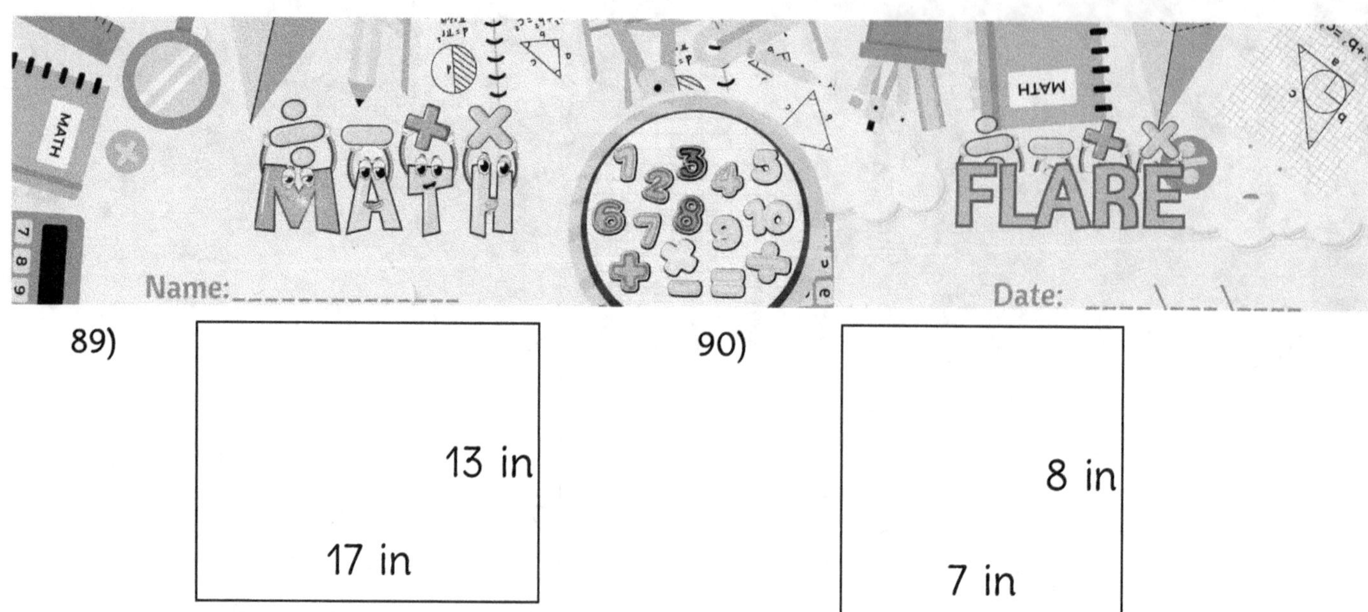

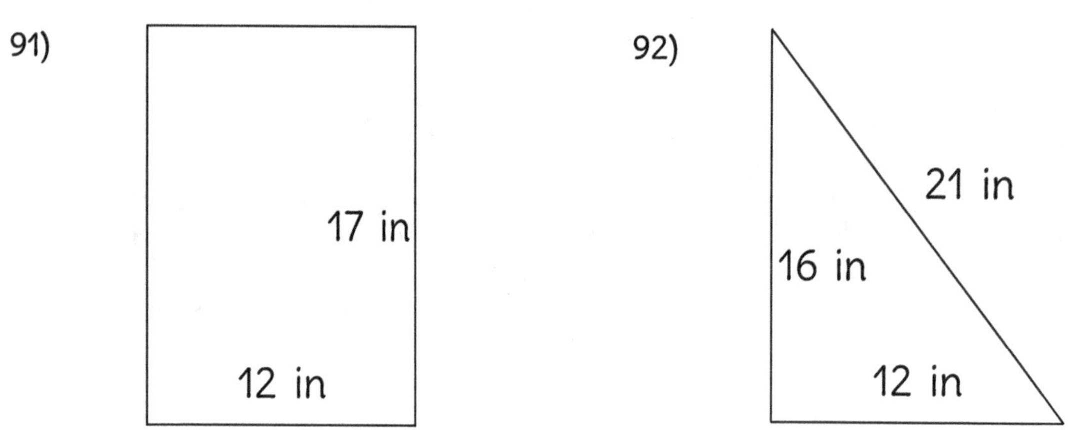

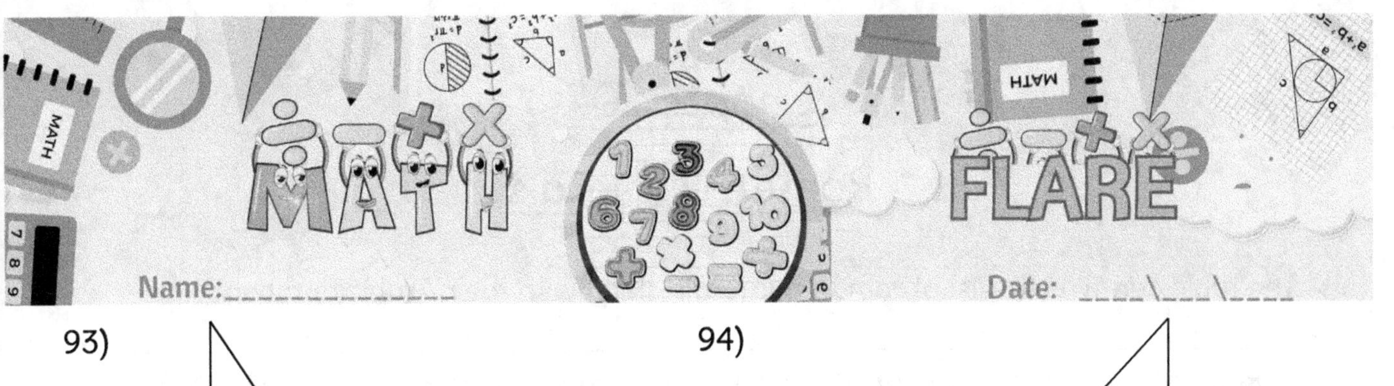

93)

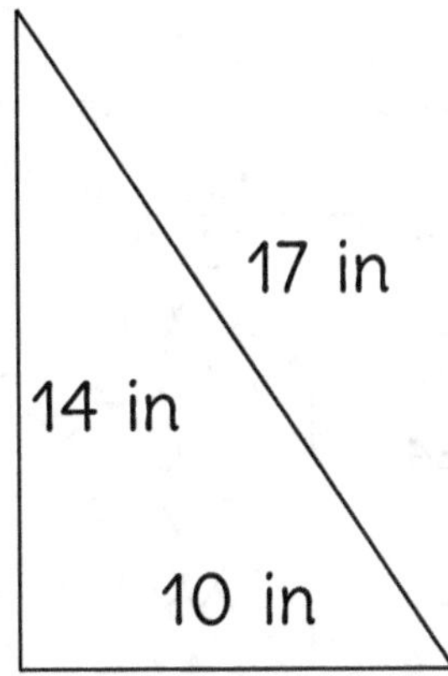

94)

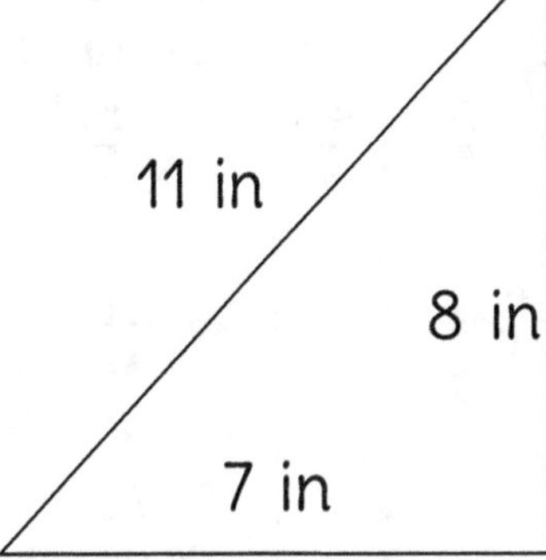

95)

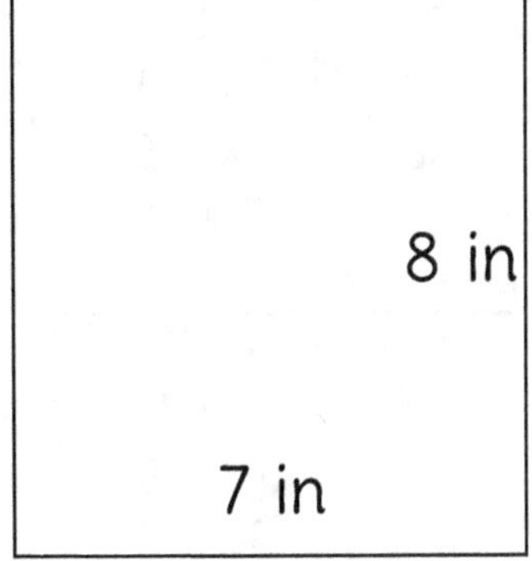

96)

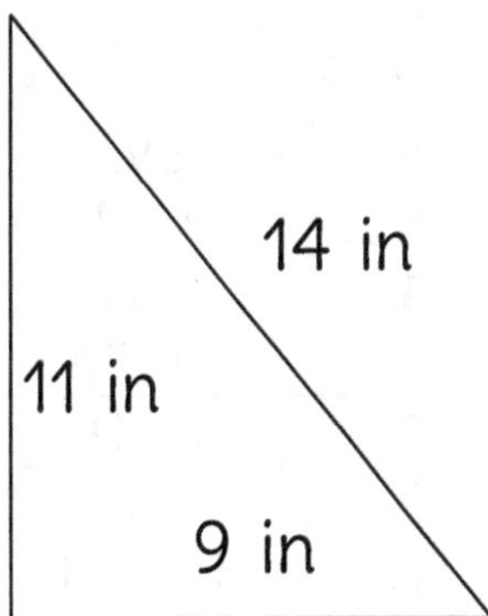

Chapter. 07

Roman Numerals

The table contains the list of roman numerals along with their Arabic number.

Roman Numeral	Arabic Number	Roman Numeral	Arabic Number	Roman Numeral	Arabic Number	Roman Numeral	Arabic Number
I	1	XI	11	XXI	21	XXXI	31
II	2	XII	12	XXII	22	XXXII	32
III	3	XIII	13	XXIII	23	XXXIII	33
IV	4	XIV	14	XXIV	24	XXXIV	34
V	5	XV	15	XXV	25	XXXV	35
VI	6	XVI	16	XXVI	26	XXXVI	36
VII	7	XVII	17	XXVII	27	XXXVII	37
VIII	8	XVIII	18	XXVIII	28	XXXVIII	38
IX	9	XIX	19	XXIX	29	XXXIX	39
X	10	XX	20	XXX	30	XL	40
XLI	41	L	50	LI	51	LXI	61
XLII	42	LI	52	LX	60	LXII	62
XLIII	43	LII	53	LXI	61	LXIII	63
XLIV	44	LIII	54	LXIV	64	LXIV	64
XLV	45	LIV	55	LXV	65	LXV	65
XLVI	46	LV	56	LXVI	66	LXVI	66
XLVII	47	LVI	57	LXVII	67	LXVII	67
XLVIII	48	LVII	58	LXVIII	68	LXVIII	68
XLIX	49	LVIII	59	LXIX	69	LXIX	69
L	50	LIX	59	LXX	70	LXX	70
LXXI	71	LXXX	80	LXXXI	81	XC	90
LXXII	72	LXXXI	81	LXXXII	82	XCI	91
LXXIII	73	LXXXII	82	LXXXIII	83	XCII	92
LXXIV	74	LXXXIII	83	LXXXIV	84	XCIII	93
LXXV	75	LXXXIV	84	LXXXV	85	XCIV	94
LXXVI	76	LXXXV	85	LXXXVI	86	XCV	95
LXXVII	77	LXXXVI	86	LXXXVII	87	XCVI	96
LXXVIII	78	LXXXVII	87	LXXXVIII	88	XCVII	97
LXXIX	79	LXXXVIII	88	LXXXIX	89	XCVIII	98
LXXX	80	LXXXIX	89	XC	90	XCIX	99
LXXXI	81	XC	90	XCI	91	C	100

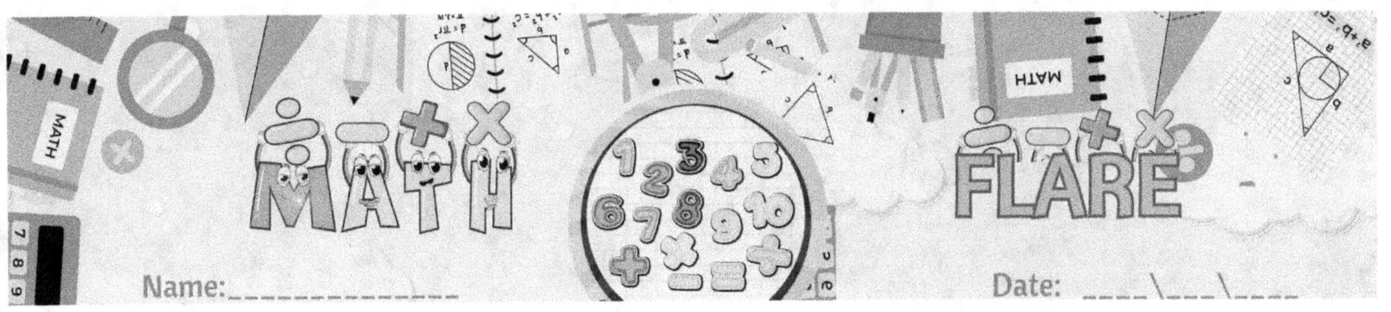

Roman Numerals

1) IV = _____4_____

2) V = __________

3) VII = __________

4) VI = __________

5) II = __________

6) XXXV = _____35_____

7) XXVIII = __________

8) III = __________

9) XXXII = __________

10) IX = __________

11) XIV = __________

12) XLII = __________

13) XXXIX = __________

14) VIII = __________

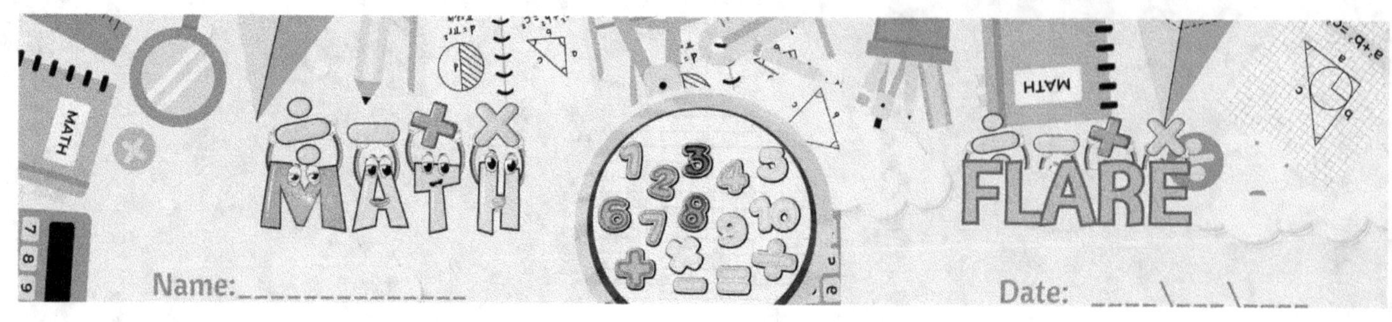

15) XX = ___________________

16) XXXIII = ___________________

17) XXV = ___________________

18) XLIX = ___________________

19) XXXIV = ___________________

20) L = ___________________

21) X = ___________________

22) I = ___________________

23) XXIV = ___________________

24) XXXVII = ___________________

25) XXVI = ___________________

26) XLV = ___________________

27) XLVII = ___________________

28) XXIII = ___________________

29) XLIII = ___________________

30) XLVIII = ___________________

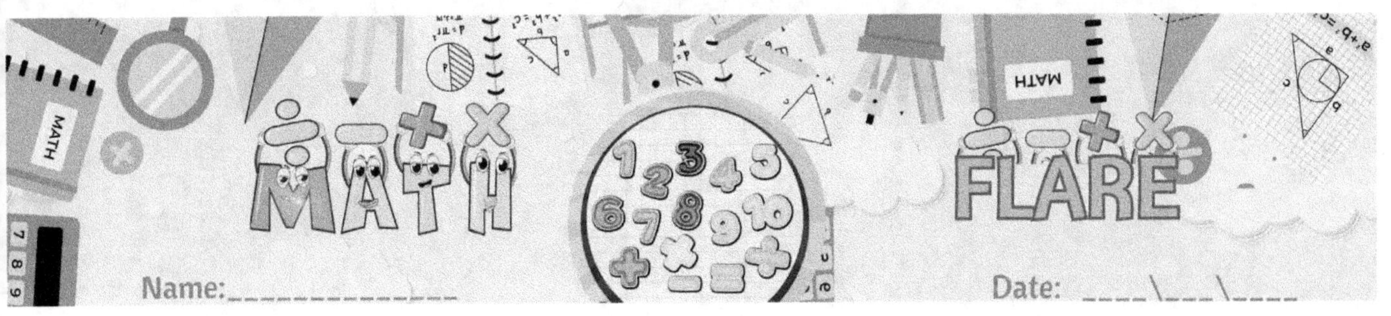

31) XLVI = _______________

32) XXX = _______________

33) XXVII = _______________

34) XXXVI = _______________

35) XVI = _______________

36) XIX = _______________

37) XVIII = _______________

38) XLIV = _______________

39) XVII = _______________

40) XL = _______________

41) XIII = _______________

42) XXIX = _______________

43) XXII = _______________

44) XXXI = _______________

ANSWERS

Page 1: Addition with Regrouping

1. 1,511	2. 1,730	3. 1,824	4. 1,510	5. 1,251
6. 1,310	7. 1,532	8. 1,573	9. 1,115	10. 1,130
11. 1,510	12. 1,174	13. 1,510	14. 1,421	15. 1,140
16. 1,451	17. 1,110	18. 1,240	19. 1,111	20. 1,222
21. 1,230	22. 1,161	23. 1,310	24. 1,211	25. 1,670
26. 1,216	27. 1,113	28. 1,240	29. 1,422	30. 1,224
31. 1,264	32. 1,160	33. 1,211	34. 1,615	35. 1,620
36. 1,140	37. 1,440	38. 1,413	39. 1,414	40. 1,410
41. 1,321	42. 1,270	43. 1,411	44. 1,953	45. 1,163
46. 1,122	47. 1,241	48. 1,524	49. 1,111	50. 1,320
51. 1,110	52. 1,121	53. 1,493	54. 1,212	55. 1,510
56. 1,212	57. 1,831	58. 1,212	59. 1,151	60. 1,111
61. 1,411	62. 1,422	63. 1,311	64. 1,232	65. 1,730
66. 1,230	67. 1,821	68. 1,331	69. 1,142	70. 1,251
71. 1,244	72. 1,110	73. 1,414	74. 1,110	75. 1,216
76. 1,370	77. 1,123	78. 1,180	79. 1,110	80. 1,321
81. 1,817	82. 1,131	83. 1,211	84. 1,311	85. 1,161
86. 1,130	87. 1,180	88. 1,311	89. 1,135	90. 1,311

91. 1,210   92. 1,934   93. 1,523   94. 1,322   95. 1,210

96. 1,921   97. 1,113   98. 1,272   99. 1,531   100. 1,360

101. 1,211   102. 1,371   103. 1,620   104. 1,212   105. 1,234

106. 1,113   107. 1,110   108. 1,410   109. 1,450   110. 1,410

111. 1,727   112. 1,360   113. 1,667   114. 1,181   115. 1,140

116. 1,410   117. 1,211   118. 1,111   119. 1,230   120. 1,112

Page 7: Subtraction with Regrouping

1. 84   2. 83   3. 177   4. 136   5. 161   6. 88

7. 163   8. 272   9. 77   10. 58   11. 381   12. 581

13. 187   14. 773   15. 176   16. 153   17. 67   18. 129

19. 53   20. 83   21. 376   22. 137   23. 73   24. 137

25. 135   26. 282   27. 687   28. 87   29. 54   30. 282

31. 24   32. 87   33. 411   34. 77   35. 84   36. 73

37. 276   38. 166   39. 484   40. 387   41. 46   42. 141

43. 85   44. 14   45. 287   46. 78   47. 86   48. 57

49. 52   50. 182   51. 133   52. 87   53. 66   54. 218

55. 482   56. 767   57. 483   58. 322   59. 83   60. 57

61. 62   62. 679   63. 51   64. 476   65. 329   66. 769

67. 171   68. 52   69. 241   70. 185   71. 47   72. 83

73. 273   74. 87   75. 283   76. 84   77. 433   78. 173

79. 54   80. 567   81. 287   82. 47   83. 138   84. 63

85. 69	86. 72	87. 151	88. 125	89. 484	90. 287
91. 85	92. 231	93. 185	94. 473	95. 27	96. 469
97. 129	98. 282	99. 486	100. 674	101. 241	102. 85
103. 89	104. 383	105. 29	106. 282	107. 69	108. 61
109. 85	110. 282	111. 77	112. 162	113. 64	114. 269
115. 388	116. 344	117. 477	118. 151	119. 61	120. 289

Page 13: Addition Word Problems

1. 114	2. 47	3. 53	4. 97	5. 138	6. 95	7. 146
8. 107	9. 37	10. 82	11. 49	12. 111	13. 56	14. 73
15. 101	16. 104	17. 45	18. 24	19. 114	20. 154	21. 106
22. 139	23. 95	24. 169	25. 98	26. 97	27. 95	28. 127
29. 137	30. 111	31. 158	32. 140	33. 169	34. 116	

Page 22: Subtraction Word Problems

1. 49	2. 27	3. 19	4. 8	5. 56	6. 5	7. 8	8. 23
9. 80	10. 0	11. 39	12. 7	13. 19	14. 58	15. 15	16. 19
17. 44	18. 18	19. 3	20. 69	21. 2	22. 5	23. 0	24. 0
25. 58	26. 14	27. 14	28. 15	29. 12	30. 34	31. 15	

Page 30: Multiplication

1. 21	2. 33	3. 0	4. 10	5. 15	6. 20	7. 20
8. 11	9. 2	10. 108	11. 28	12. 24	13. 18	14. 64
15. 42	16. 4	17. 84	18. 84	19. 27	20. 32	21. 7

22. 18	23. 48	24. 25	25. 21	26. 40	27. 63	28. 81
29. 12	30. 90	31. 45	32. 12	33. 12	34. 22	35. 55
36. 33	37. 3	38. 50	39. 9	40. 32	41. 110	42. 77
43. 88	44. 72	45. 8	46. 35	47. 35	48. 54	49. 0
50. 48	51. 8	52. 30				

Page 33: Multiplication: 2 x 1

1. 44	2. 80	3. 60	4. 33	5. 15	6. 36	7. 71
8. 88	9. 48	10. 90	11. 99	12. 66	13. 55	14. 80
15. 36	16. 40	17. 50	18. 66	19. 69	20. 39	21. 42
22. 96	23. 28	24. 84	25. 26	26. 48	27. 16	28. 93
29. 82	30. 74	31. 64	32. 62	33. 30	34. 25	35. 64
36. 86	37. 91	38. 68	39. 84	40. 24	41. 22	42. 20
43. 40	44. 88	45. 46	46. 84	47. 85	48. 37	49. 67
50. 63	51. 41	52. 38	53. 60	54. 52	55. 77	56. 94
57. 12	58. 48	59. 44	60. 83	61. 92	62. 19	63. 11
64. 28	65. 18	66. 69	67. 26	68. 89	69. 98	70. 45
71. 70	72. 10	73. 53	74. 99	75. 75	76. 93	77. 62
78. 82	79. 86	80. 68	81. 66	82. 24	83. 22	84. 61
85. 78	86. 42	87. 40	88. 50	89. 20	90. 80	91. 13
92. 60	93. 76	94. 32	95. 14	96. 47	97. 95	98. 54
99. 55	100. 57	101. 81	102. 44	103. 23	104. 34	105. 17

106. 87   107. 31   108. 35

Page 40: Division

1. 6   2. 3   3. 4   4. 10   5. 3   6. 2   7. 9   8. 1   9. 5

10. 4   11. 4   12. 8   13. 9   14. 3   15. 6   16. 6   17. 8   18. 4

19. 2   20. 8   21. 8   22. 8   23. 2   24. 5   25. 9   26. 9   27. 7

28. 2   29. 6   30. 3   31. 10   32. 9   33. 2   34. 7   35. 3   36. 4

37. 2   38. 7   39. 7   40. 5   41. 2   42. 5   43. 10   44. 6   45. 1

46. 8   47. 9   48. 4   49. 7   50. 2   51. 1   52. 8

Page 43: Long Division (double digit)

1. 8   2. 66   3. 2   4. 76   5. 12   6. 66

7. 93   8. 66   9. 10   10. 9   11. 51   12. 75

13. 56   14. 54   15. 57   16. 25   17. 38   18. 65

19. 28   20. 89   21. 62   22. 45   23. 22   24. 14

25. 50   26. 47   27. 79   28. 64   29. 84   30. 96

31. 80   32. 96   33. 19   34. 90   35. 61   36. 32

37. 16   38. 8   39. 32   40. 67   41. 6   42. 30

43. 54   44. 95   45. 30   46. 39   47. 49   48. 74

49. 18   50. 93   51. 20   52. 17   53. 68   54. 98

55. 100   56. 12   57. 78   58. 68   59. 11   60. 80

61. 40   62. 25   63. 37   64. 33   65. 8   66. 24

67. 54   68. 94   69. 75   70. 35   71. 35   72. 39

73. 29   74. 97   75. 97   76. 9   77. 40   78. 73

79. 37   80. 76   81. 21   82. 43   83. 53   84. 92

85. 3   86. 44   87. 80   88. 46   89. 71   90. 88

91. 60   92. 20   93. 90   94. 36   95. 65   96. 74

97. 90   98. 96   99. 13   100. 100   101. 91   102. 79

103. 10   104. 48   105. 62   106. 63   107. 76   108. 36

Page 50: Multiplication Word Problems

1. 120   2. 153   3. 200   4. 182   5. 104   6. 90   7. 306

8. 36   9. 162   10. 180   11. 90   12. 280   13. 220   14. 90

15. 192   16. 42   17. 45   18. 57   19. 40   20. 90   21. 8

22. 12

Page 56: Division Word Problems

1. 66   2. 70   3. 42   4. 900   5. 10   6. 45   7. 48   8. 13

9. 36   10. 60   11. 38   12. 20   13. 97   14. 59   15. 65   16. 2

17. 28   18. 61   19. 5   20. 49   21. 51

Page 63: Adding Decimals

1. 95.66   2. 90.71   3. 148.71   4. 83.77   5. 50.20

6. 94.16   7. 179.36   8. 106.17   9. 113.56   10. 99.55

11. 151.46   12. 115.14   13. 96.85   14. 59.84   15. 85.90

16. 79.59   17. 98.87   18. 54.35   19. 137.28   20. 48.30

21. 145.61   22. 119.99   23. 106.32   24. 156.50   25. 95.33

26. 75.38	27. 177.02	28. 137.60	29. 140.88	30. 142.79
31. 91.42	32. 86.99	33. 145.70	34. 120.53	35. 142.55
36. 48.73	37. 92.74	38. 95.27	39. 95.00	40. 78.63
41. 74.11	42. 89.41	43. 45.60	44. 118.14	45. 122.03
46. 80.63	47. 109.67	48. 114.44	49. 96.43	50. 108.07
51. 157.48	52. 116.20	53. 112.79	54. 60.08	55. 63.42
56. 115.64	57. 157.10	58. 83.97	59. 139.60	60. 123.61

Page 66: Subtracting Decimals

1. 75.80	2. 1.81	3. 45.78	4. 17.14	5. 9.65	6. 66.67
7. 18.98	8. 10.37	9. 46.78	10. 9.81	11. 60.09	12. 50.21
13. 73.08	14. 12.34	15. 19.58	16. 8.32	17. 28.65	18. 32.90
19. 11.09	20. 32.17	21. 49.33	22. 51.63	23. 78.61	24. 13.06
25. 26.81	26. 11.51	27. 32.12	28. 9.79	29. 18.34	30. 21.15
31. 14.03	32. 43.81	33. 32.74	34. 3.38	35. 81.16	36. 5.30
37. 19.23	38. 81.68	39. 27.87	40. 31.15	41. 58.37	42. 55.71
43. 61.44	44. 13.36	45. 28.01	46. 59.06	47. 65.09	48. 13.15
49. 3.11	50. 42.07	51. 15.89	52. 57.49	53. 54.15	54. 6.70
55. 24.39	56. 5.57	57. 0.03	58. 30.52	59. 46.70	60. 17.35

Page 69: Place Value

| 1. 3 ones | 2. 2 thousands | 3. 7 tenths |
| 4. 8 thousands | 5. 5 tens | 6. 8 ones |

7. 1 tenth

8. 5 tenths

9. 7 hundredths

10. 5 hundreds

11. 4 hundredths

12. 9 hundreds

13. 1 ten

14. 1 tenth

15. 0 hundreds

16. 2 tenths

17. 9 tenths

18. 3 hundredths

19. 6 hundreds

20. 4 hundreds

21. 1 tenth

22. 1 thousandth

23. 8 thousandths

24. 9 thousandths

25. 5 ones

26. 5 thousands

27. 2 tens

28. 1 thousand

29. 2 tenths

30. 2 hundreds

31. 2 thousands

32. 4 tenths

33. 3 thousands

34. 0 ones

35. 8 tens

36. 9 thousands

37. 9 tens

38. 1 ten

39. 8 ones

40. 7 thousands

41. 4 hundredths

42. 4 tenths

43. 4 tens

44. 0 ones

45. 5 tenths

46. 4 hundreds

47. 4 thousandths

48. 2 hundredths

49. 2 thousands

50. 9 ones

51. 1 thousand

52. 7 thousands

53. 7 hundredths

54. 3 tens

55. 1 tenth

56. 1 ten

57. 4 tens

58. 4 hundredths

59. 9 tenths

60. 9 hundredths

61. 2 tens

62. 3 ten thousands

63. 1 one

64. 4 ones

65. 5 hundreds

66. 9 hundreds

67. 0 hundredths

68. 0 tenths

69. 7 hundreds

70. 2 tens

Page 78:   Place Value: Expanded Notation

1. 7,409.3	2. 699.24	3. 144.23	4. 483.01	5. 6,603.5
6. 6,522.9	7. 736.77	8. 6,917.6	9. 92.515	10. 6,577.9
11. 511.91	12. 39,714	13. 805.75	14. 1,808.5	15. 63,224
16. 29.278	17. 96.724	18. 128.64	19. 2,951.2	20. 14,322
21. 2,804.3	22. 794.49	23. 22,820	24. 6,778.0	25. 5,132.4
26. 77.790	27. 348.34	28. 65,446	29. 76,070	30. 22,888
31. 8,008.3	32. 35.866	33. 91.630	34. 919.31	35. 79.976
36. 2,085.0	37. 671.11	38. 878.79	39. 32.811	40. 13.120
41. 15.654	42. 41.747	43. 72,377	44. 43.281	45. 63.704
46. 31,294	47. 71,859	48. 88.239	49. 9,337.5	50. 19,005
51. 13,376	52. 622.83	53. 627.37	54. 931.39	55. 85,160
56. 946.43	57. 5,710.5	58. 4,664.3	59. 9,697.6	60. 8,824.4
61. 403.95	62. 182.31	63. 9,310.5	64. 79.627	65. 85.695
66. 25.325	67. 48,083	68. 88.643	69. 3,810.8	

Page 88:   Place Value: Expanded Notation

1. 5 ten thousands + 2 thousands + 3 hundreds + 7 tens + 4 ones

2. 6 thousands + 2 hundreds + 1 ten + 6 ones + 6 tenths

3. 1 thousand + 8 hundreds + 8 tens + 4 ones + 5 tenths

4. 8 thousands + 5 ones + 2 tenths

5. 2 thousands + 6 hundreds + 3 tens + 9 ones + 2 tenths

6. 9 tens + 8 ones + 6 tenths + 6 hundredths + 7 thousandths

7. 8 ten thousands + 6 thousands + 2 hundreds + 9 tens + 6 ones

8. 1 hundred + 7 tens + 7 tenths + 2 hundredths

9. 7 thousands + 9 hundreds + 5 tens + 3 ones + 8 tenths

10. 1 ten + 4 ones + 7 hundredths + 6 thousandths

11. 3 tens + 3 hundredths

12. 1 ten thousand + 5 thousands + 9 hundreds + 3 tens + 1 one

13. 4 thousands + 6 hundreds + 5 tens + 9 ones + 4 tenths

14. 7 thousands + 2 hundreds + 7 ones

15. 6 ten thousands + 7 thousands + 6 tens + 5 ones

16. 1 ten + 9 ones + 5 tenths + 1 hundredth + 2 thousandths

17. 2 thousands + 7 hundreds + 7 tens + 9 ones + 9 tenths

18. 7 thousands + 3 hundreds + 1 ten + 2 ones + 9 tenths

19. 9 hundreds + 8 tens + 4 ones + 9 tenths

20. 1 thousand + 6 hundreds + 7 tens + 7 ones + 1 tenth

21. 8 tens + 5 ones + 3 tenths + 3 hundredths + 1 thousandth

22. 6 thousands + 3 hundreds + 7 tens + 4 ones + 5 tenths

23. 3 thousands + 4 tens + 6 ones + 8 tenths

24. 9 thousands + 9 tens + 2 tenths

25. 4 ten thousands + 4 thousands + 5 hundreds + 6 tens + 6 ones

26. 7 ten thousands + 2 thousands + 7 hundreds + 2 tens + 4 ones

27. 9 hundreds + 7 tens + 4 ones + 2 tenths + 2 hundredths

28. 4 thousands + 8 hundreds + 6 tens + 4 ones + 1 tenth

29. 9 ten thousands + 2 thousands + 7 hundreds + 4 tens + 9 ones

30. 5 ten thousands + 7 thousands + 5 hundreds + 8 tens + 5 ones

31. 4 tens + 8 ones + 3 tenths + 7 hundredths + 9 thousandths

32. 8 ten thousands + 3 thousands + 2 hundreds + 1 ten

33. 8 thousands + 3 hundreds + 2 tens + 1 one + 5 tenths

34. 6 tens + 1 tenth + 3 hundredths + 1 thousandth

35. 5 tens + 1 one + 1 thousandth

36. 5 tens + 6 ones + 8 tenths + 3 hundredths + 8 thousandths

37. 9 tens + 4 ones + 5 tenths + 3 hundredths

38. 8 ten thousands + 2 thousands + 2 hundreds + 3 tens

39. 4 thousands + 6 hundreds + 3 tens + 4 ones + 5 tenths

40. 9 hundreds + 4 tens + 4 ones + 7 tenths + 1 hundredth

41. 9 ten thousands + 8 thousands + 8 hundreds + 6 tens + 4 ones

42. 8 ten thousands + 7 thousands + 5 hundreds + 7 tens + 1 one

43. 7 tens + 7 ones + 5 tenths + 6 hundredths + 6 thousandths

44. 4 ten thousands + 2 thousands + 5 hundreds + 6 tens + 7 ones

45. 7 hundreds + 6 tens + 9 ones + 4 tenths + 6 hundredths

46. 8 tens + 2 ones + 3 tenths + 1 hundredth + 3 thousandths

47. 9 ten thousands + 3 thousands + 8 hundreds

48. 4 thousands + 6 hundreds + 1 ten + 6 ones + 1 tenth

49. 3 tens + 6 ones + 4 hundredths

50. 7 tens + 1 tenth + 1 hundredth + 5 thousandths

51. 6 thousands + 7 hundreds + 8 tens + 9 ones + 6 tenths

52. 5 tens + 2 ones + 1 tenth + 9 hundredths + 5 thousandths

53. 4 thousands + 9 hundreds + 5 tens + 9 ones + 2 tenths

54. 8 ten thousands + 1 thousand + 8 hundreds + 7 tens + 2 ones

55. 5 hundreds + 2 tens + 7 ones + 7 tenths + 6 hundredths

56. 8 tens + 8 ones + 6 tenths + 2 hundredths + 8 thousandths

57. 4 tens + 1 one + 6 tenths + 9 hundredths + 8 thousandths

58. 2 ten thousands + 7 thousands + 9 hundreds + 4 tens + 2 ones

59. 4 thousands + 5 hundreds + 4 tens + 8 ones + 6 tenths

60. 5 ten thousands + 3 thousands + 6 hundreds + 6 tens + 7 ones

Page 98: Fraction Identification

1. 2/3	2. 1/2	3. 5/6	4. 3/5	5. 2/8	6. 3/9	7. 7/8
8. 2/6	9. 5/10	10. 4/7	11. 4/5	12. 1/4	13. 3/10	14. 3/4
15. 1/7	16. 3/6	17. 5/8	18. 2/9	19. 2/4	20. 4/9	21. 1/3
22. 2/7	23. 1/5	24. 7/10	25. 3/7	26. 7/9	27. 2/10	28. 4/6
29. 3/8	30. 8/10	31. 9/10	32. 5/7	33. 6/8	34. 1/8	35. 4/10
36. 6/7	37. 5/9	38. 2/5	39. 4/8	40. 1/10	41. 1/9	42. 1/6

43. 6/9   44. 6/10   45. 8/9   46. 1/4   47. 1/9   48. 1/2   49. 1/3

50. 6/7   51. 3/5   52. 1/3   53. 2/5   54. 1/4   55. 4/10   56. 2/5

57. 4/6   58. 1/4   59. 1/2   60. 3/6   61. 4/5   62. 1/7   63. 3/4

64. 1/2   65. 2/7   66. 3/5   67. 4/7   68. 2/8   69. 2/3   70. 1/4

71. 1/2   72. 5/6   73. 2/8   74. 1/5   75. 2/4   76. 4/5   77. 5/8

78. 4/5   79. 1/3   80. 2/10

Page 107:   Compare the Fractions

1. <   2. >   3. >   4. >   5. >   6. <   7. =   8. <   9. <   10. <

11. >   12. <   13. <   14. >   15. >   16. =   17. >   18. >   19. <   20. <

21. >   22. <   23. <   24. >   25. >   26. <   27. >   28. <   29. >   30. >

31. >   32. >   33. <   34. =   35. <   36. >   37. >   38. >   39. >   40. >

41. <   42. =   43. <   44. <   45. >   46. <   47. <   48. >   49. <   50. <

51. >   52. <   53. <   54. >   55. >   56. <   57. <   58. <

Page 112:   Fractions Addition: Common Denominator

1. 8/9   2. 7/10   3. 4/5   4. 6/7   5. 1/3   6. 3/4

7. 3/5   8. 3/4   9. 2/3   10. 5/11   11. 1/1   12. 2/3

13. 2/3   14. 3/10   15. 6/7   16. 4/5   17. 5/9   18. 4/5

19. 10/11   20. 5/6   21. 11/12   22. 1/2   23. 5/8   24. 2/5

25. 5/6   26. 7/10   27. 2/7   28. 3/4   29. 5/11   30. 5/9

31. 7/8   32. 7/9   33. 5/6   34. 5/11   35. 3/7   36. 3/5

37. 1/2   38. 4/5   39. 3/4   40. 8/9   41. 2/3   42. 9/11

43. 7/12   44. 3/4   45. 6/7   46. 7/9   47. 1/2   48. 5/7

49. 1/2   50. 6/11   51. 4/5   52. 5/6   53. 9/10   54. 5/9

55. 5/6   56. 5/6   57. 7/11   58. 3/4   59. 3/8   60. 1/3

61. 5/11   62. 2/5   63. 5/7   64. 2/3   65. 2/3   66. 2/9

67. 5/12   68. 5/8   69. 5/7   70. 1/5   71. 1/2   72. 2/3

73. 7/9   74. 4/7   75. 4/7   76. 4/9   77. 3/5   78. 7/8

79. 6/11   80. 2/3   81. 8/9   82. 3/11   83. 1/2   84. 3/4

85. 4/5   86. 1/2   87. 4/7   88. 5/6   89. 3/4   90. 10/11

91. 7/11   92. 3/4   93. 1/2   94. 6/7   95. 1/3   96. 4/5

Page 120: Fractions Subtraction - Common Denominator

1. 3/8   2. 3/5   3. 1/6   4. 5/12   5. 1/3   6. 1/12

7. 1/8   8. 2/9   9. 3/10   10. 1/2   11. 1/5   12. 3/11

13. 3/7   14. 1/6   15. 1/4   16. 1/3   17. 4/7   18. 3/10

19. 1/3   20. 5/12   21. 1/4   22. 1/6   23. 1/5   24. 1/8

25. 4/7   26. 1/11   27. 2/5   28. 1/9   29. 3/7   30. 1/12

31. 1/4   32. 6/11   33. 1/9   34. 3/10   35. 1/8   36. 1/6

37. 1/9   38. 7/12   39. 1/5   40. 3/10   41. 1/7   42. 1/11

43. 1/2   44. 1/10   45. 1/7   46. 1/11   47. 2/3   48. 1/3

49. 2/5   50. 1/7   51. 1/3   52. 6/11   53. 1/2   54. 8/11

55. 1/9   56. 1/7   57. 1/12   58. 1/4   59. 3/10   60. 1/4

61. 2/5   62. 2/5   63. 1/6   64. 3/8   65. 1/3   66. 2/5

67. 3/11   68. 1/6   69. 1/5   70. 2/7   71. 1/3   72. 3/5

73. 2/11   74. 1/2   75. 2/7   76. 7/10   77. 1/8   78. 4/9

79. 2/3   80. 5/11   81. 1/4   82. 1/2   83. 1/11   84. 1/2

85. 1/12   86. 1/6   87. 1/4   88. 2/9   89. 1/2   90. 1/4

91. 6/11   92. 1/3   93. 1/11   94. 1/12   95. 1/3   96. 5/9

97. 1/8   98. 4/9   99. 1/12   100. 5/8   101. 1/10   102. 1/5

103. 1/10   104. 1/5

Page 129: Area and Perimeter: Rectangles and Triangles

1. P=45 A=84   2. P=44 A=120   3. P=44 A=84.5

4. P=46 A=91   5. P=42 A=110   6. P=36 A=54

7. P=26 A=28   8. P=45 A=84   9. P=24 A=24

10. P=24 A=24   11. P=54 A=176   12. P=56 A=136

13. P=36 A=81   14. P=34 A=72   15. P=35 A=49.5

16. P=43 A=75   17. P=33 A=45   18. P=32 A=44

19. P=39 A=66   20. P=31 A=40   21. P=19 A=15

22. P=53 A=117   23. P=30 A=56   24. P=46 A=91

25. P=34 A=49.5   26. P=23 A=21   27. P=23 A=20

28. P=26 A=28   29. P=37 A=60   30. P=26 A=28

31. P=30 A=54   32. P=40 A=99   33. P=21 A=18

34. P=50 A=156   35. P=50 A=102   36. P=54 A=182

37. P=24 A=24.5   38. P=29 A=36   39. P=54 A=182

40. P=32 A=45   41. P=26 A=28   42. P=36 A=55

43. P=28 A=48   44. P=32 A=45   45. P=25 A=28

46. P=27 A=32   47. P=45 A=84.5   48. P=29 A=35

49. P=24 A=36   50. P=29 A=36   51. P=22 A=21

52. P=47 A=91   53. P=44 A=84   54. P=43 A=77

55. P=44 A=117   56. P=61 A=162   57. P=38 A=88

58. P=26 A=28   59. P=56 A=192   60. P=34 A=50

61. P=22 A=21   62. P=41 A=72   63. P=56 A=195

64. P=60 A=221   65. P=48 A=97.5   66. P=34 A=72

67. P=52 A=169   68. P=28 A=48   69. P=38 A=90

70. P=33 A=50   71. P=32 A=63   72. P=38 A=60.5

73. P=27 A=32   74. P=26 A=28   75. P=53 A=117

76. P=24 A=36   77. P=50 A=105   78. P=42 A=77

79. P=50 A=156   80. P=40 A=100   81. P=27 A=32

82. P=32 A=45   83. P=50 A=154   84. P=62 A=240

85. P=30 A=56   86. P=22 A=21   87. P=38 A=88

88. P=31 A=40   89. P=60 A=221   90. P=30 A=56

91. P=58 A=204   92. P=49 A=96   93. P=41 A=70

94. P=26 A=28   95. P=30 A=56   96. P=34 A=49.5

Page 153: Roman Numerals

1. 4   2. 5   3. 7   4. 6   5. 2   6. 35   7. 28   8. 3

9. 32   10. 9   11. 14   12. 42   13. 39   14. 8   15. 20   16. 33

17. 25   18. 49   19. 34   20. 50   21. 10   22. 1   23. 24   24. 37

25. 26   26. 45   27. 47   28. 23   29. 43   30. 48   31. 46   32. 30

33. 27   34. 36   35. 16   36. 19   37. 18   38. 44   39. 17   40. 40

41. 13   42. 29   43. 22   44. 31

www.ingramcontent.com/pod-product-compliance
Lightning Source LLC
Chambersburg PA
CBHW080937120726
48003CB00011B/3191